Arizona

Lawrence W. Cheek
Photography by Michael Freeman
and Kerrick James

COMPASS AMERICAN GUIDES
An Imprint of Fodor's Travel Publications, Inc.

Arizona

Copyright © 1997 Fodor's Travel Publications, Inc.
Maps copyright © 1997 Fodor's Travel Publications, Inc.
FOURTH EDITION 1997

LIBRARY OF CONGRESS CATALOGING-IN-PUBLICATION DATA
  Cheek, Larry.
  Arizona/Lawrence W. Cheek; photography by Michael Freeman and Kerrick James —4th ed.
  p.   cm. —(Compass American guides)
  Includes bibliographical references and index.
  ISBN 0-679-03388-2
  1. Arizona—Guidebooks. I. Title. II. Series: Compass American guides (series)
      F869.3.C44 1997   97-15503
      917.9104'53—dc20   CIP

Editors: Barry Parr, Kit Duane, Debi Dunn
Fourth Edition Editors: Carrie Bell Sears,
  Kit Duane
Managing Editor: Kit Duane
Creative Director: Christopher Burt
Produced by Twin Age Ltd., Hong Kong

Designers: Christopher Burt, David Hurst,
  Debi Dunn
Map Design: Mark Stroud, Moon Street
  Cartography; Eureka Cartography; Bob Race

Printed in China

10 9 8 7 6 5 4 3 2 1
First published in 1991

Compass American Guides, 5332 College Ave. Suite 201, Oakland, CA 94618, USA

917.91
C HE

PHOTO AND ILLUSTRATION CREDITS

Unless otherwise stated below, all photography is by **Michael Freeman**. The Publisher gratefully acknowledges the following individuals and institutions for the use of their photographs and/or illustrations on the following pages: **Kerrick James** cover photo, pp. 3, 8-9 (all), 14-15, 32-33, 40-41, 49, 56, 76, 91, 104 (top right, bottom), 105, 107, 122, 132, 148, 152, 153, 157, 161, 172, 173, 176, 177, 180, 185, 188, 192 (top), 193 (bottom), 201, 204, 206, 215, 222, 228, 237, 262, 264-265, 269, 273, 276, 280-281; **George H. H. Huey** p. 86 (all), 114-115 (all); **Peter Bloomer** p. 52; **Patricia A. Cheek** p. 292; **Paul Chesley** p. 198; **Eduardo Fuss** p. 202 (all); **Arizona Historical Society Library** pp. 93, 100, 101, 118, 129, 152, 156, 166, 182, 183, 270; **Bisbee Mining & Historical Museum** p. 133; **Bob Race** p. 238; **Harry S. Robins** pps. 22-23.

   Compass American Guides would also like to thank **David Laird** for his careful reading of the manuscript, **Lesley Bonnet** for the index, **Kelly Duane** for fact checking, and **Julie Searle** for her editorial contributions.

To Patty, who made my life in the desert complete

CONTENTS

Topical Essays

Literary Extracts

Maps

FACTS ABOUT ARIZONA

Grand Canyon State

CAPITAL: Phoenix

STATE FLOWER: Flower of saguaro cactus

STATE BIRD: Cactus wren

STATE TREE: Paloverde

ENTERED UNION: Feb. 14, 1912

FIRST EUROPEAN SETTLEMENT: 1629

POPULATION: 4.5 million

Flower of saguaro cactus

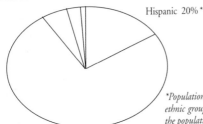

Black 3.0%

Native American 5.6%   Asian   1.5%

Hispanic 20%*

*Population of Hispanic origin is an ethnic grouping and not additive to the population racial groupings

GEOGRAPHY

Size: 114,000 sq. mi. (6th largest)

Highest point: 12,633 feet

Humphreys Peak

Lowest point: 70 feet

Colorado River, Mexican border

CLIMATE

Wettest Place	**Driest Place**	**Lowest Temp:**	**Highest Temp:**
Crown King	Yuma Valley	Hawley Lake	Parker
Yavapai County	Yuma County	Jan. 7, 1971	July 7, 1905
28.26 inches annually	2.70 inches annually	-40° F (-40° C)	127° F (53° C)

FAMOUS ARIZONANS

Cochise ♦ Geronimo ♦ Zane Grey ♦ Carl Hayden ♦ Sandra Day O'Connor

Percival Lowell ♦ Barry Goldwater ♦ Linda Ronstadt ♦ Bruce Babbitt ♦ Erma Bombeck

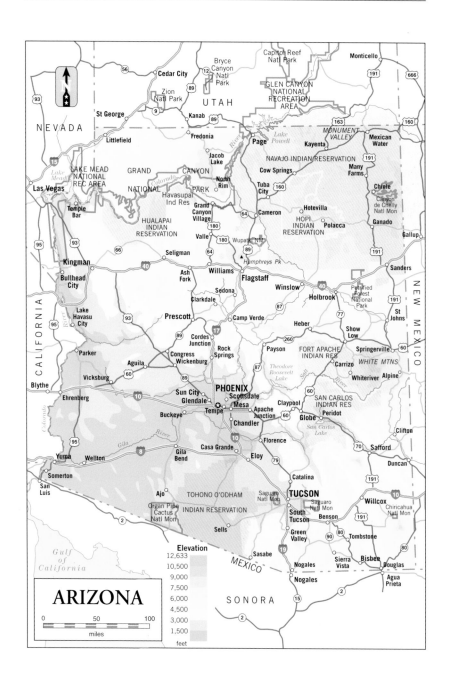

ARIZONA

Elevation	
12,633	
10,500	
9,000	
7,500	
6,000	
4,500	
3,000	
1,500	
feet	

0   50   100
miles

O V E R V I E W

ARIZONA is not the Arid Zone. Its geography comprises alpine forests, deep red sandstone canyons, rolling grasslands, and deserts that grow carpets of wildflowers in spring. Its largest city, Phoenix, flaunts its wealth and ambition, and irrigates the desert into submission. The second city, Tucson, struggles to come to terms with its desert environment and Hispanic heritage. The state's back roads lead to 16 national parks and monuments, 20 Indian reservations, and a host of resorts.

GRAND CANYON

Nothing else on earth prepares one for the sight: a vast chasm a mile deep and 277 miles long, a gallery of fantastic shapes sculpted by weather and water and repaint-

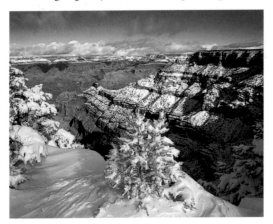

ed daily by the changing patterns of sun and atmospheric conditions. Waterfalls, rapids, fossils of trilobites half a billion years extinct, and ruins of Indians nearly a millennium old—no place on earth exposes so much history and beauty to view. No place on earth, it sometimes seems, draws such crowds.

PAINTED DESERT
SONORAN DESERT

Four deserts meet in Arizona. To the west lie the wind-sculpted dunes of the Mojave, to the north and east, the Great Basin Desert, which embraces the surreal colors of the Painted Desert and the Petrified Forest. The American West's most fecund and fascinating desert, the Sonoran, stretches from central Arizona south into Mexico, and the desolate wilderness of the Chihuahuan Desert, which stretches east across southern New Mexico and into West Texas.

ANCIENT INDIAN RUINS

Farming and village-dwelling Indian cultures flourished in the Southwest between A.D. 300 and 1450, after which they collapsed or dispersed. Their abandoned cities weren't re-discovered until the late 19th century. In Arizona visit the White

House Ruin in Canyon de Chelly and Pueblo Grande near the Salt River. The pottery of these ancient cultures can best be viewed at the Heard Museum in Phoenix and the Museum of Northern Arizona in Flagstaff.

SPANISH COLONIAL MISSIONS

Spanish conquistadors and settlers brought with them Franciscan and Jesuit missionaries who supervised the construction of churches. Most of these can be found in southeast Arizona where the Spanish first settled.

PHOENIX AND TUCSON

These are sprawling, dynamic cities with a laid-back style, bristling with great restaurants, outdoor recreation, resorts, and golf courses. Visit the Indian art collection at the Heard Museum in Phoenix or walk the Echo Canyon trail up Camelback Mountain on the city's eastern edge. Smaller Tucson is known for its dramatic mountains, the University of Arizona, and its Barrio Histórico.

BACK ROADS AND SMALL TOWNS

Follow the back-roads maps on pages 218-219 to discover colorful Sedona with its galleries and restaurants, and the polychromatic strata of nearby Oak Creek Canyon. In northern Arizona are the ancient Sinagua ruins at Wupatki National Monument and the Anasazi sites at Canyon de Chelly. Near Tucson visit the saguaro cactus forests at Saguaro National Park, or cross the border at Nogales into Mexico. Other roads lead to the mining town of Bisbee and to Tombstone, where Wyatt Earp and Doc Holliday shot it out with the Clanton gang at the O.K. Corral.

(all photos by Kerrick James)

INTRODUCTION

I FIRST STARED AT ARIZONA IN 1973 THROUGH A WINDOW of an airplane, a commercial jet cruising somewhere in the lower stratosphere. I was flying from Des Moines to Tucson for a job interview, and what I still remember with startling clarity, as I pressed my nose to the glass and looked at the Sonoran Desert seven miles below, was a feeling of hollow, gnawing alienation.

I thought: I won't take the job. I cannot live in this place.

The barren earth appeared the color of sun-bleached cardboard. It was raked and torn and furrowed by corrosive wind and bogus rivers that would flow, with luck, 10 days in a year. The mountains seemed equally desolate and hostile; from this altitude I had no inkling of their heroic natural architecture or the kaleidoscopic changes of the plant and animal environments on their slopes every few hundred feet. The entire Arizona landscape appeared to hold no life, no interest, no promise.

My reversal of heart did not come quickly or painlessly. For the first several years after I accepted a job in Tucson, I oscillated between a reporter's fascination with the place and a tentative resident's annoyance with it. I didn't like the bugs, the ferocious cutlery that poses as plant life in the desert, or the exhausting summer heat. I missed the sensation of four distinct seasons, and remembered in demented wistfulness the soft, cold feel of snow on my neck. I was peeved at the strange forces that seemed to be pulling on Arizona's political compass. I remember my astonishment one day in 1974 when I first saw a billboard demanding "Get US out of the UN!" on the Interstate between Tucson and the Mexican border. (It took 20 years for the desert sun to bleach it into illegibility, but then the John Birch Society put up a fresh one north of Tucson.) I detested Phoenix, and over time developed a modest reputation as the Tucson journalist who wrote more vitriolic essays about that other city than anyone in modern history. This mini-specialty peaked with a call from the *Arizona Republic*, Phoenix's morning paper, wanting to interview me about the tradition of hostility between the two cities. I still hadn't come to terms with Arizona, but on certain topics I was at least an authority.

Yet during my 14-year tenure at the *Tucson Citizen*, Tucson's afternoon daily, I slowly and inevitably nurtured an affection for the state.

There were some pivotal moments. One came at a time when I was beginning to indulge seriously in bicycling—this after a couple of years of mostly staying indoors, bitching about the sunshine. Finally on Sunday mornings I began a ritual of pedaling out to Saguaro National Park, a 20-mile round trip from my house, and riding the hilly eight-mile loop road through the pristine cactus forest in the foothills of the Rincon Mountains. On a spring day I was wobbling up a long and pain-inducing hill when a Buick wearing Minnesota plates swished past. Four uncomprehending faces stared at me through sealed windows; their expressions resembled anthropologists observing some primitive aborigine praying to a pine cone. I realized at that moment that by insulating themselves from the desert—from its physical demands and its miraculous beauty alike—they were failing to understand even the first thing about it. As well as missing the point, probably, of life itself.

Another came in 1975, the year after a young Phoenix lawyer named Bruce Babbitt was elected state attorney general. He opened his office once a month to any Arizonan who wanted to come in and talk about their problems. I spent one of those days with him, and his connection to the land and culture of Arizona touched me. For the first time I liked an Arizona politician.

More than most other states, Arizona tests its people. Its jagged landscapes and diverse cultures dare us to comprehend them. Its climatic extremes challenge our stamina, will, and common sense. The everyday trials of living in a place that has grown more rapidly than sensibly cause many people either to leave or withdraw into their private worlds, taking no part in the public life of the place. We have a volatile population: for every three souls who arrive, two leave. Yet, it is from this instability that opportunity is given birth. In Arizona, whether you lean to art, politics, land fraud, or journalism, you can invent yourself.

This book is partly about that act of inventing, which forms so much of Arizona's history and contemporary culture. It also is a guide to the state's attractions and eccentricities—there are enough things to experience described in here, from hidden canyons to museums of archaeology, to keep any visitor occupied for years. It does not read very much like a conventional guidebook. It is highly opinionated and occasionally cranky, and when it turns to some of the misuse and abuse my sorry species has visited on this magnificent land it bounces peevishly between anger and sorrow. It does manage to say some fairly nice things about Phoenix. (Either I have matured or that city has.) It says even more about the joy of taking part in the extravagant life of the deserts, the canyons, the mountains, and the forests that make up this amazing land. In the end, this book is about falling in love.

D E S E R T S

A SONORAN DESERT STORY:

A CROWD OF VACATIONING ISRAELIS PILES OUT OF A BUS at the Arizona-Sonora Desert Museum, the world-famous desert zoo/arboretum a dozen miles west of Tucson. They buy their tickets, then gather under the ramada that overlooks the museum grounds. Their eyes sweep across a forest of saguaro cacti interspersed with woody sprays of ocotillo wearing their flame-shaped orange flowers of spring. The spindly, green-barked palo verde trees are veiled in yellow blossoms, the velvet mesquite and ironwood trees are in luxuriant leaf, and even the homely prickly pear cacti are erupting with peach- and yellow-colored flowers, some the size of coffee cups.

Asks one of the Israelis, not joking: "So where's the desert?"

Another story:

It is June 1996, still gentle spring in the pines of northern Arizona, but already a time of soaring, searing temperatures in the Sonoran Desert. It is hotter than normal this June, but the weather does not deter five illegal immigrants from Mexico. Somewhere west of Nogales, the young men cross the border into Arizona and head north through the unforgiving desert wilderness.

With more U.S. Border Patrol agents than ever watching the border towns this year, a trek through this remote territory seems their best shot at getting work across the border.

The group walks 70 miles in five days, stopping for water in two villages on the Tohono O'odham Reservation. Their destination is a farm field near Eloy, but they never make it. With less than 15 miles to go, their hopes—and their lives—wither in the heat. All five perish amid a vast expanse of creosote scrubs near the boundary of Pima and Pinal counties, 30 miles south of Casa Grande.

It is the worst illegal immigrant tragedy in Arizona since July 1980, when 13 Salvadorans also died of exposure near the border. Unfortunately, similar deaths involving Mexican or Central American refugees occur each year.

In an effort to prevent such tragedies, the U.S. Border Patrol has issued radio and television public-service announcements warning against the dangers of desert crossings. In addition, signs are posted in the Mexican villages along the border. The words are not minced:

(following pages) To enjoy this view of Monument Valley, visitors must hire a Navajo guide and jeep and make the trip to Hunts Mesa. (Kerrick James)

<table>
<tr><td>

DESIERTO PELIGROSO
La falta de agua y las altas temperaturas
in el desierto pueden causar la
MUERTE
Por tu propia seguridad
NO INTENTES CRUZARLO

</td><td>

DANGEROUS DESERT
The lack of water and the high
temperatures in the desert can cause
DEATH
For your own safety
DON'T TRY TO CROSS IT

</td></tr>
</table>

The desert gives life abundantly, the desert revokes it disinterestedly. "Here death is like breathing. Here death simply is," wrote Charles Bowden in *Blue Desert*, a provocative collection of essays. The late Edward Abbey, who was Bowden's inspiration, frequently mused about death in the desert—though never the death *of* the desert. In the closing pages of *Desert Solitaire*, his finest book, he wrote:

> Whether we live or die is a matter of absolutely no concern whatsoever to the desert. Let men in their madness blast every city on earth into black rubble and envelop the entire planet in a cloud of lethal gas—the canyons and hills, the springs and rocks will still be here, the sunlight will filter through, water will form and warmth shall be upon the land and after sufficient time, no matter how long, somewhere, living things will emerge and join and stand once again, this time perhaps to take a different and better course.

In the desert, death is exposed, not concealed in the shadows and underbrush of a forest. An hour's walk along any trail in the desert will yield reminders of the fragility of life and the inevitability of its end: a coyote's skull, tufts of coarse, gray-brown fur still clinging to its lower jaw; a century-old saguaro fried by lightning (or perhaps strangled by air pollution) still standing, its naked, woody ribs splaying like a fountain spray and bleaching in the relentless sun. A cottontail darts across the trail and freezes in the shadow of a creosote bush, assuming it's thus invisible to predators—which, of course, it isn't; a coyote's eyes lock easily onto that fluffy white ball of a tail. The bunny adapts by breeding prolifically during its short, timorous life. Bad news for the individual, adequate protection for the species. The desert offers no regrets.

The irony is that this same *desierto peligroso* is also a place that welcomes life. It is extravagantly fecund. Because the desert's plants and animals (and at least its pre-Columbian peoples) are so keenly adapted, they impose themselves on the land with insane determination. A few thimblefuls of sediment wash into a fissure between two boulders, and inevitably a barrel cactus (or something) will sprout, seemingly growing out of rock at whatever crazy angle it needs to stake a claim for some sunlight. The cholla, bloodthirstiest of all cacti, will fight off a human armed with pliers and forceps, yet the cactus wren blithely and safely nests in it. The most common misconception about the deserts of the Southwest is that they are desolate, barren, lifeless places. In fact, they teem with life—weird, colorful, perfectly adapted, interdependent, fiercely obstinate life.

Few *Homo sapiens* fall in love with, or understand, this desert life at first encounter. It appears exotic but threatening. Arizona is home to 11 species of rattlesnake, 30 species each of scorpion and tarantula, the black widow and brown recluse spider, the giant (up to eight inches long) desert centipede and the Gila monster—this last species being one of only two venomous lizards on the planet.

People coming to Arizona from moist, green places frequently ask the natives: "How can you live here with all these rattlesnakes, scorpions, and Gila monsters?" The Arizonan, oddly, responds by *exaggerating* the menace of this terrible triad.

Even among Arizonans, who ought to know better, the Gila monster is credited with an amazing list of frightful features: The monster is poisonous because it has no rectum, so a lifetime's waste is stored in its body. When it bites, it will hold on until it hears thunder. And even its breath is poisonous.

According to an 1890 account in the *Tucson Citizen,* "A woodcutter lay down to sleep . . . they found him stone dead, and near his body a Gila Monster . . . as the body of the man bore no marks of a bite or other wounds, we must suppose that his death was caused by the mere exhalation of the lizard."

All this is fanciful nonsense, as is the belief that these shy, waddling, 12- to 16-inch lizards (hardly "monstrous") will spring out of hiding to attack an unwary human. In fact, virtually all *Heloderma suspectum* bites occur because someone is trying to harass or toy with the lizard.

"This is exactly what one will do if you approach it in the wild," explained a curator of small animals at the Arizona-Sonora Desert Museum. "First, it will pick up its pace and lumber away with as much dignity as it can manage. If there's any kind of a dark recess nearby, it will crawl inside. If it's cornered it will finally turn around and face the threat and inhale and exhale forcefully. This is its defensive posture. At this point, anything that touches its body or comes within reach of its jaws is going to get bitten."

Even then—contrary to another cherished belief—the bite is not fatal. The Gila monster's venom is chemically primitive, primarily defensive, and sub-lethal. Nature, as usual, is making perfect sense here. If a coyote were bitten by a Gila monster and died from it, the lizard would still have to fret about the next coyote. But if the predator is bitten and (narrowly) survives, it learns that the Gila monster is not part of *its* food chain. Over time, this "knowledge" becomes encoded in the species' genetic memory, and coyotes and Gila monsters give each other a wide berth, to their mutual advantage.

So even though newspaper reports continue to cite human death tolls from Gila monsters, they simply are not true. The best research has unearthed only one possible fatality in Arizona history: that of a "Col. Yearger" in 1878 who, according to reports, also had been on a continuous drunk for a month.

Why all the myths? Because the desert is a strange, and in many ways harsh, environment—and by exaggerating its strangeness and harshness, the people who live in it can convince themselves that they are braver for having conquered it. This mythology is harmless enough to us humans, but not to the rattlesnakes, scorpions and Gila monsters—which people routinely kill even in the wild for no better reason than that they are venomous animals.

Probably Arizona's lizards, snakes, arachnids, and insects get more press than they deserve, proportionately speaking. The state's deserts, especially the Sonoran, support a spectacular variety of wildlife. A complete catalog here is impossible, but consider a few.

"Parody pigs with oversize heads and undersize hams" was Abbey's classic description of the collared peccary, or javelina. He wasn't exaggerating their strangeness. If some political party were to adopt a pig as its symbol, a political cartoonist, wanting to portray it as scrappy and aggressive, would draw something like a javelina: small (about two feet high at the shoulder), with short, muscular legs, a big head tapering into a long, probelike snout, and dagger-like canine teeth. The desert's most social mammal, javelina invariably forage in groups, usually five to 15 individuals strong.

Seldom does any writer type the word "javelina" without the modifier "bad-tempered." It has become a desert cliché. Hogwash, the javelina would reply, if it could. Every desert animal has evolved some defensive strategy; the collared peccary's is to bristle, snort and stand its ground—en masse. No predator in its right mind would risk charging into such a platoon in search of a tasty youngster. With-in the group, javelinas are extremely cordial to each other, the females even nurs-ing each other's offspring—a rare phenomenon in nature. Their sociability makes javelina-watching one of the desert's great pleasures (when undertaken, as with the Gila monster, from a discreet distance).

Coyotes, even though discouraged from dining on javelina and Gila monsters, arguably are the desert's most intelligent and adaptable creatures. They will eat vir-tually anything else that can't eat them. Because of this, they are the one desert mammal that actually has benefited from the cities now sprawling through their habitat.

"Urban coyotes," as wildlife-management officials term them, are ubiquitous—and urbane. A regional supervisor for the Arizona Game & Fish Department has told of watching a coyote standing at the curb of a busy six-lane thoroughfare in Tucson, carefully monitoring the traffic in both directions, and finally loping across in safety. More often, the animals use their natural freeway system—the normally dry arroyos that cut through the desert cities—to get around and hunt for food. Garbage and household pets are most favored. A coyote can easily kill a domestic cat or a dog its own size. If a bigger dog chases a coyote, the dog often will find an unpleasant surprise waiting where its prey leads it: more coyotes.

Humans who encounter an abandoned litter of urban coyotes and "adopt" the cute, fuzzy pups also get an unpleasant surprise. At the age of about five months, they begin biting everything in sight, including the hands that feed them. They cannot be domesticated, and it's contrary to state law to try. Coyotes are best en-joyed from a distance. Open the windows on a warm spring night, and eventually, sometimes just before dawn, their uncannily melodic howling and yipping will float miles on the still desert air into the house. It sounds like a celebration, as well it may be. Nothing in the desert seems to live better than a coyote.

Most species have more to regret from the encroachment of *Homo sapiens*. No one would expect the hermit-like spadefoot toad to be among them, but because of advances in recreational technology, it may be.

Scaphiopus couchii spends nearly all its life alone in a sealed burrow three feet underground. No one is quite sure what it does down there except wait for the ground to shake from thunder. When the summer storms come, the spadefoot is thus reminded to burrow to the surface to feed and mate in the shallow ponds that collect on the desert floor after heavy rains. The tadpoles then begin a frantic race to adulthood before the ponds evaporate.

Arizona State University zoologist John Alcock, author of two gracefully written books on Sonoran Desert life, described an experiment in which tape recordings of loud motorcycles were played above spadefoots buried in a terrarium. The toads mistook the din for thunder, and burrowed to the surface—a waste of energy that could prove fatal in their marginal existence in the desert. Thus, fumed Alcock, off-roaders enjoying their "trivial human inventions" may endanger one of the least-seen and most elegantly adapted of all the desert's animals.

The desert's plants are no less strange, no less strategically endowed to cope with their environment, and in some sad cases, no less threatened by the humans around them.

Of the four distinct deserts that extend into Arizona, the Sonoran (again) features the most extravagant community of plants. This is a function of climate. The Sonoran is fairly wet, for a desert, with annual rainfall averaging 7.5 inches in Phoenix, 12 inches in Tucson, and 8.82 inches at Organ Pipe National Monument. Fragile plants also are not in much danger of a hard freeze, at least not below elevations of 3,000 feet. Tucson, at 2,630 feet, records an average of 17 freezing lows per year, but it very rarely falls below 25 degrees and never for more than a few hours. If it did, its signature plant, the giant saguaro, would not exist.

The saguaro inhabits a more-or-less horseshoe-shaped chunk of southern Arizona that includes Tucson, Phoenix, and the 4,335-square-mile Tohono O'odham Reservation. They then march south into the Mexican states of Sonora and Baja California. But even though their range is tightly restricted by climate, they have come to serve as a symbol of all Arizona and even the entire frontier West. So essential is their emblematic value that in *Broken Arrow,* the classic 1951 James Stewart western, the film crew scattered plaster-of-Paris saguaro among the red rocks of Sedona. A saguaro would no sooner grow in cool Sedona than in San Francisco.

An average human lifetime, about 75 years, expires before it occurs to a saguaro to perform the act that makes it so impressive to humans, which is to grow its first arm or two. Thus outfitted, the still-adolescent cactus takes on an anthropomorphic character. Some individuals seem to raise their arms in surrender, others in supplication, a few in bewilderment. One monster in the foothills of the Santa Catalina Mountains currently sports 21 arms curling in a swirl around its trunk, like a mutant green Baryshnikov in a pirouette frozen for eternity. The sentient human, wandering about a forest of these 30-foot creatures, feels like an explorer in the midst of a race of strangely still and silent alien beings. This eerie sensation is multiplied tenfold in the moonlight.

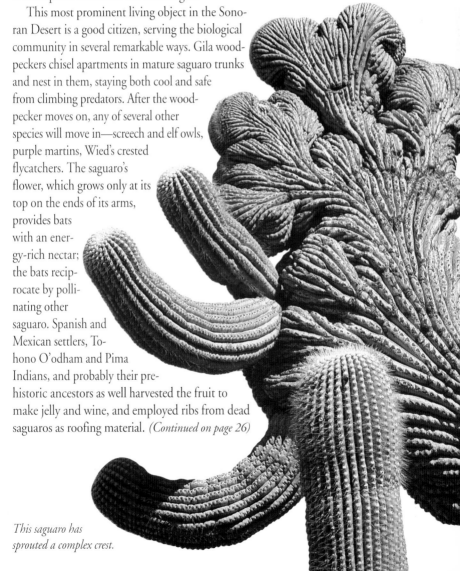

This most prominent living object in the Sonoran Desert is a good citizen, serving the biological community in several remarkable ways. Gila woodpeckers chisel apartments in mature saguaro trunks and nest in them, staying both cool and safe from climbing predators. After the woodpecker moves on, any of several other species will move in—screech and elf owls, purple martins, Wied's crested flycatchers. The saguaro's flower, which grows only at its top on the ends of its arms, provides bats with an energy-rich nectar; the bats reciprocate by pollinating other saguaro. Spanish and Mexican settlers, Tohono O'odham and Pima Indians, and probably their prehistoric ancestors as well harvested the fruit to make jelly and wine, and employed ribs from dead saguaros as roofing material. *(Continued on page 26)*

*This saguaro has
sprouted a complex crest.*

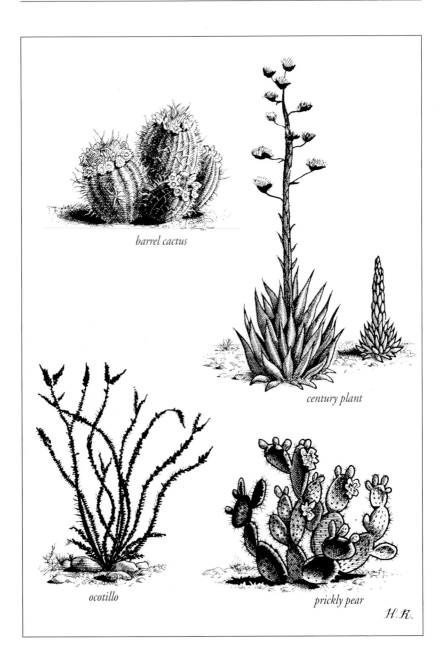

barrel cactus

century plant

ocotillo

prickly pear

H.R.

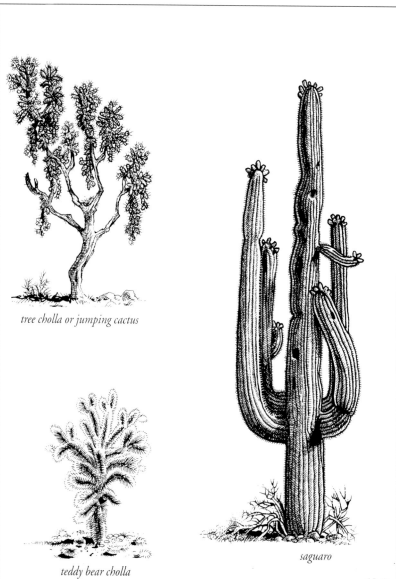

tree cholla or jumping cactus

teddy bear cholla

saguaro

H. K.

FEROCIOUS FLORA

*T*ree, bush, plant and grass—great and small alike—each has its sting for the intruder. You can hardly stoop to pick a desert flower or pull a bunch of small grass without being aware of a prickle on your hand. Nature seems to have provided a whole arsenal of defensive weapons for these poor starved plants of the desert. Not any of the lovely growths of the earth, like the lilies and the daffodils, are so well defended. And she has given them not only armor but a spirit of tenacity and stubbornness wherewith to carry on the struggle. Cut out the purslain and the iron weed from the garden walk, and it springs up again and again, contending for life. Put heat, drouth, and animal attack against the desert shrubs and they fight back like the higher forms of organic life. How typical they are of everything in and about the desert. There is but one word to describe it and that word—fierce—I shall have worn threadbare before I have finished these chapters.

—John C. Van Dyke, *The Desert*, 1901

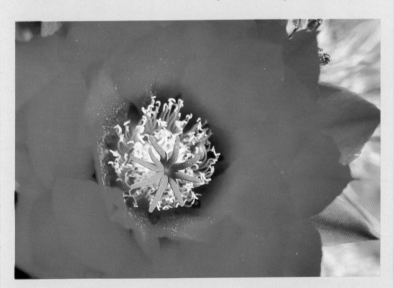

The brilliant scarlet hedgehog blossom is a springtime ornament for the Sonoran Desert.

Saguaro are prized both by cactus bandits and legitimate landscape architects, but century-old individuals like this seldom survive transplanting.

Yet people also abuse the saguaro. As early as 1854, a pioneer explorer, J. R. Bartlett, found arrows sticking into saguaros in the Yuman Indian lands of far west Arizona. In the early 1980s, a Phoenix man fired a shotgun into a saguaro until it toppled, killing him. Sometimes even *good* intentions doom the plants. Mature saguaros, which landscape architects love to use in their designs, usually die when transplanted. The Arizona-Sonora Desert Museum has seen a 95 percent mortality rate among transplanted saguaros 12 or more feet high, and has quit moving them. Landscapers haven't, because they don't connect the transplant with the cactus's demise. A mature saguaro, perfect symbol of both the desert's perseverance and fragility, takes three to five years to die.

Heat and light also shape the character of Arizona's deserts. Most people naturally think of them as excessive, as a dismaying drawback to year-round residence in at least half of Arizona. A few—Abbey was prime among them—welcome the heat because it discourages at least some people from moving here.

Summer comes early to the low desert and holds it in relentless lock for five long months. On average, Phoenix endures 91 days of 100+ readings per year. Buckeye, Gila Bend, and Casa Grande all have been brutalized by 100-degree marks in March. The first 100 usually strikes Phoenix by mid-April; Tucson by early May. (In the latter city, the first 100 of the year is hailed as the day "the ice breaks on the Santa Cruz." This is doubly dry humor; the Santa Cruz is a dry riverbed.) By June, the desert is under siege. June 26, 1990, was especially memorable, a torrid day that toppled more weather records than any other date in modern history. A sampler:

CITY	ELEVATION (in feet)	TEMP: HIGH (F)	TEMP: LOW (F)
Bisbee	5,490	106°	68°
Phoenix	1,092	122°	91°
Sedona	4,240	110°	76°
Safford	2,920	112°	68°
Tucson	2,630	117°	80°
Yuma	141	122°	85°

Note the predawn "low" of 91 for Phoenix. This was a ghastly demonstration of what meteorologists have begun to call the "heat island" effect: the metropolis's immense size is making its summer climate worse. Heat absorbed by asphalt and concrete and roof tiles during the day is radiated at night and trapped by atmospheric inversions. Lows in the 90s are no longer unusual in Phoenix.

Chambers of Commerce struggle to put the best possible spin on these numbers. "But it's a *dry* heat!" is their mantra. True, but it's also a relentless heat. A T-shirt popular around Phoenix depicts a couple of bleached skeletons lounging in patio chairs, taking the sun. One remarks, cheerfully, to the other: "But it's a *dry* heat."

According to the U.S. Geological Survey, Arizona has more "hell" place names than any other state—a total of 55. (Utah places second with 46.) Hell Hole Valley, Hellgate Mountain, Hell's Neck Ridge, no fewer than four Hell Canyons—it is a creative list, but no one who has endured a few desert summers would call it fanciful.

Outside on a 115-degree midsummer day it is difficult to be conscious of any sensation but the heat. It is like a pressure that pushes on every square inch of the body. Even in shade, the face reddens, the torso moistens, the will to do anything productive—except lurch toward the nearest air-conditioned building—vanishes. Tempers seem shorter; police answer more domestic-disturbance calls in the summer. It isn't unlike Alaskan cabin fever; the seasons are simply reversed.

With the heat comes a quality of light unique in North America. Observed Reyner Banham in *Scenes in America Deserta*, "The full sun of the desert—the Mojave in particular—gives a spectral, hurtful light that is a close brother to heat, and strikes equally hard." John C. Van Dyke, a much earlier essayist, felt that with the pain came an incomparable reward: "In any land what is there more glorious than sunlight! Even here in the desert, where it falls fierce and hot as a rain of meteors, it is the one supreme beauty to which all things pay allegiance." Either interpretation is most true in June, when none of Arizona's deserts can hope for rain, or clouds, or even enough humidity to soften the light. The sky is not quite blue; it appears bleached, almost white. Mountain ranges on the horizon lose both dimension and color; they appear as flat, washed-out cardboard cutouts propped against the sky. Even buildings become painful to look at.

But in other months the desert's light is miraculous. In July, August, and early September come the summer storms, romantically if inaccurately termed "monsoons" in Phoenix and Tucson. Even in the mornings, the humidity is higher, diffusing the sun's glaring fury (while rendering evaporative coolers worthless). In the afternoons, platoons of gray, overweight cumulus clouds rumble in from the south. Inside an hour, the sky turns to charcoal and dumps torrents on the desiccated land. Then after maybe 15 minutes, the storm begins to break up and slivers of late-afternoon sunlight scythe through the clouds, selectively highlighting a few acres of mountain, desert or city with golden fire.

In the winter—what passes for winter in the desert—the light is softer still but no less dramatic. Early morning sun will backlight a forest of saguaros in such a way that the light squeezes through their spines, glinting and diffusing on its way, so that each cactus seems to wear a glowing yellow halo. Afternoon light is penetrating and incisive, and if the air is particularly still and dry one can see astounding details in the landscape at preposterous distances. I have stood on a peak near Hannagan Meadow at the eastern edge of the state and traced ridgelines in the Santa Catalina Mountains near Tucson, a straight-line distance of 130 miles —with naked eye.

It is the evening light that is the most spectacular, even startling. Arizona's winter sunsets are clichéd *ad nauseam* in curio and commerce—sweat shirts, bus benches, even automatic teller machines are decked out in painted sunsets—but the real thing, the nightly ballet of light in the western sky, is so unpredictable and varied that nobody grows jaded. We do lose perspective. Former Gov. Bruce Babbitt has told a story about watching a group of tourists one evening as a world-class sunset unfolded. Someone snapped a Polaroid, and all turned their backs on the real sunset to watch the photo of it develop. The anecdote may illustrate a peculiar truth about Arizona's light and landscapes: sometimes the reality is so overwhelming that image is easier to comprehend.

Four deserts, distinctly different in climate, biology and scenery, extend into Arizona. Combined, they make up something between half to two-thirds (scientists quibble about the definition of a "desert") of the state's 113,508 square miles.

■ PAINTED DESERT

The Colorado Plateau, which sprawls north and east of the city of Flagstaff, includes portions of the high Great Basin Desert—its Arizona appendage more commonly called the Painted Desert. It is strange, haunting country, its geology as bizarre as the Sonoran Desert's more abundant biology. The land is scored by jagged canyons and punctuated by heroic sandstone skylines of cliffs, mesas, buttes, and spires up to a thousand feet high. The visitor experiences a palpable,

Agatized sections of tree trunks are scattered around Petrified Forest National Park in the Painted Desert.

sometimes uncomfortable sensation of insignificance out here; the scale of everything seems too gigantic to comprehend.

Most people assume that water, over a few hundred million years, carved spectacles such as Canyon de Chelly, while wind-whipped sand abraded the buttes of Monument Valley. The truth is a little more disquieting, particularly if one is standing on the rim of a canyon or at the base of a butte. Rivers started the erosion process, and runoff abetted it, but natural weaknesses in the rock formations also allowed pieces to crumble and fall away. Monument Valley, which used to be a solid plateau of sandstone roughly as high as the tops of the "monuments" today, literally is crumbling away in huge splinters and sheets. The reassuring news is that geologic time, like the monuments themselves, is so vast as to be almost irrelevant to the puny humans standing around, gaping in awe.

For the most part, the Painted Desert curves along the lower reaches of the Navajo Reservation. Its rounded, soft-looking formations are visible from US 89 as you drive south from Lake Powell; and looking north from I-40 as you drive east from Holbrook. Its eroding layers of clay, siltstone, and sandstone are represented in an array of subtle colors ranging from off-white to russet to several shades of gray.

MONUMENT VALLEY

A Navajo tribal park that straddles the Arizona-Utah border near the town of Kayenta, Monument Valley is a dramatic landscape of towering sandstone monoliths and buttes. Over time, each formation has been carved by wind and rain into its own unique shape. Though the dozens of Westerns filmed here since the 1930s given the impression that such formations are ubiquitous throughout the West, that is hardly the case. Monument Valley is a quirk of nature that looks best in the golden light of early morning or late afternoon.

Visitors usually take the 17-mile unpaved loop drive through the park, but some of the valley's most fascinating and eerie sandstone totems lie well away from the road. The Navajo strictly forbid hiking, rock climbing, and off-road driving. Guided tours with more intimate photo opportunities may be booked at the visitor center. However, Valley of the Gods, a similar cluster of enormous spires and buttes only 30 miles to the north, can be visited without restrictions. Consult a Utah map for directions. *Take US 163, 22 miles north from Kayenta, turn right at the junction and follow signs five miles to the visitor center; (520) 871-7371 or (801) 727-3287.*

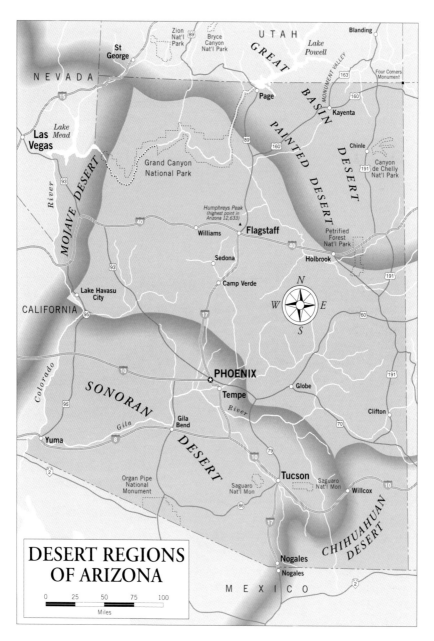

DESERT REGIONS
OF ARIZONA

0   25   50   75   100

Miles

(following pages) Rainbow over the Mitten and Merrick Buttes in Monument Valley. (Kerrick James)

PETRIFIED FOREST NATIONAL PARK

Conveniently, the best stopping place to view the Painted Desert is Petrified Forest National Park, a dry, barren landscape strewn with something rare in nature: prehistoric petrified logs. A spectacular 27-mile drive leads through a garden of mineralized logs and Anasazi petroglyphs. Eight overlooks at the park's northern end offer the best Painted Desert vistas, whereas the most impressive clusters of petrified wood lie in the park's southern section. Backcountry hiking is permitted here, but anyone leaving the road should pack a plentiful supply of water, even in winter. *North entrance, Painted Desert Visitor Center: take I-40 to exit 311, 30 miles east of Holbrook. South entrance, Rainbow Forest Museum: take US 180, 19 miles southeast from Holbrook; (520) 524-6228.*

■ MOJAVE DESERT

The Mojave, at Arizona's northwestern edge, is Arizona's driest desert. Only 4.52 inches of rain falls in an average year at Lake Havasu (a man-made lake, of course). This skimpy precipitation does not nourish much plant life, but what manages to thrive is fiercely tenacious. The ubiquitous creosote bush, a spindly, scruffy shrub, is believed to live as long as 11,000 years, making it the oldest living thing on earth. The Joshua tree, which may see 500 years, is as distinctive a signature plant to the Mojave as the saguaro to the Sonoran. A member of the yucca genus, it grows as high as 30 feet, sending out a grotesque tangle of arms that terminate in fists spiked with green daggers.

From its jagged peaks to its coarse valleys, the Mojave seems the harshest of Arizona's deserts. Sculpted daily by the wind and baked hard by the sun, the land's architecture seems to hold itself up as a challenge to human survival. The Mojave is most often seen by travelers on US 93 between Wickenburg and Las Vegas. Along the way are a Joshua tree forest, miles of creosote, and mountains that look as friendly as saw blades.

■ SONORAN DESERT

The Sonoran is the desert of superlatives. It is more colorful, more varied, more lovely, more crowded, more dangerous, and more threatened than any of the others. More species of birds, some 300, make their homes in the Sonoran Desert than in any other arid region on the continent. More rain falls in the Sonoran Desert than any other in North America; there literally are forests—called bosques—

THE HORRIBLE "ESCORPION"

Strangest of all was the uncouth, horrible "escorpion," or "Gila monster," which here found its favorite habitat and attained its greatest dimensions. We used to have them not less than three feet long, black, venomous, and deadly, if half the stories told were true. The Mexicans time and time again asserted that the escorpion would kill chickens, and that it would eject a poisonous venom upon them, but, in my own experience, I have to say that the old hen which we tied in front of one for a whole day was not molested, and that no harm of any sort came to her beyond being scared out of a year's growth. Scientists were wont to ridicule the idea of the Gila monster being venomous, upon what ground I do not now remember, beyond the fact that it was a lizard, and all lizards were harmless. But I believe it is now well established that the monster is not to be handled with impunity.

—John G. Bourke, *On the Border with Crook,* 1892

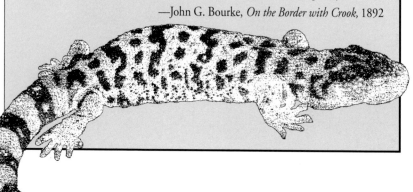

(following pages) The jumping cholla so luxuriates with needles that Sonoran Desert dwellers like to claim it "jumps" to attack unwary passers-by. It doesn't.

of mesquite in this desert. It is a noisy desert, and not just because of the intrusions of humans and our mechanized contraptions. Cactus wrens screech at each other in an appalling tenor rasp, cicadas lay down an omnidirectional drone, coyotes yelp, crickets tick, the ubiquitous Western whiptail lizards swish from bush to bush, rattlers helpfully advise stray humans to buzz off. Except in the midday summer sun, when most of these creatures are sensibly taking a snooze, it is hard to feel alone in the Sonoran Desert. And it is becoming harder all the time. In large part because of its beauty and lushness, more Arizonans live in the Sonoran Desert than in any other geographic region of the state: more than three-fourths of our total 4.5 million people. This crush of bodies, with the pressures they impose on the desert's modest resources, is the state's most ominous problem.

The Sonoran is celebrated, studied, and preserved in several parks and museums in central and southern Arizona. In summer, early-morning visits are recommended.

Desert Botanical Garden, Phoenix
A lovely botanical garden featuring 10,000 desert plants from the Sonoran and other deserts. Its exhibits explain historic uses of plants in the Sonoran Desert, and a demonstration garden struggles (without apparent success) to convince Phoenicians that water-saving desert landscaping is an idea whose time is here. *1201 N. Galvin Parkway; (602) 941-1225.*

Arizona-Sonora Desert Museum, Tucson
This museum regularly appears on lists of the world's ten best zoos. Its world is the animals, plants, and natural history of the Sonoran Desert, but its exhibits also encompass this desert's forested mountains, rivers and seacoast on the Gulf of California. The full range of Sonoran Desert animals is on display here, from the one-tenth-ounce calliope hummingbird to the black bear. Docents work the grounds, continually giving demonstrations on topics such as the differences between the jaws of herbivores and carnivores. Allow three hours for a complete visit. *Take Speedway Boulevard west across Gates Pass to Kinney Road. The museum is at 2021 N. Kinney in Tucson Mountain Park; (520) 883-2702.*

Saguaro National Park, Tucson

The desert's saguaro forests can be explored at close range at Saguaro National Park, which is split into two units: one is 15 miles west of Tucson, while the other lies on the city's eastern edge in the foothills of the Rincon Mountains. The west unit has a vastly denser population of saguaros and is the more interesting place to visit. The east park offers a paved eight-mile loop road popular with runners and cyclists. *For directions and information call (520) 733-5100.*

Boyce Thompson Southwestern Arboretum, Southeastern Arizona

This arboretum superficially resembles the Arizona–Sonora Desert Museum, but there is an important difference: grown on its thousand acres are cacti from all around the world. Sixteen inches of rain annually turn this into one of the most extravagantly lush areas of the Sonoran Desert. *55 miles east of Phoenix on US 60, three miles west of the mining town of Superior; (520) 689-2811.*

Organ Pipe Cactus National Monument, Southwestern Arizona

Though common in northern Mexico, the organ pipe cactus occurs naturally in only one place in the United States: at Organ Pipe National Monument, a 516-square-mile preserve on the Mexican border. The cactus is a spectacle sprouting a cluster of huge vertical arms (up to 12 feet) that resemble—vaguely, at least—the pipes of an organ. Quitobaquito Spring, a historic natural watering hole, attracts more than 260 species of birds. *The monument headquarters is just off Route 85, 22 miles south of Why; (520) 387-6849.*

■ CHIHUAHUAN DESERT

The Chihuahuan is Arizona's overlooked desert. Many travelers head east out of Tucson on Interstate 10, not even noticing the gradual change that marks the transition from the Sonoran into the Chihuahuan Desert, which will remain their host across the lower edge of New Mexico and on into the high, barren badlands of West Texas. Most of the Chihuahuan Desert lies in the Mexican state of Chihuahua; only its northwestern sliver edges into Arizona.

About 50 miles east of Tucson, the Interstate traveler has climbed some 1,500

feet, probably without realizing it. The saguaro have given way to yucca, the shrub cover to rolling hills of straw-colored grass. This edge of the Chihuahuan Desert receives only eight to 10 inches of rain a year, which is less than Tucson gets, but because it is higher, it is also cooler, and that makes the rain more efficient. Hence the grass.

Two remarkable features mark the edge of the Chihuahuan Desert: **Texas Canyon,** a mountain range literally made of boulders, and the **Willcox Playa,** visible from I-10 just southwest of Willcox. The playa looks like a vast lake shimmering in the distance, but it is a permanent mirage, a cruel optical joke surrealistically imposed on a 50-square-mile basin that *used* to be a lake. Now it is one of the strangest places in Arizona, a parched, table-flat wasteland where absolutely nothing grows from one horizon to another, as far as the eye can see. A writer for *The Arizona Daily Star* once described it like this: "To walk on the playa is to travel through another dimension. At times, its vast emptiness seems like a gateway to the Twilight Zone." Yet even this most desolate region of the desert supports life. Eggs of three species of miniature shrimp lie dormant below the lake bed for as long as 30 years, and then after an extravagant summer rain, when water puddles into a soupy mud on the playa, the crustaceans hatch. If the water holds out they may last two weeks, which is just long enough to mate, deposit more eggs and then die—having miraculously assured, a shrimp's eon later, the eventual appearance of their offspring.

Life forms indigenous to the Chihuahuan Desert are easier to find at Chiricahua National Monument. Though best known for its acres of magnificent column-shaped rock formations, it also is home to many plants and animals uncommon north of the Mexican border. Birders flock to the park to spot rare Mexican chicadees, sulfur-bellied flycatchers, and coppery tailed trogons. Also from the south of the border are mammals such as the Apache fox squirrel, and trees such as the Chihuahua pine and the Apache pine. *The park entrance is 120 miles east of Tucson and 36 miles southeast of Willcox off Route 186. Drive eight-mile Bonita Canyon Drive to the crest of the Chiricahua Mountains and spend some time on the more than 17 miles of hiking trails; (520) 824-3560. (Also see page 57.)*

(previous pages) Montezuma Canyon in the Coronado National Monument overlooks classic Chihuahuan Desert scenery. (Kerrick James)

DESERT ETIQUETTE

 few tips on desert etiquette:

1. Carry a cooking stove, if you must cook. Do not burn desert wood, which is rare and beautiful and required ages for its creation (an ironwood tree lives for over 1,000 years and juniper almost as long).

2. If you must, out of need, build a fire, then for God's sake allow it to burn itself out before you leave—do not bury it, as Boy Scouts and Campfire Girls do, under a heap of mud or sand. Scatter the ashes; replace any rocks you may have used in constructing a fireplace; do all you can to obliterate the evidence that you camped here. (The Search & Rescue Team may be looking for you.)

3. Do not bury garbage—the wildlife will only dig it up again. Burn what will burn and pack out the rest. The same goes for toilet paper: Don't bury it, burn it.

4. Do not bathe in desert pools, natural tanks, tinajas, potholes. Drink what water you need, take what you need, and leave the rest for the next hiker and, more importantly, for the bees, birds, and animals—bighorn sheep, coyotes, lions, foxes, badgers, deer, wild pigs, wild horses—whose lives depend on that water.

5. Always remove and destroy survey stakes, flagging, advertising signboards, mining claim markers, animal traps, poisoned bait, seismic exploration geophones, and other such artifacts of industrialism. The men who put those things there are up to no good and it is our duty to confound them. Keep America beautiful. Grow a Beard. Take a Bath. Burn a Billboard.

—Edward Abbey, *The Journey Home:
Some Words in Defense of the American West,* 1977

M O U N T A I N S

It is the summer of 1927, a decade before even rudimentary evaporative air conditioning will begin to become common in Tucson. Editors of *The Arizona Daily Star* and the rival *Tucson Daily Citizen* simmer in their downtown offices, heckling each other and churning out dueling editorials. The issue: how to move Tucson to the cool top of 9,157-foot Mt. Lemmon for the five long months of summer.

The forward-looking *Star* predicts that by the 1940s, highways and automobiles will be obsolete. It proposes creating a municipal "air line" and shaving the mountaintop for an airstrip.

> An air line would bring the cooling breezes and tall pines to within 30 minutes of Congress Street. Summer vacationers could breakfast on top of the range, fly to Tucson for a shopping trip, and be back in the mountains in time for lunch. The poor tired businessman could live at home beneath the pines and be at his office or store for the full eight- or ten-hour shift.

The *Citizen* ridicules the *Star's* aeronautical reverie and presses for a highway up the mountain. "Experts" parade daily across the front page, predicting economic calamity unless the road is built. The *Citizen* even recruits the local Roman Catholic bishop for its cause, publishing a pro-highway interview with him under the ominous headline:

> TUCSON DOOMED TO BE 8 MONTH TOWN
> UNLESS MOUNTAIN ROAD BUILT

But cost-conscious voters balk, rebuffing $500,000 bond issues in 1928 and again in 1930. The *Citizen's* publisher, Gen. Frank H. Hitchcock, won't give up. In 1933 he hears that the director of the federal Bureau of Prisons wants to experiment with employing prisoners on highway construction to help "rehabilitate" them. A flurry of meetings ensues, and work begins on the highway within three months.

The Mt. Lemmon Highway turns out to be a more daunting project than anyone imagines. By the time the 25-mile road punches into the cool Ponderosa pine country, it has taken 18 years, 8,003 federal prisoners, and—even with all that free labor—nearly $1 million. But the result is a road that, mile for mile, is arguably Arizona's most scenic—and one that remains controversial even today.

■ An Archipelago of Rocks

The popular image of Arizona is that of a parched, wrinkled landscape of hostile desert plants set off by a distant backdrop of cardboard-cutout mountains propped against the sky. The nature of those mountains, in this image, remains something elusive and mysterious. This is as it always has been. In the theology of many of Arizona's Native Americans, the spirits dwell in the mountains.

In less mystical terms, the mountains are the reason for Arizona's great environmental diversity. Biologists call them "sky islands," a fitting metaphor. The environment at the summit of a 10,000-foot Arizona mountain is as radically different from that of the desert floor 7,000 feet below as that of Hawaii from the water around it. Early boosters of the Mt. Lemmon Highway liked to tout it as being the equivalent of driving from Mexico to Canada in an hour.

On an average Arizona mountain, the temperature falls three to four degrees F, while precipitation increases four to five inches for every 1,000-foot gain in elevation. These profound variations create dramatically evolving laminations of biotic communities on the mountains. As many as six of these distinct life zones occupy the sky islands of southern and central Arizona. Biologists sometimes disagree on the names and boundaries of these zones, but here is an attempt to sort them out:

Desert Shrub, 2,000-3,500 feet, essentially an extension of the plant and animal communities of the desert floor rising into the mountain foothills. Generous rainfall and runoff from higher elevations, however, produce more lush growth than in the flat basins. Forests of saguaro, mesquite and palo verde dominate, and in years of above-average winter precipitation, these elevations wear spring carpets of wild poppies, mustard flowers and other colorful blooms.

Chaparral, 3,500-6,000 feet. This is a temperate zone dominated by tall grasses, tough-leafed evergreen shrubs and one remarkably unfriendly succulent, the self-descriptive shindagger agave. The manzanita is its signature plant, a shrublike tree that grows only five or six feet high and sports a distinctive and lovely glossy, cherry-red bark.

Oak woodland, 4,500-6,000 feet. The dominant species is Emory oak with some Arizona oak and Mexican oak—and still the occasional yucca and prickly pear cactus—interspersed. Not yet dense enough to be considered forest, the trees are fairly sparse except in riparian habitats.

Piñon-juniper woodland, 5,000-7,000 feet. Substantial snow falls at these elevations even in the southernmost ranges. The piñon, or Mexican pine, is a tree too

NATURAL ATTRACTIONS

If you have limited time to tour Arizona, which of its more spectacular natural wonders should you see? My indispensable six, traveling (roughly) north to south:

Monument Valley, straddling the Utah–Arizona border and resplendent with red-gold sandstone towers, has been carved by the forces of nature for millions of years. You can get a good overview of the weathered natural skyscrapers by following the 17-mile loop road into the valley. Off-road trips are led by Navajo guides *(see pages 30 and 117).*

The Grand Canyon is one of the wonders of the natural world—277 miles long, four to 10 miles wide and 5,000 to 6,000 feet deep. Your eyes can get lost in the canyon's rich colors and varied textures. There are many ways to enjoy a visit here. You can simply sit atop the rim and watch as the shadows and colors in the canyon change throughout the day. You can walk the rim trails or hike from rim to river and back. Or sign up for a week-long white water rafting adventure on the canyon's Colorado River *(see pages 60-72).*

Canyon de Chelly, quieter and more intimate than the Grand Canyon, is almost as beautiful, with its vermillion cliffs, ancient Anasazi ruins, and small Navajo farms. Access is limited by the Navajo people, but you may drive its rim, walk down to one Anasazi ruin, or hire a Navajo guide to take you inside *(see pages 72-74).*

The Petrified Forest is a rarity in nature—clusters of mineralized wood believed to be more than 220 million years old, and scattered in the wild and beautiful landscape of the multi-hued Painted Desert. A spectacular 27-mile drive passes wood, desert, and Anasazi petroglyphs *(see page 34).*

Oak Creek Canyon is a juxtaposition of intense colors—vibrant reddish-pink rocks, deep green oaks and conifers, and bright blue sky. Just north of Sedona in central Arizona, it has dozens of hiking trails and five campgrounds *(see page 75).*

Chiricahua National Monument in southeast Arizona is rich in both history and scenery. The ancestral hideout of the Chiricahua Apaches, it is known for its acres of column-shaped rock formations and its unusual desert plants and animals *(see page 57).*

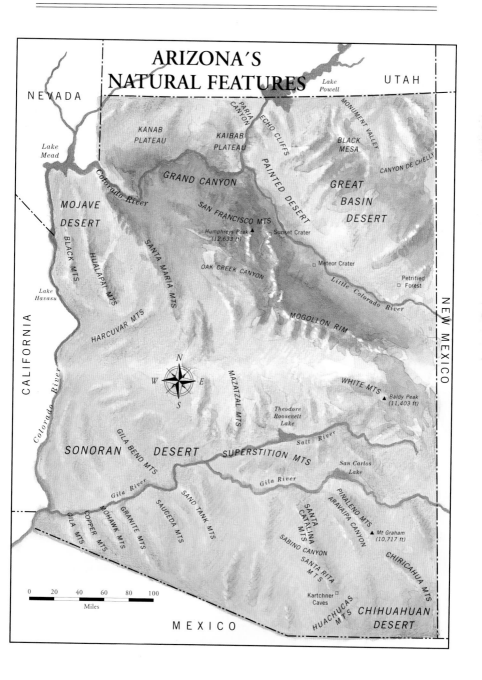

diminutive and gnarled to be of interest to the timber industry, but its abundant nuts provide food for large communities of birds. The Clark's nutcracker, a jay that has evolved a special nut pouch under its tongue, has been found flying with as many as 95 piñon nuts at a time.

Ponderosa pine forest, 7,000-9000 feet. These are authentic forests, dominated by the gigantic ponderosa. Mature trees probe up to 125 feet into the sky, fighting for sunlight, and the winners live 200 to 400 years. The world's largest stand of ponderosas is in northern Arizona, girdling the San Francisco Mountains, but the forests are profuse enough in the desert sky islands to the south that logging operations have been carried out since the 1880s.

Canadian life zone, 7,500-10,000 feet. The common name of this zone is not at all misleading; its dark, mossy forests of Douglas fir, white fir and quaking aspen—and its abundant black bears—closely mimic the biology of Canada's forests 2,000 miles to the north.

The higher one ascends through these life zones, the more compelling the "island" analogy becomes. A squirrel happily adapted to crunching nuts at 9,000 feet will spend its entire life on that one mountain, as will its extended family. Even if something were to happen on that mountain that threatened its survival (such as a forest fire), it would have no options; it could not survive a 50-mile trek through open desert to another "island."

This is true of most other mountain-dwelling creatures, although bears, provoked by the intervention of *Homo sapiens,* have tried it, and periodically the Arizona Game & Fish Department will try moving a "problem bear" from one mountain to another. The extradited bear, guided by an amazing homing instinct, may strike out for his old home, crossing deserts, highways and suburban back yards en route. One such bear was discovered in a tree in a Tucson yard a few years ago; it had been trying to return to the Huachuca Mountains from the Santa Catalinas—a trek of 80 miles.

For many plants and animals, confinement to one mountain island means that the species inbreeds. As long as the pool of available mates is large, this by no means spells trouble for it. Over time, however, it may well become a unique subspecies, different in important characteristics from its relatives on the next mountain over. If the gene pool is too small, however, the animal will edge toward extinction: the Mexican gray wolf and the grizzly bear both disappeared from Arizona's mountains in this century (although a controversial reintroduction of the

The trail from Lockett Meadow is a favorite place to view aspens in the San Francisco Peaks.
(Kerrick James)

gray wolf got underway in eastern Arizona in early 1997). As more and more human beings cluster around and increasingly settle in the Arizona mountains, the problem of saving these island environments for their original inhabitants is producing a swarm of controversies.

■ HUMANS AND MOUNTAINS

"The spirit of the mountain is a woman, and she is troubled," Berniece Falling Leaves explained.

Black Mountain is a strange knob of brown granite and black schist that rises abruptly out of the desert 35 miles northeast of downtown Phoenix. Two small communities, eccentric Cave Creek and affluent Carefree, curl around it and press into it. Mansions worth as much as $3 million cling to its sides. According to Berniece Falling Leaves, a half-Sioux mystic/metaphysicist, the spirit of the mountains is troubled: all those houses are unwelcome.

To prove her point, she offers a story: one day some time ago, when development around the mountain was just beginning to accelerate, Falling Leaves and a Canadian medicine man named Buffalo Dreamer invited some sympathetic believers to a ceremonial dance in honor of the mountain's spirit. It was a mild, sunny day, she recalls, without a cloud anywhere in the sky. Suddenly, as the dance drew to a close, an enormous shudder of thunder erupted in the *blue sky* over Black Mountain.

"Everyone's eyes were the size of manhole covers," claims Falling Leaves. "But we knew our energy had been transferred to the spirit of the mountain."

The concept of mountain spirits is an ancient one in Arizona. Many Native American cultures regard mountains as sacred. Baboquivari Peak, 60 miles southwest of Tucson, is one: I'itoi, the protective Elder Brother of the Tohono O'odham people, is said to live there. For a desert people, this is an elegantly logical theology. Rainfall was and is their most vital resource, and in the desert, thunderstorms almost always begin over the mountains.

Likewise in modern Anglo culture, mysteries tend to reside in the mountains. By far the most durable is that of the Lost Dutchman mine in the Superstition Mountains 40 miles east of Phoenix.

The legend of the Lost Dutchman dates from the 1870s, when two German-born prospectors named Jacob Waltz and Jacob Weiser supposedly made a sensational strike somewhere deep in the craggy Superstitions. Every time they showed up in Florence, the little desert town to the south, they paid for their supplies from pouches bulging with gold nuggets—or so the story goes. Somehow, Weiser met with an untimely demise. One account suggests that Waltz did it; another, suspiciously colorful, reports him crawling out of the mountains stuck full of Apache arrows and dying in a doctor's office. Waltz continued mining, eventually retired to Phoenix, and, shortly before he died, dictated some enigmatic directions to the mine to a bakery woman who had become his close friend. That was in 1891, and people have been combing the Superstitions in search of the Lost Dutchman for an entire century since.

Some of the fortune hunters are kooks, some are casual hobbyists, some are serious and indefatigable. Among the latter is Bob Corbin, once the state's attorney general, who has been systematically searching for the mine since 1957. The Superstitions, however, seem determined to preserve their secret. A curiously large number of people have died in these mountains. Some have been weekend hikers and climbers who simply fell to their deaths, but many others were on the trail of the Lost Dutchman when they were mysteriously shot or just disappeared. One ghostly corollary to the mine legend says that Waltz is doing it. More likely—in fact, this has been documented—at least some of the murders have been committed by prospectors who feared that a rival would find the mine first. For whatever reason, according to *Arizona Highways*, at least 36 people are known to have perished in the Superstitions since Jacob Waltz departed with his terrible and compelling mystery.

In the 1970s and 1980s, a movement to protect Arizona's mountains gained considerable public support. Pima County and the city of Scottsdale passed the state's first hillside ordinances to halt the steady creep of subdivisions up the suburban mountain slopes. Rep. Morris K. Udall, once dean of Arizona's congressional delegation, managed to jam 3,750 square miles of pristine Arizona land, much of it mountainous, into a 1990 wilderness bill. Udall, who served 15 terms in Congress, once said that wilderness protection for his home state was one of the achievements of which he was most proud.

In 1980, the University of Arizona first approached the U.S. Forest Service about leasing a few acres on top of 10,717-foot Mt. Graham (near Safford) for a cluster of new observatories. When environmental studies commenced, scientists found a unique rodent inhabiting the site—the Mt. Graham red squirrel, one of those subspecies that had been evolving in isolation for an estimated 10,000 years.

A 15-year-long string of studies ensued, accompanied by lawsuits and demonstrations. By 1994, the university and environmentalists had become bitter enemies, and construction of the observatories began. The interminable battle illustrated the depth of the passions that now swirl around Arizona's mountains.

There is another interesting example. *Frog Mountain Blues*, a 1987 book by environmentalist Charles Bowden, argued from beginning to end to close that most spectacular of Arizona roads, the Mt. Lemmon Highway.

Politically, it is unlikely the highway ever will be closed. It has many defenders and caretakers, and all it takes is a clear summer day, a good friend, a picnic basket and a convertible with the top peeled back to convince most of us that the mountain may be asked, gently, to please suffer this one intrusion. However, it is even more unlikely that were this highway just being proposed today that it would ever be built. The mountain would remain wild, and would almost surely be the better for it.

■ MOUNTAINS OF NORTHERN ARIZONA

SAN FRANCISCO PEAKS

Just north of Flagstaff Arizona's highest mountain range reaches 12,643 feet at the summit of Humphreys Peak. The San Francisco Peaks are "stratovolcanoes," composed of alternating layers of lava and ash. During the summer the lower reaches of these peaks, are an Eden of sunny meadows and shady forests of pine and quaking aspen. The challenging summit trail up Humphreys Peak is well maintained and affords tremendous vistas of northern Arizona. (Lightning is a constant hazard in July and August.) During the winter, Nordic and downhill skiers enjoy **Arizona Snowbowl Ski Resort,** which has four chairlifts and 32 trails slicing down the peaks. *Take US 180 north of Flagstaff to the Snowbowl turnoff on the right. Drive another seven miles on the paved road to the ski area and the trailhead to Humphreys Peak. Snowbowl; (520) 779-4577.*

Snow on San Francisco Peaks north of Flagstaff. (Peter Bloomer)

SUNSET CRATER

More than 400 Arizona mountains are the remnants of volcanic activity. The most recent known volcanic eruption in Arizona was in the winter of 1064-65, when a volcano 10 miles north of present-day Flagstaff blanketed 120 square miles of countryside with lava, cinders, and ash. The most prominent memento of that drama is Sunset Crater, a 1,000-foot-high cinder cone that is now a national monument. Trails lead among the lava flows, but not up the cone,. The adjacent campground is excellent. *Take US Highway 89, 15 miles north of Flagstaff; (520) 526-0502.*

HUALAPAI MOUNTAIN PARK

Located 14 miles southeast of Kingman, lush Hualapai Mountain Park rises unexpectedly out of northwestern Arizona's desolate Mojave Desert landscape. Most people driving through Kingman enroute to Las Vegas or Laughlin, Nevada, can't even imagine that an inviting alpine oasis could exist in such country. It's too bad, because this county park has thick forests, stellar views, hiking trails, picnic areas, rustic cabins—and no crowds. *Take Hualapai Mountain Road southeast out of Kingman until you reach the park. For information call Hualapai Ranger Station at (520) 757-3859.*

■ MOUNTAINS OF CENTRAL ARIZONA

MOGOLLON RIM

The most sublime natural attraction running northwest of the White Mountains is the Mogollon Rim, a weird and spellbinding escarpment that plunges 2,000 feet in one vertical slash from the undulating mountain country to the Tonto Basin. Spectacular and vertiginous views are best from the Rim Drive (Forest Road 300), a good but lonely gravel road closely paralleling the rim for 43 miles. *Take Route 260 east from Payson 30 miles to the Woods Canyon Lake turnoff. Turn left and follow paved lake road a few miles to unpaved Rim Drive. Payson Ranger Station; (520) 474-7900.*

WHITE MOUNTAINS

The White Mountains, 120 miles northeast of Phoenix, comprise Arizona's best-known and most intensively developed mountain vacationland. Recreation is the strong suit in these mountains, not solitude.

Twenty-five lakes are scattered around the mountains. Most are small, but are generously stocked with fish, rainbow and brown trout being most common. Cross-country skiing and snowmobiling are everywhere. Downhill skiers can choose from 65 trails laced across three mountains at the Sunrise Park Resort, owned and operated by the White Mountain Apache Tribe; *(520) 735-7600.*

The incorporated community of Pinetop-Lakeside offers small theater, guided full-moon ski tours, and frequent golf tournaments; the nearby town of Show Low has such recreational oddities as a summer Grand Prix for bathtubs on wheels.

APACHE-SITGREAVES NATIONAL FOREST

Arizona's least-known high-country scenery lies in the Apache-Sitgreaves Forest, whose peaks range up to 10,995-foot Escudilla Mountain. For an introduction, take US Route 191 from Clifton to Alpine, a federally designated Scenic Byway. There is not one town along the winding 95-mile route, but wildlife is abundant: deer, elk, wild turkeys, mountain lions, black bears. *(520) 333-4301.*

SUPERSTITION WILDERNESS

The 235-square-mile Superstition Wilderness is Phoenix's nearest great, wild mountain area. A jagged, forbidding range, the Superstitions can be admired from the base at Lost Dutchman State Park or attacked on trails. The Superstitions are not a remarkably high range; the tallest peak is Mound Mountain at 6,266 feet. This is, however, a truly intimidating range; after scouring it for the Lost Dutchman for more than 30 years Arizona's one-time attorney general Bob Corbin confessed to the *Arizona Daily Star* that he had vast canyons left to search. "You'd need ropes to get into some of these areas," Corbin said. "The place we're messing with now, I can't get a horse within half a mile of it." *From Phoenix take the Superstition Freeway (US 360) east to the Apache Trail (AZ 88) in Apache Junction. For a day's adventure looping around the Superstitions, take AZ 88, 75 miles from Apache Junction to Globe, and then follow US 60 west back to Phoenix.*

■ Mountains of Southern Arizona

PICACHO PEAK

Picacho Peak, located between Phoenix and Tucson, masquerades very effectively as a volcanic cone, but it actually is the eroded remains of other lava flows. The precipitous climb up Tunter Trail to the summit, a 1,500 foot elevation gain, erodes the remains of many hikers' courage. The view, however, is spectacular. *Off I-10 at exit 219, 74 miles southeast of Phoenix; 46 miles northwest of Tucson. Picacho Peak State Park; (520) 466-3183.*

SANTA CATALINA MOUNTAINS

The Santa Catalinas on Tucson's north edge are one of the few major Arizona ranges to be probed by a paved road, the Mt. Lemmon Highway. Picnic grounds, campgrounds and awesome geologic spectacles occur every couple of miles along the two-lane road, which climbs 5,293 feet in 25 miles. At the end is Ski Valley,

Cochise stronghold in the Dragoon Mountains. (Kerrick James)

the southernmost developed ski area in the U.S., and Summerhaven, a community with a few unpretentious inns and boutiques. On holiday weekends in summer, the Mt. Lemmon Highway is best avoided. *(See page 75 for Sabino and Romero canyons in the Santa Catalinas.)*

KITT PEAK

A road also curls to the summit of 6,882-foot Kitt Peak 55 miles southwest of Tucson. This is the nexus of astronomical research in Arizona, with more than a dozen telescopes clustered on the mountaintop. There is a visitor center and small museum open daily (free) with guided tours of the observatories given on weekends and holidays. *Kitt Peak National Observatory. Take AZ 86, 56 miles west of Tucson; turn south on AZ 386; (520) 318-8726.*

CHIRICAHUA MOUNTAINS

The Chiricahua Mountains in Arizona's southeastern corner are rich both in history and scenery. These were the ancestral homelands of the Chiricahua Apaches, and when their leader, Cochise, negotiated peace with the U.S. Army in 1872, he was promised the mountain range as a reservation. Cochise died two years later, and in 1875 the promise evaporated and his people were herded north to the San Carlos Reservation. In 1924, President Calvin Coolidge designated the most spectacular part of the range as a national monument.

A graded road, Bonita Canyon Drive, crosses over the north end of the Chiricahuas, but the best way to appreciate them is on foot. There are more than 111 miles of developed trails in the Chiricahua Wilderness, and maps are available in the monument visitor center. The most ambitious can take the Morse Canyon Trail to 9,357-foot Monte Vista Peak and 9,795-foot Chiricahua Peak. One of the most interesting features in the Chiricahuas is erosion-sculpted volcanic rocks bearing names such as "Duck on a Rock." Another is black bears, which, thanks to the Chiricahuas' protected status, thrive in this range. There are bears on most of Arizona's high mountains, but in the Chiricahuas there is a mob of them. *Chiricahua National Monument. Take AZ 186, 37 miles southwest of Willcox; (520) 824-3560.*

KARTCHNER CAVERNS

For most of their adult lives, Randy Tufts and Gary Tenen secretly have cared for a baby—a helpless creature more than two miles long and Lord knows how many millions of years old. A *baby*? Yes: the metaphor surfaces again and again in any conversation with Tufts and Tenen, who discovered Arizona's largest known cave near Benson in 1974 and didn't tell anyone until 1988. "The cave is defenseless," explains Tufts. "It can't speak for itself. It can't make decisions for itself. It's like a child that's forever two years old. It has to have people who will love it, who will protect it, who will argue on its behalf."

Balanced against the straining engines of full-throttle development in Arizona are people such as Tufts and Tenen, people whose dreams are not to transmute the land's resources into personal wealth, but to preserve those resources for future generations. These people are no longer rare, but the state's unexploited treasures are.

Kartchner Caverns will be one of Arizona's most spectacular attractions when it opens as a state park in 1998. One of its rooms could swallow a football field. There are calcium carbonate drapes that look like thin-sliced bacon or billowing waves of translucent rice noodles. Some stalactites are several feet long and yet thin as a pencil. Tufts believes it is the most pristine wet cave in the country. And the way he and his friend have worked to keep it that way is as unusual as the cave itself.

The two businessmen have been avid cavers most of their lives. "When I was a freshman at the University of Arizona," recalls Tufts, "my idea of a good time was going to the library on Saturday afternoons and scanning dissertations about Arizona geology for mentions of limestone. Then I'd go out with a topo map to areas that seemed like good prospects for caves to see if I could find anything."

One day in 1974, the two were out on one of these prospecting forays when they discovered an intriguing opening. They tossed in a rock, checking for rattlesnakes, then slithered in.

"Imagine a passage about 10 by 24 inches, surrounded by boulders that weren't quite nested together," Tenen says. "Our legs were out at one angle and our bodies at another, and we squirmed about 20 feet while the boulders wobbled around us. I guess there's a period in your life when you're young enough that you have no fear."

This rocky passage opened onto a succession of small, dry rooms, typical of Arizona caves. Then they came to another crawlway, and at its end was a small hole. Moist air was squirting through it. They chiseled at the hole for two hours until they could scrape through. Then, as Tenen recalls, "with every step we took, the fantasy unfolded. The dream of every caver was coming through. The third room was better than the first two, and it was wet."

They explored 500 feet of the cave that day, so enraptured that they were ignoring caving's prime rule. "Suddenly we realized that nobody knew where we were," says Tenen. "In an unexplored cave you can get lost, or you can step on a floor that's nothing but a crust with a pit below it . . . ."

They systematically explored the cave over the next six months, never finding any sign that other humans had preceded them. They corked the entrance with a removable concrete plug to conceal it. They traced the land ownership to the J. A. Kartchner family of nearby St. David, then quietly investigated the Kartchners. They feared two things for the cave. One, that its owners might turn it into a tourist trap, slicing stalactites into souvenir ashtrays. Or two, that news of its existence might seep out, and people would start "exploring" it without regulation. A cave not far away is full of trash, and visitors such as "FRANKIE" and "DANNY" have autographed its walls. But the Kartchners, an extended family of Mormon farmers, seemed like people who could be trusted. When Tufts and Tenen finally approached them and took them on a tour of the unsuspected cave on their own property, the family immediately saw themselves as trustees of an environmental treasure.

Tufts and Tenen prepared a detailed proposal for the Kartchners to operate the cave as a private park. The family considered it for two years and finally decided they didn't have the resources. Then the discoverers wrote a plan to move the cave into state hands. In 1988, the Kartchners sold the property to the State Parks Board.

The state has been equally painstaking in caring for the baby. "It's a live cave, and we need to make sure we know exactly what keeps it alive," says a Parks Board spokesman, explaining why it has taken several years to get the caverns ready for tourism. "I like to use this analogy: when we go in, we're like a virus invading a living organism, and we need to be certain we don't do irreparable damage to that organism."

Tufts and Tenen say it will be a $22 million-dollar state-of-the-art cave development with airlock doors and carefully routed trails. Yet, even as they describe it, one senses that they regret it has to be "developed" at all. It is like caging an animal: inevitably, its wild character is lost forever.

"The entrance is close enough to a major highway that you can hear the cars, so we knew early on that the cave was in trouble," explains Tenen. "We made a choice between controlled change of its environment and the probability of uncontrolled, haphazard, and probably spiraling destruction. If one factor had been different—if it had been hidden deep in the mountains, or if it had a thousand-foot rappel to get into it—there would still be a concrete plug in it, and we'd still be keeping it secret."

C A N Y O N S

CANYONS ENCLOSE AND DEFINE WORLDS. They nourish unique biosystems and work unpredictable magic on the pliant human mind. A canyon can fill one with wonder or fright, or both at once.

There are literally thousands of canyons in Arizona, far too many to canvass here. There are V-shaped mountain canyons, formed more by volcanic upheavals than by erosion. There are sandstone "slot canyons" on the Colorado Plateau only a few feet wide and hundreds of feet deep. There are urban canyons that flood with people every weekend, and canyons so remote that only the most determined backpackers ever get into them. Following are the best canyons I know, including, inevitably, the Grand Canyon.

■ GRAND CANYON

Shortly after the end of World War I, Marshal Ferdinand Foch, the Allies' supreme commander, visited the Grand Canyon as a guest of Jack Greenway, former Rough Rider and Arizona mining magnate. A contingent of reporters hovered around, waiting to record Foch's reaction. He stared into the great chasm for a moment, then turned to Greenway and said something in French. Greenway turned to the reporters and translated: "Marshal Foch says that the canyon is the most beautiful manifestation of God's presence on the entire earth." What Foch actually had said was, "Let's have a cup of coffee."

U.S. Secretary of the Interior Bruce Babbitt, a former Arizona governor, recounts this story in his excellent *Grand Canyon: An Anthology*. As Babbitt interprets it, Foch wasn't being indifferent; he just wasn't comprehending what he was seeing. His brain had no precedent for processing visual information on this scale. John Muir, who had visited the canyon in 1898, articulated the problem perfectly:

No matter how far you have wandered hitherto, or how many famous gorges and valleys you have seen, this one, the Grand Canyon of the Colorado, will seem as novel to you, as unearthly in the color and grandeur and quantity of its architecture, as if you had found it after death, on some other star . . . .

I have been to, and into, the Grand Canyon many times, and my senses, too, keep failing me. My notes, scribbled in a hip pocket notebook, always seem later as limp and banal as a televangelist's sermon. I am irritated with myself, but also consoled by the observation that many other people fail to come to terms with the canyon: in its presence, all human endeavor seems banal.

Nature carved the canyon with the Colorado River, then enlarged it over time with relentless whittling winds, geologic uplifts, and erosive rains and runoff. The gorge is young compared with the strata of its rock walls. The youngest layer, the Kaibab limestone at the top, is around 250 million years old. The rock at the bottom may be 2.6 billion years old. Human beings have lived around and inside it for at least 4,000 years. John Wesley Powell, a courageous and fascinating man who had lost his right arm in the Civil War, led the first thorough U.S. expedition through the canyon in 1869. He set out from the Colorado tributary of Green River in Wyoming on May 24 with 10 men and a flotilla of four 16- and 21-foot rowboats. The tattered remains of the expedition—two boats, seven men—arrived more than three months later at the mouth of the Virgin River (now somewhere under Lake Mead in Nevada's southeastern corner). Powell's dramatic and meticulous chronicle, published by the U.S. Government Printing Office in 1875, ranks among the most compelling and literate explorers' journals ever written.

Three of Powell's companions died on the expedition—the ones, ironically, who balked at running the stupefying Separation Rapid (also now inundated by Lake Mead) and tried to walk out of the canyon. Three days later, Shivwits Paiute Indians encountered them on the North Rim and killed them.

Powell's reports from this and a subsequent expedition in 1871 introduced the Grand Canyon to an astonished country, but tourism took hold slowly. Even to settlers in Utah and Arizona Territory, the canyon seemed remote and inaccessible. However, John Hance, an itinerant miner and raconteur, built a log cabin on the South Rim about 1883, and soon began leading paying guests into the canyon on trails. Hance, it could be said, was the father of Grand Canyon marketing. In 1886 he advertised in the Flagstaff newspaper:

> Being thoroughly conversant with all the trails leading to the Grand Canyon of the Colorado, I am prepared to conduct parties thereto at any time. I have a fine spring of water near my house on the rim of the Canyon, and can furnish accommodations for tourists and their animals.

It wasn't until 1901, when the 64-mile railroad punched through from Williams to the South Rim, that tourists began flocking to the canyon in serious numbers. By 1905 the luxurious El Tovar Hotel was complete, and in 1922 Phantom Ranch—then as now the only accommodation on the canyon floor—opened for guests. Today's routine amusement of river running, however, remained an exotic and frequently deadly venture for a long time: After Powell's first successful river trip through the canyon in 1869, it was 80 years before 100 people, including the Powell parties, had done the same. What turned the Colorado into the relatively benign stream it is today was the completion of Glen Canyon dam in 1963. Environmentalists still consider the dam an unspeakable outrage, a crime against nature. Interestingly, Theodore Roosevelt, who visited the Grand Canyon in 1903 and proclaimed it a national monument five years later, would surely have agreed. In a speech he made at the South Rim during that 1903 visit, he said:

> In the Grand Canyon, Arizona has a natural wonder which, so far as I know, is in kind absolutely unparalleled throughout the rest of the world. I want to ask you to do one thing . . . . to keep this great wonder of nature as it now is . . . . I hope you will not have a building of any kind, not a summer cottage, a hotel or anything else, to mar the wonderful grandeur, the sublimity, the great loveliness and beauty of the Canyon. Leave it as it is. You cannot improve on it. The ages have been at work on it, and man can only mar it. What you can do is keep it for your children, your children's children, and for all who come after you, as the one great sight which every American . . . should see.

VISITING THE GRAND CANYON

No single mode of exploring the Grand Canyon is enough to fully appreciate and comprehend it, and standing on the rim and staring in is the most inadequate of all. One needs to engage the canyon with all the senses. Hike its trails, feel its walls, challenge its river. Fly over it—at twilight, if possible, when its vivid afternoon colors of auburns, greens, purples, and browns slowly converge into a deep, mist-like, saturating blue, and its sharp edges melt away in the faint light, the sensation of mystery growing as bottomless as the chasm itself.

FROM THE DIARY OF JOHN WESLEY POWELL, GRAND CANYON

*A*nd now we go on through this solemn, mysterious way. The river is very deep, the canyon very narrow, and still obstructed, so that there is no steady flow of the stream; but the waters wheel, and roll, and boil, and we are scarcely able to determine where we can go. Now, the boat is carried to the right, perhaps close to the wall; again, she is shot into the stream, and perhaps is dragged over to the other side, where, caught in a whirlpool, she spins about. We can neither land nor run as we please. The boats are entirely unmanageable; no order in their running can be preserved; now one, now another, is ahead, each crew laboring for its own preservation. In such a place we come to another rapid. Two of the boats run it perforce. One succeeds in landing, but there is no foothold by which to make a portage, and she is pushed out again into the stream. The next minute a great reflex wave fills the open compartment; she is water-logged, and drifts unmanageable. Breaker after breaker rolls over her, and one capsizes her. The men are thrown out; but they cling to the boat, and she drifts down some distance, alongside of us, and we are able to catch her. She is soon bailed out, and the men are aboard once more; but the oars are lost, so a pair from the *Emma Dean* is spared. Then for two miles we find smooth water.

—John Wesley Powell, 1869

CHOOSING WHICH RIM TO VISIT

The Grand Canyon is a 277-mile furrow cut by the Colorado River into the Kaibab Plateau of northwestern Arizona. While you can see across the canyon, the drive from the South Rim Village to the North Rim Overlook is long, the shortest route being 235 miles via the Navajo Bridge. Most visitors choose one rim from which to see the canyon, and then figure out how to get down into it.

The South Rim of the canyon can be reached by driving north from Flagstaff, Arizona, on scenic US 180 to Grand Canyon Village or north off I-40 from Williams on AZ 64. Here are lodgings, restaurants, thousands of visitors, and few places to park. Yet with a little effort and ingenuity you can get away from the crowds and enjoy the canyon. **The North Rim,** located south and east of St. George, Utah, off US 89 and AZ 67, is more remote, has fewer amenities, and

(following pages) "The prudent keep silent"—John Muir

draws fewer visitors. Because its elevation at 8,200 feet is 1,500 feet higher than the South Rim, it's also colder and gets more precipitation. Thanks to the abundant snow, it is open to visitors only mid-May through mid-October.

DRIVING

Roads follow both the North and South rims of the canyon for short distances. Overlooks are marked, and it's quite possible to simply drive along, park your car, get out, and look. *(Refer to the map on pages 68 to 69.)* At the South Rim orient yourself at the **Park Headquarters and Visitors Center,** four miles into the park from the South Entrance Station. Less than a mile farther is the **Yavapai Geologic Museum,** which explains the geologic history of the canyon. East Rim Drive has numerous extraordinary views along its 25-mile route from Grand Canyon Village to Desert View—from which you can see all the way to the Painted Desert.

The North Rim's Cape Royal Scenic Drive will take you (follow the signs) to Point Imperial, which at 8,803 feet provides views of the Painted Desert, Vermilion Cliffs, and Navajo Mountain.

HIKING

The best times to hike are morning and evening, when the air is cool and the colors enhanced by angled light. Easy walks and hikes along maintained trails are the best way for most people to get a sense of the canyon's majesty. Hiking to the bottom is memorable, strenuous, and best undertaken by people in excellent physical condition who take the precautions necessary in a desert landscape. The elevation change is dramatic, there is little or no water, and midday summer temperatures are often over 100 degrees. Hiking shoes or boots are a must for comfort.

Ambitious hikers should consult the hiking guides available in the stores, visitors centers, or the Backcountry Reservations Office. Talk to rangers and buy maps. Backpackers will need permits; day hikers do not.

The alternative to the busy maintained trails are the "secondary trails," which are not maintained by the National Park Service: Hermit, Grandview, Tanner, Boucher, New Hance, Thunder River, and others. They range from moderately difficult to very difficult; some may require route-finding skills. It goes without saying that they also are more rewarding. Hikers or mule riders staying overnight at Phantom Ranch may want to reserve an extra day for the lovely **Clear Creek**

Trail (18 miles round trip), which passes Anasazi ruins and Cheyava Falls, the canyon's highest (usually a trickle, however, except during spring runoff). Clear Creek is relatively level and easy.

Many hikers prefer professionally guided overnighters. The **Grand Canyon Field Institute** offers three- and four-day educational programs on a variety of topics including geology, wildlife, and photography; *(520) 638-2485.*

South Rim Hikes. An easy walk along the South Rim is via the **West Rim Trail**—a partially paved, fairly level trail that begins at Bright Angel Lodge (just to the west of Grand Canyon Village) and ends eight miles later at Hermit's Rest. The wonderful overlooks along the way aren't as crowded as those that can be driven to, and from May through September the road adjacent to the trail is closed to all vehicles but shuttle buses—which stop at various points along the way picking up anyone who wants to hop aboard. Many people walk to Hermit's Rest, get something to eat at the snack bar, and take the shuttle back to the Village.

South Kaibab Trail begins at Yaki Point four miles east of the Village. An excellent day hike is the three-mile round trip from Yaki Point to Cedar Ridge, which has magnificent views all along the way. The elevation drops 1,500 feet. Early morning is the best time to go, when the air is still cool, and the colors, as the sun comes up, are magnificent. From Cedar Ridge you will get a sense of the depth and majesty of the canyon; the hike to the bottom of the canyon is six miles long, descends 4,620 feet, and is exceedingly hot, dry, and grueling.

Bright Angel Trail is the easiest and most overused rim-to-river trail in the canyon. One way it drops 7.7 miles and 4,420 feet. A strenuous day trip along this trail takes you to the magnificent river views at **Plateau Point.**

North Rim Hikes. Uncle Jim Trail is a fairly easy walk through forest with little elevation gain. It leads to several quiet canyon overlooks. Begin by following the Ken Patrick Trail at the North Kaibab trailhead.

North Kaibab Trail follows an exceedingly beautiful route, beginning in the forest on the North Rim and descending along Bright Angel Creek to the Colorado River. A good day trip on this route is to go as far as the Roaring Springs picnic ground—about 4.6 miles each way. The trailhead leaves from a parking lot two miles north of Grand Canyon Lodge.

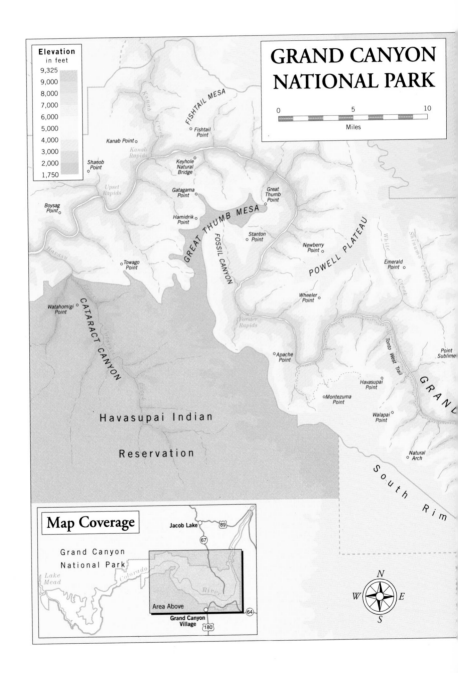

Elevation
in feet
9,325
9,000
8,000
7,000
6,000
5,000
4,000
3,000
2,000
1,750

GRAND CANYON NATIONAL PARK

0   5   10
Miles

FISHTAIL MESA
Fishtail Point

Kanab Point
Kanab Rapids
Shanob Point
Keyhole Natural Bridge
Gatagama Point
Upset Rapids
Boysag Point
Hamidrik Point
GREAT THUMB MESA
Great Thumb Point
Stanton Point
Newberry Point
POWELL PLATEAU
Emerald Point
Towago Point
FOSSIL CANYON
Wheeler Point
Watahomigi Point
CATARACT CANYON
Wonder Rapids
Apache Point
Point Sublime
Havasupai Point
GRAND
Montezuma Point
Walapai Point

Havasupai Indian

Reservation

Natural Arch

Tonto West Trail

White Creek

Shinumo Creek

South Rim

Map Coverage

Grand Canyon
National Park

Lake
Mead

Jacob Lake   89
67

Colorado
River

Area Above

Grand Canyon Village   180

64

N
W   E
S

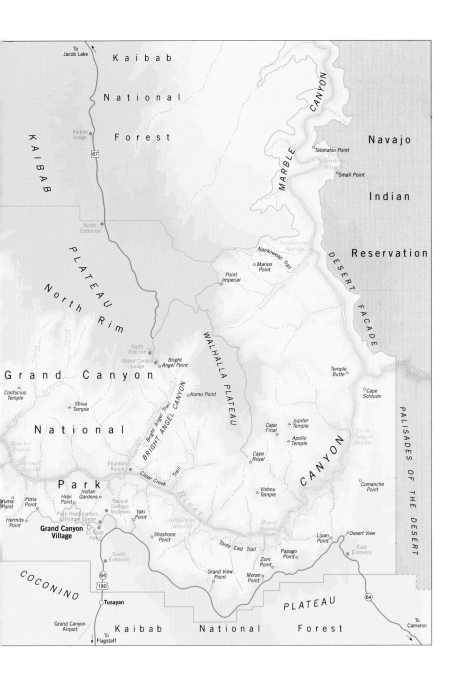

To
Jacob Lake

K a i b a b

N a t i o n a l

F o r e s t

Kaibab
Lodge

67

North
Entrance

K
A
I
B
A
B

P L A T E A U

North   Rim

G r a n d   C a n y o n

Confucius
Temple

Shiva
Temple

N a t i o n a l

Boucher
Rapids

Hermit
Rapids

Dragon Creek

Bright Angel Trail

BRIGHT ANGEL CANYON

North
Rim Inn
Grand Canyon
Lodge

Bright
Angel Point

Komo Point

WALHALLA PLATEAU

MARBLE   CANYON

Tatahatso Point

Harding
Rapids

Small Point

DESERT   FACADE

N a v a j o

I n d i a n

R e s e r v a t i o n

Nankoweap
Rapids

Nankoweap Trail

Marion
Point

Point
Imperial

Nankoweap Creek

Little Colorado River

Temple
Butte

Cape
Solitude

PALISADES   OF   THE   DESERT

P a r k

Yuma
Point

Pima
Point

Hopi
Point

Indian
Gardens

Phantom
Ranch

Clear Creek   Trail

Bright Angel Trail

River

Grapevine
Rapids

Hermits
Point

Park Headquarters
& Visitors Center

Yavapai
Geologic
Museum

Yaki
Point

El Tovar
Hotel

Grand Canyon
Village

Shoshone
Point

South
Entrance

64

180

Tusayan

Grand Canyon
Airport

To
Flagstaff

Cape
Final

Jupiter
Temple

Apollo
Temple

Cape
Royal

Vishnu
Temple

C A N Y O N

Lava
Canyon
Rapids

Comanche
Point

Horse
Rapids

Tonto   East   Trail

Zuni
Point

Papago
Point

Grand View
Point

Moran
Point

Lipan
Point

Desert View

East
Entrance

K a i b a b   N a t i o n a l   F o r e s t

C O C O N I N O

P L A T E A U

64

To
Cameron

MULE TRIPS

Wrangler-guided trips ranging from seven hours to three days are available. The concessionaire requires that riders weigh less than 200 pounds and be fluent in English. Warns the brochure, "Those who are disturbed by heights or large animals should reconsider." Reservations are necessary up to 11 months in advance for the South Rim; for the North Rim, one day or two. Two-day trips include an overnight stay at Phantom Ranch near the bottom of the canyon. *For reservations call (303) 297-2757.*

RAFTING

The raft trip down the Grand Canyon is one of the great wilderness adventures in the world, but not for the faint of heart. Rapids such as the 19-foot drop at the Sockdolager are terrifying but, like other terrifying experiences, definitely unforgettable. Once you've done it, you'll probably spend the rest of your life hoping to run into other people who've done it so you can relive your experience with them.

Rafting from Lee's Ferry 277 miles to Lake Mead is about a 12-day trip. Shorter trips go to Phantom Ranch (three days, 89 miles) and to Bar 10 Ranch (seven to ten days, 188 miles). Along the way you can swim in turquoise pools, shower under waterfalls, and hike the side canyons. The canyon changes dramatically as you travel forward: cliffs rise thousands of feet overhead and it's possible to see bighorn sheep, beaver, mule deer, and peregrine falcons.

A half-day or a full-day float trip (i.e. no rapids) can be taken on Zodiac rafts from Glen Canyon Dam and to Lee's Ferry. *For float trips call Aramark Outfitters (800) 528-6154. Seventeen companies offer white water trips that range from one to 19 days. Whether you choose wooden dorries, small oar-powered rafts, or large motorized rafts, the average cost of a guided trip is $200 per day per person; (800) 473-4576.*

STEAM TRAIN

Since 1989, South Rim visitors have had the intriguing option of driving to Williams, then riding a vintage steam locomotive to the South Rim. The Grand Canyon Railway ceased regular service in 1953 but now, after restoration and a very popular revival, it slices through 64 miles of scenic high plateau country and the Kaibab National Forest. Reservations are strongly advised. One big advantage to visitors who arrive by train is that they do not have to search for scarce parking spaces. *Grand Canyon Railway; (520) 773-1976 or (800) 843-8724.*

HELICOPTER OR AIRPLANE TOURS

Grand Canyon Airport is now Arizona's third busiest, and the canyon's airspace is hazardous. Try **Scenic Airlines** *(702) 739-1900;* **Air Nevada** *(702) 648-9778;* **Sierra Nevada Airways** *(702) 631-3119;* or **Helicop-Tours Choppers** *(702) 736-0606.*

HAVASUPAI INDIAN RESERVATION

The Havasupais ("People of the Blue-Green Water") number about 600 people and are the most isolated of any Arizona tribe—even their mail arrives by mule train. Havasupais farm a side canyon to the Grand Canyon and operate a store, lodge, and campground available to visitors. To visit their one village, Supai, you'll leave your car on the Coconino Plateau and hike or take a mule to the bottom of the gorge. Once there, you'll find a red-rock canyon, a stream, and a series of magnificent water falls that plunge 100 feet into a turquoise pool.

To reach Supai from Grand Canyon Village, travel south on US 180 for 57 miles to Williams, then take I-40 west 44 miles to Seligman. Continue 34 miles west on AZ 66 until you reach Indian Route 18. Finally, head north 60 miles on AZ 66 through the Hualapai Reservation, park at Hualapai Hilltop (elevation 5,200), and either walk or ride a mule 11 miles further into Havasu Canyon (3,200). Reservations at the campground and lodge must be made in advance; (520) 448-2121.

■ PARIA CANYON

Paria Canyon, a water-tortured gash in the Paria Plateau just west of Lake Powell, may offer the most spectacular canyon trek of any in the state—but it's not for the timid, inexperienced, or claustrophobic. Backpackers, who sometimes must wade through waist-deep water, tell many "thrilling" stories of their experiences in the narrow, twisting canyons of the Paria River. In places, Paria is 1,100 feet deep and 10 feet wide. Flash floods roar through on occasion, drowning some and stranding others for days, and late summer hiking (July-September) is discouraged. This is also quicksand country.

Paria Canyon is as wildly beautiful and isolated as any spot in the the Southwest. If it's blistering hot up on the desert floor, in the shade of the vermilion cliffs it's cooler. The narrow band of sky overhead is a brilliant cerulean blue, and the smallest hint of greenery seems like a miracle. High overhead, the jumbled sticks that look like bird nests are really flash flood flotsam.

Before setting out on the four-to-six-day adventure through Paria Canyon, hikers should call the BLM weather service in Kanab, Utah, (801) 644-2672. The trailhead is reached from US 89 between Kanab and Big Water in southern Utah. Turn in at the ranger station to pick up the required (free) permit and maps, then follow the dirt access road south to the campground. The trail begins there and follows the canyon for 35 miles until it ends at the Colorado River adjacent to Lee's Ferry. (Refer to maps on pages 7 and 47.)

■ CANYON DE CHELLY

Canyon de Chelly (pronounced "d'shay") in northeast Arizona earned its pseudo-Spanish name from the inability of early 19th-century Spaniards to pronounce the Navajo word *tsegi,* which means "rock canyon." A more elegant solution might have been for them simply to call it el cañón exquisitó, for it is arguably Arizona's most exquisite canyon.

There actually are several adjoining canyons here, with the largest tributary—Canyon del Muerto—stretching nearly as long as Canyon de Chelly's 27 miles. While the greatest depth is only about 1,000 feet, the walls themselves form an astonishing spectacle. Generally even steeper and sheerer than the Grand Canyon's walls, some appear to have eroded in layers, like a flaking biscuit, while others look as though they were sliced by a 600-foot knife. One remarkable feature is Spider Rock, a needle-like sandstone monolith shooting 800 feet out of the canyon floor. In autumn, particularly, Canyon de Chelly is a festival of color, with the auburn walls playing off the lime-green and golden cottonwoods snaking along the river at the bottom.

Humans have occupied Canyon de Chelly for almost 2,000 years. The Anasazi left some 400 ruins beginning with primitive pit houses and ending with the construction of a three-story masonry high-rise around A.D. 1284. They also left thousands of paintings on the canyon walls, and when their Navajo successors

(opposite) Some 400 Anasazi ruins huddle under the walls of Canyon de Chelly. This, the White House Ruin, is the only one accessible without a Navajo guide.

began to move into the canyon in the mid-1700s, they added their pictorial stories. One Navajo canyon painting quite literally depicts the Spanish military expedition of Antonio Narbona in 1804-05, and behind it lies a tragic story.

On a chilly January morning in 1805 Narbona and his men discovered more than a hundred Navajos hiding in a remote cave 600 feet above the canyon floor. Narbona later claimed that after a battle "with the greatest ardor and effort," his valiant troops killed "90 warriors" along with a few women and children holed up in the cave, but Navajo oral history holds that the victims were *all* women, children, and old men. The Navajo version has more of the resonance of truth: the first Spaniard to climb to the cave that day was attacked by a *woman* defender armed with a knife. The massacre gave Canyon del Muerto its haunting Spanish name: it means "Canyon of Death."

Canyon de Chelly became a national monument in 1931, although the Navajos, who still farm the canyon floors, restrict access to most of it. Today about 30 Navajo families still live in the canyon in summer.

You may pick up maps and directions, and sign up for ranger-led tours (summers only) or guided hikes at the visitor center on the mesa rim near the entrance. *Canyon de Chelly Visitor Center; (520) 674-5500.*

You may drive around the north and south rims to overlooks that gaze down thousand-foot red cliffs, to cottonwood trees, a stream winding in a swath of sand, a few farms, and Navajo hogans. **South Rim Drive** begins at the visitors center, passes White House Overlook—from which an unrestricted trail winds down to the White House Ruin—and continues to Spider Rock Overlook. **North Rim Drive** also begins at the visitor center, then follows Canyon del Muerto, and ends at Massacre Cave Overlook where 115 Navajo were killed by Narbona's party.

Near the entrance to the canyon (follow signs) is the venerable **Thunderbird Lodge** from which jeep tours are led by knowledgeable Navajo guides. Both half- and full-day tours lead you into Canyon de Chelly and Canyon del Muerto. In the cooler months remember to take a jacket, as the canyon can be bitterly cold even on a very sunny day; *(520) 674-5841.*

■ OAK CREEK CANYON

Its juxtaposition of intense colors—vibrant reddish-pink rocks, deep green forests, bright blue sky—makes central Arizona's Oak Creek Canyon one of the prettiest places in the state.

The U.S. Forest Service maintains about 10 hiking trails into Oak Creek's tributary canyons, all of which are spectacular. One deserves special mention: the **West Fork of Oak Creek**, poetically and accurately described in an *Arizona Highways* article by William E. Hafford as "the canyon the moon cannot find." Even in the daytime, West Fork can seem dark. Some of its walls are actually concave, sculpted by a creek into forms that look like frozen ocean waves. The trail crosses the creek repeatedly, so expect to get wet.

Oak Creek Canyon, like the Grand Canyon, is to be avoided during peak vacation times. Its top attraction, Slide Rock State Park (so named for a natural sandstone slide leading into a pool on Oak Creek) draws crowds like a Southern California beach on a warm summer afternoon. Fall is the best season in the canyon anyway, because of the color show staged by its forests of oak, mountain mahogany, sycamore, and sumac. From mid-October to early November, Oak Creek Canyon near Sedona is the most colorful place in Arizona.

Located along US 89A between Flagstaff and Sedona. For information on campgrounds and hiking trails call Sedona Ranger station (520) 282-4119. For accommodations in the canyon call (520) 282-7722. Refer to maps on pages 7 and 47.

■ CANYONS IN THE SANTA CATALINA MOUNTAINS

The rugged Santa Catalina Mountains on the north edge of Tucson include seven major canyons—Bear, Sabino, Esperero, Ventana, Finger Rock, Pima, and Romero. **Sabino,** highly accessible by road-going tram, is by far the best known. Most visitors walk or ride along the canyon bottom, although the easy 4.2-mile Phoneline Trail, which is in effect a man-made ledge 400 feet up on the canyon's

south wall, is much more engaging. The **Esperero Canyon Trail** leads 5.5 miles to a lovely seasonal waterfall named **Bridalveil Falls**; unfortunately the trail rises about 3,500 feet en route. On a warm day, Esperero feels rather more like a death march than a day hike. *(Refer to maps on pages 7 and 47.) Sabino Canyon lies 13 miles northeast of Tucson's downtown. Take Tanque Verde Road to Sabino Canyon Road and turn north 4.5 miles to the canyon. Sabino Canyon Visitor Center; (520) 749-3223. A trail through Romero Canyon is accessible from Catalina State Park, 14 miles north of Tucson on US 89. Santa Catalina Ranger District; (520) 749-8700.*

■ ARAVAIPA CANYON

Aravaipa is the connoisseur's canyon of southern Arizona, an enclosed wilderness whose lush riparian habitat harbors seven species of fish, eight amphibians, 46 reptiles, 46 mammals and more than 200 species of birds. To preserve them, the U.S. Bureau of Land Management strictly regulates the number of humans allowed in. For a hiking permit, contact the BLM Safford District Office; I have not known anyone who doesn't think this lovely canyon is worth that small bother. *(Refer to maps on pages 7 and 47.) 711 14th Avenue, Safford, AZ 85546; (520) 428-4040.*

■ RAMSEY CANYON

Located in the Huachuca Mountains just south of Sierra Vista near the Mexican border, Ramsey Canyon is a hummingbird haven from spring to early fall. A lush riparian area with a year-found stream, the canyon ranges in elevation from 4,200 to over 6,200 feet. The best place to see hummingbirds (14 species have been spotted here) and other wildlife is the Nature Conservancy's Ramsey Canyon Preserve, which has a bird observation area, short nature trail, and a longer trail to an overlook in the Coronado National Forest. Day visitors must register at the visitor center and need parking reservations for weekends and holidays. The only accommodations are a handful of rental cabins that must be booked as much as 12 months in advance. *Ramsey Canyon Preserve; (520) 378-2785.*

One of northern Arizona's water-sculpted "slot canyons," hundreds of feet deep and only a few feet wide. (Kerrick James)

THE FIRST ARIZONANS

HE WAS A CONSTRUCTION WORKER, SHORT BUT WITH a mountain-man build, a sand-colored beard, and a direct, guileless manner of speaking. He seemed mildly intrigued that I had spent two days tracking him down, so he agreed to tell me firsthand what happened to him one night at an 800-year-old Sinagua Indian ruin near Sedona—so long as I would identify him only by his nickname, "Ropes."

He had worked occasionally as a wilderness guide, and had poked around this little-known cliffside ruin for 15 years. Twice he had lingered after dark, and had found that the place spooked him. "I got a real uneasy feeling," he said. "Like I was intruding."

Finally, he packed in with a sleeping bag, determined to spend the night. He watched the red mountains turn violet in the twilight, then a smoky purple, then black against an indigo sky. He was about to drift into sleep. And then he began to hear crying.

"At first I tried to tell myself it was bats. Then I thought, well, it's jackrabbits. Finally I realized I was hearing children. Crying, in *this room*. I kind of chilled out, let the hair come back down on my neck, tried to go to sleep again. And every time I was on the verge of sleep, I'd be awakened by these ungodly sounds. Children crying. It felt like tears in there. All night, it felt like tears."

In the next morning's light, Ropes investigated the room. He found tiny fingerprints that had been pressed into wet mortar nearly a millennium ago. He traced the sun's path and realized that this room would have been the first to receive the winter light and the last to relinquish it, so it would have been the warmest room in the village. It had been some kind of a nursery.

I did not scoff at Ropes' story. I had heard too many others. An *Arizona Highways* editor told me about a night near Sycamore Canyon, 20 miles south of Sedona, when a little Indian kid materialized inside his camper and stared at him through the darkness for several minutes. Indians haven't lived in Sycamore Canyon for hundreds of years. A Tucson restaurant owner, also a credible source, was hiking in Anasazi land when he spotted a crow that seemed to be trying to get his attention. He followed the bird, which eventually fluttered down beside a prehistoric stone ax. The restaurateur took the ax home and began to suffer an inexplicable string of misfortunes. His health unraveled. Business at his little crêperie, for no apparent reason, fell off 70 percent. Then one night at home he got out of bed in the dark, stumbled over the ax, and it severed a tendon in his foot. There was, he said, *a lot* of blood. Yet the ax had been wrapped securely in plastic and stashed *on top* of a table. The next week he took it back.

■ PALEO-ARIZONA

Arizona's prehistory lies literally on the surface of the land, exposed to view in the abundant ruins and potsherds and skeletons and ancient trash dumps. It tempts the imagination.

Possibly the spiritual residue of these civilizations still abides. If not, we may be excused for imagining it. We are steeped in prehistoric mystery.

The place we now call Arizona has been populated for about 12,000 years. The first 10,000 did not produce anything we would recognize as civilization. The original Arizonans, whom archaeologists call Paleo-Indians, were nomadic big-game hunters who roamed what then were grasslands, killing mammoths, bison, bears and other big game with stone-tipped spears. They probably had some form of social organization based on cooperative hunting. A pile of mammoth bones found on a southeastern Arizona ranch in 1955 had more than a dozen chipped flint projectile points in it, confirming what archaeologists had suspected: a lone Paleo-Indian could only have irritated a mammoth by flinging one spear at it. Not much more is known about these people. Living in nomadic bands, probably on the ragged edge of survival, they left no art, no architecture, no ritual objects for our examination. Looking at the monstrous bones of the slain mammoth, we can imagine that they had steely nerves.

By 6000 B.C. the big game had begun to thin out because the climate was drying, and a new people, the Archaic, either evolved from or replaced the Paleo-Indian culture. They were small game hunters and foragers, and their trash dumps ("middens" to archaeologists) suggest that they were more resourceful than their predecessors. They made fishhooks and awls from bones and armed their spears with sharp antler tips—an intriguing *offensive* recycling of their own quarry's *defensive* arsenal.

The turning point in Arizona prehistory was not the employment of increasingly clever tools, however, but agriculture.

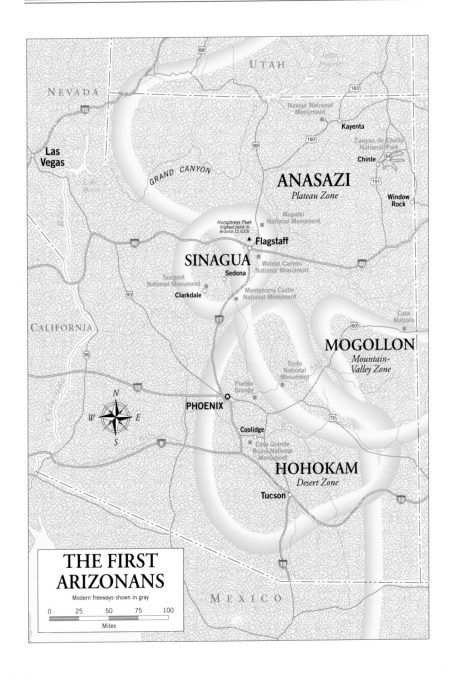

THE FIRST ARIZONANS

Modern freeways shown in gray

0 25 50 75 100

Miles

The idea of cultivating food arrived in southern Arizona from Mexico about 300 B.C. It was a revolutionary change from hunting and gathering, and eventually it triggered profound changes in primitive society. It required that people live communally and stay in one place, which led to the dawn of architecture and villages and, presumably, some system of managing those villages—in other words, government. It was accompanied by new, more complex rituals to coax rainfall and productive crops—that is, religion. It provided people with more security and leisure time, which finally allowed art and recreation to flourish. It yielded foods that could be stored and transported, such as beans and corn, and that meant they could be traded. Ideas could travel with the traders, so the pace of technological development quickened: one culture, for example, might learn from another how to weave yucca fiber into sandals. By A.D. 1000, the archaeological record tells us, prehistoric Arizona was undergoing an information revolution.

By this time several important cultures lived in Arizona: the low-desert Hohokam, the mountain Mogollon, the high-desert Anasazi, and the Sinagua of the Verde Valley and southern Colorado Plateau. In every case, their art, architecture and perseverance astonish us.

■ "ALL USED UP"

One November day in 1867, a prospector and speculator named Jack Swilling rode into the Salt River Valley of Arizona and saw something that must have astounded him: the windswept remnants of a vast system of irrigation canals, tendrils probing into the desert as far as 15 miles from the mother river. Swilling couldn't have had any idea how old they were, nor who had dredged them, but he understood their implication: people had successfully farmed this desert before, on an enormous scale, and therefore it could be done again—profitably. He organized the Swilling Irrigation and Canal Company, dredged one of the prehistoric ditches, and began attracting homesteading farmers. Thus the city of Phoenix was born, inspired by the successes of the Hohokam a thousand years earlier.

Most archaeologists think the Hohokam migrated up from Mexico, bringing the knowledge of irrigated desert farming with them. Eventually the Hohokam world sprawled across a third of Arizona, from the San Pedro River in the southeast to the central Verde Valley. Wherever they settled, they adapted. Around what is now Phoenix, where the Salt River provided a reliable year-around water source, they irrigated their corn, beans and squash by canals. In the Tucson basin, which probably received more rain but had no major river, they farmed the flood plains of the arroyos and built small check dams on slopes to manage runoff. Everywhere they built pit houses, constructed by digging a pit one to two feet deep, then raising a wood frame above the pit and filling in the walls with brush and sticks and a plaster of mud.

Not all their architecture was so modest, however. Around A.D. 1000 they began to build platform mounds, some as large as football fields and 10 to 20 feet high, with storage rooms inside and free-standing houses on top. Around 1350 they began to build high-rises. The ruin of just one remains outside the modern town of Coolidge; it is a four-story building made of solid adobe. When the Spaniards discovered it, they called it the *Casa Grande*, or Big House. Its purpose is still in dispute, but it seems to offer some tantalizing clues to the great Hohokam mystery—about which there will be more later.

The Hohokam arts were, if anything, even more impressive than their architecture and engineering. Their pottery sizzles with life. Scorpions, fish, lizards, turtles, snakes, birds, rabbits and deer parade in tight formation around ceramic vessels of all forms and sizes. Some are so highly stylized they look like animals molting into geometry, such as a bird in flight that resembles the Greek letter Σ with a bow tie. They made primitive trumpets by cutting off the spires of large conch shells. They turned other shells into jewelry by etching patterns on them, probably by using the mild acid of fermented saguaro cactus fruit. This was centuries before Europeans thought they invented acid etching in the 1400s.

And then something cataclysmic happened in the Hohokam world. Around A.D. 1400, its archaeological record begins to evaporate. Datable artifacts, such as pottery, become rare. By A.D. 1450, the line goes flat. The Hohokam literally vanish. A century later, when the first Spanish expeditions trek into Arizona, the explorers find the Pima Indians, a more modest culture of desert farmers, occupying the Hohokam lands. The Pimas supply the word for their predecessors. "Hohokam," in the Piman language, means "all used up."

"Used up" how? And why? All the theories are perforated with holes. And when we consider the contemporaneous neighbors of the Hohokam, the mystery only deepens.

Navajo petroglyphs chronicle the arrival of Spanish cavalry. (Paul Chesley)

■ "ENEMY ANCESTORS"

The high badlands of northeastern Arizona are gouged by canyons where immense ocher and auburn sandstone cliffs soar hundreds of feet over long-dry riverbeds. Here and there huge alcoves lie at the bases of the cliffs, scooped out by water and wind. In these shelters huddle the Anasazi cities, the most scalp-tingling prehistoric ruins in North America.

The Anasazi first appeared as a coherent culture in the Four Corners area (where Arizona, New Mexico, Colorado and Utah now meet) some 2,500 years ago. Today, more than any other prehistoric culture, it is these people who command our fascination. Their architecture is the prime reason. The cities—yes, cities, because these are dense, complex, urban habitats—seem like a metaphor for a relationship of perfect harmony between man and nature: they borrow protection from the cliffs, but do not deface their dramatic sites. No architecture in modern Arizona evokes the mood and power of the land so thoroughly. Half a millennium after the Anasazi, Frank Lloyd Wright developed his philosophy of "organic architecture," buildings with forms and colors and textures inspired by their sites. But Wright never designed anything so organic as did the Anasazi.

And their spirits seem restless. The Navajo, who presumably moved later into Arizona, never occupied abandoned Anasazi sites; they had the forbidding air of ghost towns. Archaeologist Alfred V. Kidder originally picked up the word "Anasazi" from the Navajo language back in 1936, believing it meant "the ancient ones." The more accurate translation is also a more ominous one: "enemy ancestors."

Given all this, it is easy to romanticize Anasazi culture, but the cold evidence is that their lives were hard and short. Their physical environment, for all its beauty, was more difficult than anything faced by the Hohokam—hot in summer, dismally cold in winter, with unpredictable rainfall and unreliable running water. Anthropologists analyzing Anasazi remains have found pitting of some bones, which suggests poor nutrition and anemia. They were short people, the men no taller than about five feet three inches, and they rarely lived more than 35 years. The cliffside pueblos, hauntingly beautiful in ruin, would have been decidedly less engaging as actual dwelling places—dark, cold, claustrophobic, and smoky.

But the social and artistic achievements of the Anasazi are a legitimate source of wonder. The architecture suggests that an entire pueblo of hundreds of people functioned as an extended family. Quite probably they were able to make a primeval form of communism work. Wrote New Mexico anthropologist Linda S. Cordell, "Our notions of personal independence and privacy would be completely foreign to the Anasazi."

The detached, single-family dwelling disappeared from Anasazi society after A.D. 1000, and the apartment-like pueblos were built in compact plans to make the most efficient use of space. Most Anasazi pueblos have multiple kivas—large, circular rooms—which implies that a different communal activity took place in each one: religious ritual here, social gatherings there. Or maybe concerts. Anasazi wood flutes as old as 1,400 years have been found in playing condition in Arizona caves. (For those into Anasazi arcana, their musical scale was A#, C, C#, D, F, G, A. Improvise on this strange scale and the music seems hauntingly open-ended; it never wants to conclude.)

Like the Hohokam, the Anasazi cultivated corn and squash, although their arid land may have given it reluctant nourishment. To supplement their diet, they devised remarkably inventive hunting techniques. Nets as long as 200 feet were woven from yucca fiber and human hair, then stretched across gulches by a few people while others chased rabbits toward them. If it wasn't the most dignified style of hunting, it must have been effective. The laboriously woven nets attest to that.

The Anasazi culture was strong enough to influence its neighbors. The Mogollon, who inhabited the mountain lands of eastern Arizona and western New Mexico, learned stone masonry and pueblo-style architecture from them. Some of the pueblos of the Sinagua, who staked out the Verde Valley and parts of the Colorado Plateau, look strikingly like the Anasazi's. Yet the Anasazi did not endure.

The peak of Anasazi civilization, the period of its most ambitious buildings and strongest trade with other cultures, spanned only two centuries—from about 1100 to 1300. Then they abandoned their canyon cities and drifted away, gradually mingling into the Pueblo people occupying the high mesas of northern Arizona and New Mexico. There is little doubt that the modern Hopi are the descendants of those Anasazi.

The mystery is *why* the Anasazi left their traditional lands. And then why did the Sinagua and Mogollon follow them into that same black hole of lost civilizations, along with the Hohokam, only a century later?

■ THE ABANDONMENT

Archaeologists term it "the abandonment." Between A.D. 1300 and 1450, every one of the dominant cultures of prehistoric Arizona either straggled away, died off or reverted to simpler, less urban lives. This does not have the whiff of random coincidence.

The lifeline of any civilization is water. When an arid-land people disappear, archaeologists logically focus their first suspicions on the water supply.

And in northern Arizona, these suspicions pay off. Tree-ring studies reveal a devastating drought that lasted from 1276 to 1299—more than half an Anasazi lifetime.

Tree trunks cut and used for ceiling beams in the houses at Betatakin, one of those Anasazi cities on today's Navajo reservation, form a story line that meshes precisely with the cataclysmic-drought theory. The first three suites at Betatakin were built in 1267. The population expanded to a peak of about 125 in the mid-1280s. The last tree used in construction at Betatakin was cut down in 1286. By 1300, the settlement was abandoned to the spirits.

ANCIENT ARIZONA POTTERY

Potters of the Southwest have been experimenting with clays, slips, and forms, both useful and decorative, for 1500 years. Designs common in the pots shown below are still part of the pottery tradition today.

HOHOKAM POT

This sacaton red-on-buff style pot was found at Casa Grande National Monument in Arizona. Its sloping shoulders make it typical of this period of pottery-making among the Hohokam people. A.D. 1100.

ANASAZI POT AND BOWL

Found at Canyon de Chelly, the cooking pot to the right was made for everyday use by the Kayenta Anasazi. The corrugations are made by pinching coils of clay.

SINAGUA BOWL

The redware bowl to the left was made by the paddle and anvil technique and was found near Flagstaff, Arizona. The Sinagua culture, whose name means "without water," flourished between A.D. 500–1450.

(all photos this page by George H. H. Huey)

HOHOKAM BUILDING

Casa Grande, a four-story adobe building south of Phoenix is now under a protective roof.

ANASAZI VILLAGE

White House Ruin at Canyon de Chelly in northeast Arizona is a long-abandoned village, set in a protective natural alcove, deep in a canyon.

SINAGUA TOWER

This sandstone masonry building at Wupatki National Monument north of Flagstaff has endured for 800 years.

The Hohokam present a much thornier problem. There is no way to tell whether this drought affected their lands as severely; the desert trees they used in their building provide no reliable ring calendar. In any event, the Hohokam persisted for another 150 years after most Anasazi cities were deserted. Water, or the lack of it, does not explain their disappearance.

What about an epidemic? One anthropologist has wondered whether some European disease, such as smallpox, leapfrogged up the trade routes from Mexico ahead of the Spaniards' march into Arizona. Not likely, since Hernando Cortes, the original *conquistador*, was born 35 years after the Arizona abandonment was complete.

Warfare? The evidence itself is in conflict. For hundreds of years, the entire Southwest and northern Mexico was a vast melting pot, with the different cultures all trading, learning from each other and even adopting each other's customs. Hohokam ballcourts, for example, began turning up in Sinagua settlements around 1100. Some archaeologists have speculated that Anasazi intermarried and merged with Mogollon. There is much more evidence suggesting interdependence than large-scale conflict.

By about 1200, though, some kind of unease appeared to be spreading across the land. Anasazi and Sinagua settlements from this period onward clearly show a defensive posture. Look at the ruin of Tuzigoot, whose 86 rooms sprawl over a Verde Valley hilltop. They have no windows or doors; the Sinagua who lived in them would have climbed ladders to drop through the roofs into dismal, pitch-dark rooms. Still, a team of archaeologists who in 1933-34 excavated 411 Tuzigoot burials found little evidence of violent deaths.

Further south in Hohokam lands, villages after 1300 tended to be larger, more urban, and apparently defended by rings of rockpile walls called *trincheras.* Casa Grande has the unmistakable air of a primitive fortress. One archaeologist has wondered, rather exotically, whether this and the other Hohokam high-rises were the castles of conquering warlords ruling over Hohokam villages. Not likely: the problem, said archaeologist David R. Wilcox of the Museum of Northern Arizona, is that no iconography of Hohokam warfare—that is, rock art or images on pottery—has ever been found. Why wouldn't the extravagantly expressive Hohokam have left some hint of epic war in their art? Since they regularly drew pictures of people hunting, dancing and making love, wouldn't they also have left some pictorial record of fighting and killing?

Question archaeologists about the abandonment late into the night, and eventually you'll hear an interesting but elusive phrase: "worn cultural patterns." Press for elaboration, and you may hear something like this:

Think about the Hohokam irrigation system, which as time wore on became increasingly extended and complex. A 15-mile-long canal would have served numerous settlements, and that would require some sort of centralized authority to control and maintain it. Over time a network of authorities might have developed special status and knowledge, passing it on from generation to generation, guarding its privilege through mystic ritual, and living apart from the proles atop mounds or in the big houses. The parallel with the Roman Catholic priesthood on another continent at the same time, the Middle Ages, is exact.

There is an engaging sliver of evidence at Casa Grande: a small hole in a wall on the fourth story aligns precisely with the sunset on the summer solstice. Knowledge of the seasons would have been critically important to the Hohokam farmers, yet this information was kept in a special and probably well-guarded place.

Now stir in a second speculative ingredient, which might be termed the USSR Analogue. Centralized authorities, aloof and isolated from the real world in their kremlins or *casas grandes*, almost always prove poor at responding to problems. They resist change. When they make a mistake, it's a grand one, affecting a large population.

There is also evidence that the Hohokam were stretching the land's natural resources alarmingly thin. Archaeologists estimate that by the 13th century, there were between 20,000 and 50,000 people living in the valley where Phoenix sprawls today. Over several centuries, this throng probably denuded the valley of trees for building and firewood, and found themselves having to walk farther and farther to harvest mesquite—which in turn would have demanded more human energy on a diet that was becoming less nourishing. Archaeologists examined 600 burials in the Phoenix area from A.D. 1250 to 1450 and found proof of serious malnutrition. Women were developing osteoporosis as soon as they were of childbearing age and had it the rest of their short lives—unborn children were literally mining the minerals from their mothers' bodies. The average adult died in his mid-thirties (not so different from life expectancy in Europe at the time).

With fewer natural resources to go around, old trading patterns probably fell apart. Hohokam trade with other cultures such as the Sinagua and Mogollon were abandoned. And thus the very complexity and interdependence of these peoples led to their demise. Once they had grown too advanced to be self-sufficient, the unforgiving environment snuffed them out.

Where did the Hohokam go? Nowhere, most archaeologists agree. Those who survived stepped backward in time, so to speak, and became the Pima and Tohono O'odham that the Spaniards found inhabiting the Sonoran Desert a century later.

The Hohokam threw off their worn cultural patterns, retreating into a simpler, more self-sufficient, more marginal lifestyle. The evidence for this continuity is persuasive—for example, some twentieth-century Pima houses resemble thousand-year-old Hohokam dwellings excavated in the same villages. But those Hohokam villages shrank, authority disintegrated, the great canals shut down, the big houses slowly weathered into dust. Life surely became harder: by 1450, decorated pottery was no longer made, which suggests there was no longer the luxury of leisure time. This was a prehistoric perestroika, the only way a suffering, beleaguered people could think of to survive. The complex lifeway was considered *hohokam*, all used up, and therefore expunged from its peoples' cultural memory.

The fascinating question: will this same desert land support *our* way of life in modern Arizona for another millennium?

MUSEUMS OF ANCIENT INDIAN ARTIFACTS

Heard Museum, Phoenix. A world-class museum with a staggering collection of more than 75,000 artifacts and artworks that document prehistoric and modern Native American cultures. Changing exhibits are consistently first-rate. *22 E. Monte Vista Rd.; (602) 252-8840.*

Pueblo Grande Museum, Phoenix. This museum houses the best remaining Hohokam mound, along with excavations and interpretive exhibits. *4619 E. Washington St.; (602) 495-0900.*

Arizona State Museum, Tucson. Enormous holdings of Native Americana and an excellent research staff of archaeologists and ethnologists make this one of the finest museums in the state. Changing exhibits are open to the public. *University of Arizona campus; Park Ave. and University Blvd.; (520) 621-6302.*

Museum of Northern Arizona, Flagstaff. This museum has staked out a special turf interpreting the natural and cultural history of the Colorado Plateau. Its quarterly magazine, *Cañon Journal*, is well worth the subscription price. Changing exhibits are open to the public. *3101 N. Fort Valley Rd., (Hwy. 180 leading out of town toward the Grand Canyon); (520) 774-5211.*

Amerind Foundation in Dragoon in southern Arizona was founded in 1937 by archaeologist William Fulton to do research in Southwestern and Mexican archaeology. Housed in Spanish-colonial revival buildings built among the rock formations of Texas Canyon, the museum exhibits an outstanding artifact collection. *Take I-10 to exit 318, 60 miles east of Tucson; (520) 586-3666.*

ANCIENT INDIAN RUINS

HOHOKAM

Hohokam architecture was mostly mud and sticks, so little remains.

Casa Grande Ruins National Monument—the one "big house" Hohokam ruin is indispensable to anyone struggling to understand the Hohokam. *About 50 miles southeast of Phoenix. Take AZ 87, just miles north of Coolidge. 1100 Ruins Dr.; (520) 723-3172.*

SINAGUA

The Sinagua, a mysterious culture that borrowed Anasazi architecture and traded avidly with the Hohokam, left hundreds of dramatic ruins scattered throughout the Verde Valley and the southern edges of the Colorado Plateau.

Montezuma Castle National Monument is an astonishingly graceful pueblo with smooth, concave facades that fill in much of a huge cave high in a limestone cliff. It does not, by the way, have anything to do with Montezuma; 19-century Verde Valley settlers gave it this name, blithely assuming that the Aztecs had preceded them. *Take I-17 to exit 289, 87 miles north of Phoenix; (520) 567-3322.*

Tuzigoot National Monument is a very different sort of development, demonstrating Sinagua adaptability; its 86 rock-walled rooms flow over the crest of a low hill in the lee of Mingus Mountain. *Follow signs 3 miles east of Clarkdale (south of Flagstaff); (520) 634-5564.*

Wupatki National Monument north of Flagstaff exhibits still another architectural style. These soft, red sandstone houses bud from rocky outcroppings with such grace and logic that nature and architecture seem to become one. *Take AZ 89, 24 miles north of Flagstaff; (520) 679-2365.*

Walnut Canyon National Monument just east of Flagstaff is unusual in that visitors are welcome to walk inside any of the 24 Sinagua ruins in this gorge. A few moments inside one of the cramped, dark dwellings offers memorable insight into the lives of the people who once lived there. Finally, private jeep-tour

*Wupatki National Monument
(photo by Kerrick James)*

firms in Sedona offer visits to little-known Sinagua ruins around the Red Rocks, and the guides generally are knowledgeable and entertaining. *Take I-40 to exit 204, seven miles east of Flagstaff; (520) 526-3367.*

ANASAZI

Anasazi ruins are scattered throughout the deep and forbidding canyons of northern Arizona, particularly on the Navajo Reservation.

Canyon de Chelly National Monument adjacent to the town of Chinle is the most abundant site both in ruins and astounding scenery. Visitors may hike unescorted to only one of the ruins in the canyon, the White House, but Navajo guides offer horseback and four-wheel-drive tours to others. *Take Navajo Rt. 64 through Chinle to the visitor center; (520) 674-5500; jeep tours (520) 674-5841.*

Navajo National Monument near Kayenta includes the huge and poetically graceful 135-room **Betatakin**, a three-hour guided walking tour from the monument headquarters, and the 160-room **Keet Seel**, a 16-mile round-trip hike or horseback ride from headquarters. Though not the most easily accessible, these are the two most spectacular prehistoric ruins in Arizona. *Take US 160, 18 miles south of Kayenta, then AZ 564 north to monument. Call in advance; limited number of visitors allowed. Ranger-guided tours; (520) 672-2366.*

MOGOLLON

The Mogollon people stretched from northern Chihuahua (Mexico) to northern Arizona, but they exhibited many different arts and lifestyles.

Casa Malpais, a Mogollon ruin at Springerville, startled the archaeological community in 1991 when word went out that there was a complex of catacombs for burials under the pueblo. Nothing of the sort has been found at any other site in the Southwest. The above-ground ruins are open to visitors, but the catacombs are absolutely off-limits. Springerville is on US 60 on the Mogollon Plateau near the New Mexico border. Ruins may only be visited by guided tour. *Meet at the Casa Malpais Museum at 318 Main Street in Springerville; follow guide in your car to the ruin. Takes about one and a half hours; (520) 333-5375.*

HISPANIC ARIZONA

ONE SPRING MORNING IN 1981 A DELEGATION of Mexican journalists arrived in Tucson bearing a startling gift to commemorate our international friendship: a 14-foot-high bronze equestrian statue of Pancho Villa, guerrilla general of the second Mexican Revolution. A controversial figure even in Mexico, Villa is best remembered north of the border for leading the only invasion of the United States mainland in this century. On March 9, 1916, Villa and his band sacked the small town of Columbus, New Mexico, killing 19 American citizens. President Wilson, probably overreacting, sent 10,000 troops into Mexico to chase him. They never caught him, but the failed manhunt elevated Villa into a hero in the eyes of some Mexicans.

Back in Tucson, City Hall checked the diplomatic wind, concluded it would be bad form to reject the gift, and nervously installed Villa and his mount in a small but prominent downtown park. Tucsonans reacted as if it were the statue from hell. The mayor himself boycotted the dedication ceremony. Historians growled that Villa was hardly a revolutionary Robin Hood, but a bandit and terrorist who also massacred his own people on whim. One midnight commentator slipped into the park with a can of paint and left a yellow stripe cleaving Villa's back.

But the statue stayed, and eventually the uproar subsided. Four years later, the *Tucson Citizen*, the evening newspaper, polled its readers on the best public sculpture in Tucson. The winner: Pancho Villa. Following that, however, a local anthropologist began an annual one-man protest, pounding 19 white crosses into the grass beside the statue on every anniversary of the Columbus raid. Several Tucsonans of Mexican ancestry now regularly turn out to protest his protest. A story in *The Arizona Daily Star* quoted one of them as saying it was proper to honor Villa in Tucson, because Tucson ought still to be a part of Mexico.

"This was all our land," she told a reporter. "Your people stole it."

■ SPANISH ROOTS

The first Spaniards entered Arizona around 1540, lured by fables of the Seven Cities of Cibola, legends redolent of riches. Francisco Vásquez de Coronado, the most persistent of the early explorers, probably led his party north along the San Pedro River and around the Mogollon Rim to the Hopi villages of the Colorado Plateau. There they learned that the rumored cities were made of sun-dried mud and not gold. Worse still, two Franciscan missionaries who stayed behind among the natives were murdered, beginning a pattern that would endure for more than a century between the persistent Franciscans and recalcitrant Hopis.

More than 300 miles to the south, Jesuit missionaries led by the tireless Italian-born Father Eusebio Kino temporarily found a warmer reception among the Pimas and Papagos (now called the Tohono O'odham). In 1701 Kino established missions at Guevavi, near modern Nogales, and at Bac, eight miles south of today's downtown Tucson. These were the northernmost outposts in a chain of 22 missions he stretched across the deserts and grasslands of the *Pimería Alta* of New Spain, the Land of the Upper Pimans. Kino had no further successes in Arizona,

SPANISH COLONIAL ARIZONA

✝ MISSION   ● PRESIDIO

0   25   50   75
Miles

Gila

Santa Cruz River

San Pedro

ARIZONA

Tucson 1776-1821

SAN XAVIER DEL BAC ✝

Santa Cruz de Terrenate
1776-1780

*N
W   E
S*

Tubac
1751-1776,
1787-1821

SAN JOSE DE TUMACACORI ✝

GUEVAVI

River

191

U. S. A.
MEXICO

SANTA MARIA SOAMCA ✝

Santa Cruz
1787-1821

Las Nutrias
1775, 1780-1787

San Bernardino
1775-1779

SARIC ✝

Terrenate
1742-1775

Altar
1753-1821

Rio Altar

✝ *TUBUTAMA*

✝ *COCOSPERA*

Fronteras
1692-1775,
1779-1821

SAN IGNACIO ✝

✝ *REMEDIOS*

Bacoachi
1784-1821

Bavispe
1778-1821

Rio San Ignacio

✝ *DOLORES*

Rio Montezuma

Rio Bavispe

Map Area

SONORA

but some 80 years after his death in 1711 the great church of San Xavier del Bac would be completed, and to Kino would go the credit both of introducing Christianity and European civilization to Arizona.

Kino is venerated today in Arizona and our neighbor Mexican state of Sonora. Many Catholics on both sides of the border are campaigning for his canonization. He appears to have been a man of boundless endurance, great charisma, and principle. His contemporary, Capt. Juan Mateo Manje, left a profile of him that in our century could as easily describe Gandhi:

> When [Kino] publicly reprimanded a sinner, he was choleric. But if anyone showed him personal disrespect, he controlled his temper to such an extent that he made it a habit to exalt whosoever maltreated him. . . . He was so austere that he never took wine except to celebrate Mass, nor had any other bed than the sweat blankets of his horse. . . . He never had more than two coarse shirts, because he gave everything as alms to the Indians.

There is a statue of Kino in modern Tucson, as well as a Kino Boulevard, Kino Hospital, Kino Paving Repairs and Kino Termite & Pest Control. There is no controversy around him today.

Possibly there should be. In the *Pimería Alta* of the eighteenth century the growing Spanish presence was a dubious blessing. The Spaniards introduced cattle ranching and improved agriculture, but also exotic European diseases such as measles and smallpox. And the more Spaniards that trickled in, the more the natives seemed to grasp the implications. In 1751 the normally peaceful Pimans rebelled, killing more than 100 Spanish ranchers, miners and priests in an astonishing uprising that ranged from Caborca, near the Sonoran coast, to Bac, near present-day Tucson. The Spanish government responded with a show of force, beginning by building a presidio (fort) at Tubac, 40 miles south of Bac. What followed was grimly precursive of the U.S. Cavalry campaigns that would follow a century later. As Juan Bautista de Anza, the captain of Tubac, reported in 1767:

> When I took over my present command in 1760, my section of the frontier was faced with an uprising of over a thousand Papagos [Pimans]. After launching various campaigns to subjugate them, I attacked them personally . . . and took the lives of Ciprian, their captain, and nine others. All the rest then capitulated and renounced the inconstancy that has been plaguing the Piman nation.

The Apaches were still more "inconstant," staging hit-and-run raids and ambushes on Spaniards and Pimans alike. They never did come fully under Spanish control, despite long and bloody warfare. In another eerie foreshadowing of the American struggles, the Spaniards resorted to trickery. In 1776, Spain's new Minister of the Indies, José de Galvéz, ordered that Apaches who agreed to make peace were to be rewarded with "defective firearms, strong liquor, and other such commodities as would render them militarily and economically dependent."

In our modern Southwest, we love to romanticize the Spanish Colonial era, recalling it as a time when simple Indians learned civilized ways under the tutelage of kindly priests, and manly dons ruled over their vast *rancheros* from tiled and arcaded *haciendas* recalling the great mansions of baroque Iberia. This is such nonsense that it qualifies as hallucination. For all the respect showered on Kino, and the rich cultural heritage left in Arizona by its Hispanic past, the raw truth is that the 17th and 18th centuries were ugly times in what is now Arizona. The Spaniards, even those marching in alleged humility under the cross, were not welcomed guests, but invaders.

■ THAT "MOSTLY MEXICAN" TOWN

Sam Hughes, a Welsh immigrant who had been working as a baker in gold-rush California, clattered into the southern Arizona desert aboard a stage one spring day in 1856. Hughes had tuberculosis and was desperately trying to make Texas, where he hoped the warm, dry air might prolong his life. The driver, afraid that Hughes would cause him the annoyance of dying en route, kicked him out in Tucson. Hughes must have felt like he was being abandoned in Neverland. Of the 500 or so people living in this isolated desert town, the driver assured him, five spoke English.

Tucson, along with the rest of Arizona, had flown the Mexican flag since 1810, the year Mexico began its violent break from Spain. Then in a dozen bloody years, 1836 to 1848, the Texas Revolution and Mexican War severed Texas, California, Nevada, Utah, and most of Arizona and New Mexico from Mexico's upper body. In 1853, the United States, strong-arming its hemorrhaged rival, bought the southern third of Arizona and the last sliver of New Mexico for a fire-sale price of $10 million and incorporated them into a U.S. territory the following year.

Despite all this, the heart and soul of Tucson, the largest and most important town in the Gadsden Purchase, would remain essentially Mexican until the first trains rumbled into town in 1880. Until then, nearly all of Tucson's cultural ties, communication and trade clung to Mexico.

Gringos who stumbled through Tucson in those days were not enchanted. The most frequently quoted description of Tucson, which dogs the Chamber of Commerce even today, is that of journalist J. Ross Browne in 1864. Modern travel writing is pallid fluff compared with this:

> . . . [The traveler] emerges to find himself on the verge of the most wonderful scatteration of human habitations his eye ever beheld—a city of mud-boxes, dingy and dilapidated, cracked and baked into a composite of dust and filth; littered about with broken corrals, sheds, bake-ovens, carcasses of dead animals, and broken pottery; barren of verdure, parched, naked, and grimly desolate in the glare of a southern sun. Adobe walls without whitewash, inside or out, baked and dried Mexicans, sore-backed burros, coyote dogs, and terra-cotta children . . . .

It's easy to dismiss Browne's raving as gringo bigotry. Yet, other early descriptions are not very different. The Tucson of the 1860s, though the largest settlement in Arizona, was severely isolated, still under periodic assault by Apaches, and simple survival, not civic beautification, headed the priorities. It was not a charming place.

It began to change with the arrival of Anglos who would become entrepreneurs, such as Hughes, and professional-class Mexicans fleeing the political tumult to the south, such as Federico Ronstadt. We can sketch the cultural history of pre-1880 Tucson through these two men.

Hughes had no formal education but a deep reservoir of determination. In photos from throughout his long life—he died in 1917, at the age of 88—his eyes, shadowed by bushy, steel-woolly brows, glow with confidence and intensity. Such a man could improvise without a blueprint in Tucson; his career eventually comprised ranching, real estate, banking, and politics.

There was one problem for men such as Hughes: women. The 1860 census of Tucson on the opposite page graphically explains.

Four years after he was dumped in Tucson, Hughes married a Mexican girl named Atanacia Santa Cruz. Eyebrows surely arched skyward all over town. Sam was 32 years old, Atanacia 12.

TUCSON'S 1860 CENSUS

	AGE	NUMBER
Mexican males	15-39	168
Mexican females	15-39	163
Anglo males	15-39	132
Anglo females	15-39	6

While the bride's age was unusual, the union across the ethnic line wasn't. Until the railroad came, there was a chronic dearth of Anglo females. The list of Anglo men who took Mexican brides reads like a who's who of territorial Tucson; it includes most of the successful merchants, ranchers and politicians. Hiram Stevens, who became the territorial delegate to Congress, married Atanacia's sister, Petra. It is unimaginable that the Mexican men weren't angered, yet oddly there is no record, not even an oral history, of trouble. One reason, suggested by University of Arizona anthropologist James E. Officer, is that the spurned Mexican men of Tucson simply brought in a fresh supply of young women from Sonora. However, none of the pre-1880 Spanish-language newspapers of Tucson survive—and if there had been resentment against the gringos, this was one outlet where it might have been vented.

In fact, Anglos and Mexicans lived in remarkable harmony in territorial Tucson. They went into business together, fought Apaches together and partied together—more so than in any other old town in the Southwest. One reason was that the Hispanic *Tucsonenses* were not mainly peasants and laborers, as they were in early Los Angeles and Phoenix. Many came from ambitious, upper-class families in Sonora.

Ronstadt, an engineer's son, was one of them. He arrived in Tucson in 1882, when he was only 14, signed on as an apprentice wainwright with the firm of Dalton and Vásquez, and eventually built up a coachworks of his own that employed 65 people. The business enjoyed a fine regional reputation; Ronstadt supplied wagons and carriages to ranchers from Colorado to the Sonoran capital of Hermosillo. While Sam Hughes endowed schools, Ronstadt generated culture. He founded the *Club Filarmónico*, one of Tucson's earliest orchestras, and launched a family musical dynasty. His daughter, Luisa Ronstadt Espinel, went on to an international career singing both opera and Spanish folk music. His great-great granddaughter, who started her career singing in Tucson coffeehouses in the 1960s, is Linda Ronstadt.

The dominance of Mexican culture in Tucson began to shrivel the day the first train wheezed into town. We can still read the story today in the architecture of the two oldest neighborhoods, El Presidio and Barrio Histórico, which huddle immediately north and south, respectively, of downtown's modern towers. The oldest houses, dating from the 1860s and 1870s, are pure Sonoran: simple, box-like shapes with plastered adobe walls two feet (half a meter) thick, a wide entry hall called a *zaguán*, and ceilings fashioned of saguaro or ocotillo ribs. By 1880, some of these adobes began to sport porches and peaked roofs of corrugated steel, the Anglo newcomers' stopgap efforts to make traditional Mexican architecture into something that felt more like home to them.

Luisa Ronstadt Espinel, great aunt of Linda Ronstadt. (Arizona Historical Society)

By the late 1880s, all but the poorest Anglos had abandoned the adobe neighborhoods and were building modest Victorian houses with yards and fences on tree-lined streets. In Florence, another essentially Sonoran town 70 miles north of Tucson, a newspaper editor in 1887 seemed to sum up Anglo attitudes—and not only about architecture—in an editorial: "The adobe does not make an attractive or a clean building, and Eastern people (that is, eastern U.S.) find it somewhat repulsive in appearance. . . . It is hoped that all new building of any pretensions will be built of brick and the unsightly adobe discarded."

With the discarding came discrimination. University of Arizona ethnohistorian Thomas E. Sheridan studied courthouse records in Tucson from 1882-89 and found that convicted murderers with Spanish surnames drew average sentences of 3.58 years; Anglos one year. Mexicans convicted of grand larceny served 3.9 years; Anglos 1.88. (The fact that stealing was punished more severely than killing, whatever one's ethnic persuasion, says something else about life in frontier Arizona.) As late as the 1950s, speaking Spanish in some Tucson schools was

(From left) Hiram and Petra Stevens, Samuel and Atanacia Hughes. (Arizona Historical Society)

punished with a soapy rinse of the offender's mouth—a sad irony in a town that owed its founding and first hundred years to Spanish-speaking people.

Yet after the railroad and even to the present, prominent Hispanic businesspeople, journalists and artists retained their status, Anglos and Hispanics continued to marry each other, and Tucson avoided the worst of the ethnic segregation that plagued so many other cities.

Those early days had set the stage. As James Officer once put it, "How were you going to tell a Ronstadt that his kid can't go to your school?"

■ HISPANIC ARIZONA TODAY

Every year on September 16, a crowd gathers at sunset on the still-hot concrete of the Phoenix Civic Plaza. *Ballet Folklórico* dancers swirl across a stage, the aroma of *carne asada*, flame-broiled beef, drifts through the air, and here and there Mexican flags flutter in celebration. The party leans on well into the night, until all at once the merriment abates and a speaker takes the stage. In Spanish, he recites the *Grito de Dolores*, that spine-prickling call to arms from a parish priest on September 16, 1810, that launched the Mexican Revolution: "My children, a new dispensation comes to us this day. Are you ready to receive it? Will you be free?" As he finishes, fireworks streak through the Phoenix sky, the national anthems of Mexico and the United States swell, and the revelers shout *¡Viva México!* The celebration of *el dieciseis de septiembre*, the Sixteenth of September, Mexico's independence day, is as colorful, noisy and passionate in Arizona as anywhere in Mexico.

About 20 percent of Arizona's population is Hispanic, and these people celebrate their heritage with pride. Not everyone embraces the troubling Pancho Villa, but certain traditions, such as the *quinceañera*, seem to be observed more faithfully now than ever. The *quinceañera* is a special Mass to bless a girl turning 15, followed by an elaborate coming-out party. In Phoenix, some priests have started to complain that their churches' schedules are being overrun with *quinceañeras*.

Some of the more internal aspects of Hispanic culture also remain firmly rooted —for one, the tradition of closely entwined, extended families. There is no shortage of Hispanic yuppies in Phoenix and Tucson, but it is still a little unusual even for well-educated, professional young Hispanics to bounce from city to city to pump up their careers. In Tucson, a city where Anglos joke that anyone who's been around at least 10 years qualifies as a native, fifth- and sixth-generation Hispanic natives are not uncommon.

Anglos like to immerse themselves in the more colorful, accessible aspects of Hispanic culture; it is a way of loosening the jacket of our stiffer Puritan heritage. Mexican food is a virtual Arizona religion. Once a year the Phoenix weekly *New Times* and the *Tucson Weekly* poll their readers, not even asking which is the best local Mexican restaurant—the question seems too epic to face—but which has the best *fajitas*, best *salsa*, best *enchilada*, even the best beans. Tucson's former mayor, Lewis C. Murphy, officially trumpeted the city as the "Mexican Food Capital of the World," apparently not pausing to consider how such a proclamation might play to the south. For years, Phoenix, Tucson, El Paso, and Santa Fe sent their top chefs to battle in an intercity Mexican Food Cookoff. When Santa Fe won in 1987, irritated Arizonans wrote letters to their editors complaining, in all seriousness, that the godless New Mexicans had used revisionist ingredients such as crab meat in their *chiles rellenos*.

But when Arizona joined the Official English movement in 1988, with a majority of voters approving a law that required all government and legal business to be conducted in English, Hispanics generally saw it as an effort to keep their culture in its place—that is, under the Anglo heel—and as a signal that the gringos, at heart, didn't want to understand or absorb anything more significant than what distinguishes a good *chile relleno*. If Arizona is good because it is multicultural, they wondered, why isn't it good that it is multilingual?

In practice, the law had hardly any effect, and two years later it was found constitutionally defective and thrown out by the courts. A little damage, however, had been done. A little more acrimony was left hanging in the air, and a few more Arizonans of Mexican lineage seemed willing to say out loud what had been held locked in their hearts before: this, after all, had been their land.

■ EXPLORING HISPANIC CULTURE

Most of the "Spanish" architecture the visitor sees in Arizona is the product of Anglo architects unearthing and romanticizing the state's past. *(See a more detailed discussion on pages 190-191.)* Two authentic Spanish missions, however, **San Xavier del Bac** and **San José de Tumacácori** survive south of Tucson. *San Xavier*

Experts began restoring the interior of San Xavier del Bac south of Tucson in 1990, a project which consumed several years and a million dollars. Above on the left is a detail of the interior prior to restoration and on the right, after restoration. The dome crowning San Xavier's east tower was never completed; the best theory is that the builders simply ran out of money (above). (Photos top right and above by Kerrick James)

The restored altar and retablo of Mission San Xavier del Bac. (Kerrick James)

del Bac, is located about 10 miles south of Tucson is off I-19, exit 92, and is open daily; (520) 294-2624. San José de Tumacácori, 45 miles south of Tucson, is also off I-19; (520) 398-2341.

Although some gentrification has occurred in Tucson's **Barrio Histórico**, a stroll along Meyer or Convent streets offers a remarkably intact impression of pre-1880 Hispanic Tucson; just mentally blot out the power lines and parked cars.

Every Arizona town and city that has a substantial Mexican-American population also has public fiestas on both September 16 and *cinco de mayo* (May 5), the latter celebrating Mexico's rout of the French occupation force at Puebla in 1862. These festivals are wonderful introductions both to Hispanic culture and Mexican history.

Mariachi music traces its roots to the *son*, a sometimes ribald or seditious Spanish song-and-dance form of the 18th century. Today the mariachi band is a virtual national emblem of Mexico, and it has gathered in ethnic influences from European classicism to American pop and country. A good mariachi band knows a thousand songs and will stamp its personal imprint on anything from one of Brahms' Hungarian Dances to that famous love anthem to Guadalajara, "*Ay, Jalisco no te rajes.*" The best Mariachi bands in the Americas can be heard annually at the **International Mariachi Conference**, held each April in Tucson.

Other museums around the state frequently schedule exhibits of Mexican or Hispanic–American art. Finally, to contemplate the checkered history of Mexican-U.S. relations, park at the fringe of downtown Tucson and walk to *Veinte de agosto* Park at Church and Broadway: there, atop a prancing horse, is that concomitant hero and villain, **Francisco "Pancho" Villa.**

(below) San Jose de Tumacácori, constructed 1773–1822. The mission's roof and walls are sealed with mortar of sand, lime, and cactus juice.

The Great Cathedral of Alamos in Sonora, Mexico was built in the 1780s and is a splendid example of Spanish colonial architecture. (Kerrick James)

MODERN INDIANS

FOURTEEN NATIVE AMERICAN TRIBES and 20 reservations occupy nearly one-third of Arizona's land and represent a variety of languages, traditions, and lifestyles. Museums and shops in Phoenix, Tucson, and Flagstaff display exquisite tribal artwork, jewelry, and crafts, but to understand the people who made these objects, you have to venture away from the cities and onto the reservations.

There is no monolithic "Indian culture" in Arizona. If you've seen one reservation, you have not seen them all. There is no comparing the windswept tablelands of the Navajo sheepherder with the flat desert fields of the Pima farmer, for example. It is also difficult to compare languages: The state's tribes speak a total of 18 distinct tongues, some of which are as unrelated to each other as French is to Russian.

Though many Native Americans wish to live a simpler more traditional life than that lived in Arizona's big cities, achieving that goal on the verge of the 21st century is not easy. Through television, computers, telephones, and tourism, Arizona's reservations have become increasingly imprinted with the ways of mainstream America. In many respects, the practices of the outside world collide with traditional Native American values and customs. Sometimes the consequences are tragic: alcoholism has bedeviled the reservations for generations; now drugs do, too. At other times the fusion only causes the Native culture to do something not necessarily destructive, but antithetical to its nature. Gambling casinos, now operating on 14 Arizona reservations, seem out-of-place amid the vast expanses of underdeveloped reservation land, yet they have become an economic boon for many tribes. For the Tohono O'odham in southern Arizona, for instance, gambling revenues now account for nearly 60 percent of the tribe's total budget.

Some tribes are seeking to benefit from contact with the outside world in other ways. The Navajo tribe, Arizona's largest, has rejected gambling but is trying to increase tourism on its sprawling reservation. The trick for the Navajo, as for other Arizona tribes, is to be connected with the world beyond the reservation without sacrificing tribal culture and language.

A decade ago, the older generation of Navajo lamented that their traditional way of life was dying. They feared for the survival of their native tongue. While such concerns still exist, tribe members have reason to be more optimistic about

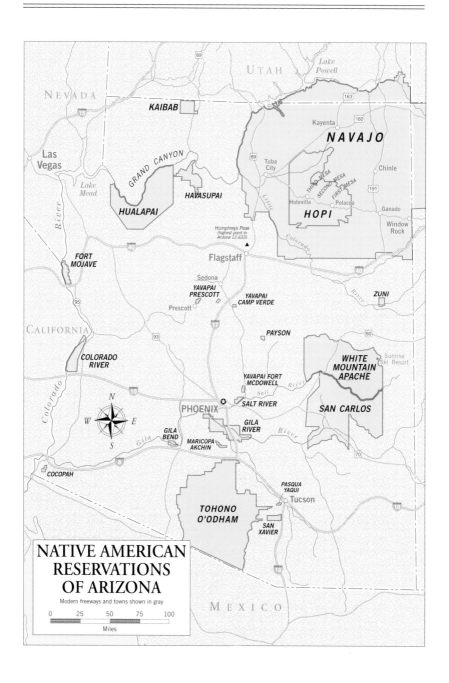

UTAH

Lake
Powell

NEVADA

KAIBAB

89

163

Kayenta

160

NAVAJO

Las
Vegas

GRAND CANYON

89

Tuba
City

Chinle

Lake
Mead

HAVASUPAI

THIRD MESA
SECOND MESA
FIRST MESA

191

River

HUALAPAI

Hotevilla

Polacca

HOPI

Ganado

Window
Rock

FORT
MOJAVE

40

Humphreys Peak
(highest point in
Arizona 12,633)

Flagstaff

Colorado

40

95

Sedona

YAVAPAI
PRESCOTT

YAVAPAI
CAMP VERDE

ZUNI

Prescott

River

CALIFORNIA

93

17

PAYSON

60

COLORADO
RIVER

WHITE
MOUNTAIN
APACHE

Sunrise
Ski Resort

Colorado

N

W   E

S

10

YAVAPAI FORT
MCDOWELL

PHOENIX

SALT RIVER

Salt   River

SAN CARLOS

GILA
BEND

GILA
RIVER

River

70

Gila

MARICOPA
AKCHIN

8

COCOPAH

PASQUA
YAQUI

Tucson

10

TOHONO
O'ODHAM

SAN
XAVIER

19

NATIVE AMERICAN
RESERVATIONS
OF ARIZONA

Modern freeways and towns shown in gray

MEXICO

0   25   50   75   100

Miles

ANOTHER WORLD

For many native people the cultural chasm between their lives and that of urban America has been too deep to be bridged. A letter written by a Tohono O'odham and published in the Tucson Citizen *a quarter of a century ago explains this poignantly.*

I am a Papago Indian [Tohono O'odham], very proud to be one, and what I want to say I hope you'll understand for I don't know much about the so-called English grammar.

The main problem I'm concerned with is unemployment for Papago Indians. Some of the problems I have in keeping a job I will discuss. I have worked with white people, but couldn't get along with them or maybe they didn't get along with me.

The people I worked with were all non-Indians. They talked behind my back (luckily I had a nosey friend to tell me all this).

They criticized the way I dressed. A great many Papagos disapprove of the white shirt and necktie bit. This is one reason why the Papago turns away clerical jobs, or vice versa. The Papago tries to be neat in every way —if he can afford it.

They criticized how quiet I was. They wished they hired someone else who'd be a little more lively. Well, this Indian isn't concerned about how much he should open his mouth, but rather how he should get his work done.

They criticized how rude I was not to say: good morning, good afternoon, hi, goodbye, etc., to every one of them. To the Papago it is silly to greet each other with the same word day after day after day, because it will only become meaningless.

The Papago, when greeting on a morning or anytime, will say what he wants to, but it is no greeting like "good morning." At times he will ask "Are you feeling fine," which I think has a little more meaning than the word, "Hi."

They criticized how rude it was not to introduce myself to a new person on the job. If a Papago wants to know who somebody is, he will ask someone else or he'll hear his name mentioned. You know, to the Papago it's quite funny to see people shake hands when introduced. Shaking hands is done only for religious purposes. When meeting a new person a smile shows the person is already accepted as a friend. They criticized how rude I was not to say thank you when done a favor. To the Papago there is no such word. When a favor is done or a gift is given, he shows appreciation by returning something of equal value to the giver. (Those people never saw the favors I returned which meant thank you.)

These are some of the reasons I was told to quit my job. So now I'm looking for another, knowing I'll face the same problems in the white society.

the future. Navajo leaders have made a commitment to preserving the Navajo ways—using the schools and media technology to keep both the culture and the language alive. Now at least 90 minutes of each day in the reservation's primary and secondary schools are devoted to a standardized curriculum focusing on the "Navajo Perspective." "You can't put the native and the Anglo perspectives together because they are too different," explains Irvin James, a cultural education specialist for the Navajo Nation. "But the Navajo Nation Tribal Education Policy requires that schools compare the two ways of learning."

On a broader front, Navajo Nation Television 5 broadcasts in the Navajo language to nine communities across the reservation at least one hour per day Monday through Thursday. Special events such as the quarterly Navajo Nation Council meetings, the Navajo Nation Fair, high school basketball games, and the Miss Navajo Pageant are broadcast live. As for how the mother tongue is faring: Nearly three-quarters of Navajos age five and up speak their native language, and the majority are bilingual.

If Western culture has made inroads on the reservations, Arizona's Native people have also made their contributions to the life of the state and the nation, influencing art, culture, and attitudes toward the land and animals. The Navajos take justifiable pride in their unique role in World War II, which began when a California engineer who had grown up in a missionary family on the reservation had the idea of using the Navajo language as a code. He was certain that no Japanese had ever been exposed to enough Navajo to learn it, and equally confident that unlike codes that merely rearranged English, the enemy would have no linguistic foundation for cracking it. To confound the enemy cryptologists still further, the 400 young Navajos who enlisted in the program scrambled words around in their own language, devising a crypto-Navajo that not even their own mothers could understand. It worked flawlessly. The entire invasion of Iwo Jima, for one, was directed by orders that crackled over shortwave radios in Navajo. More than 800 messages were transmitted and translated for the marines, not one was in error, and the Japanese never deciphered the code. Years after the war, when the Japanese chief of intelligence finally was told that the code had been based on a Native American language, he reportedly sighed and said, "Thank you. That is a puzzle I thought would never be solved."

What Native Arizonans still are contributing is an understanding and respect for the natural world that is as alien to us as Navajo speech was to Japanese cryptologists. A newspaper reporter from Tucson learned about it one scorching August day as he walked across the desert with a Tohono O'odham friend.

The Tohono O'odham noticed that the white man was wheezing from asthma, and he mentioned that his people successfully treated the problem by drinking a hot tea made from the leaves of the creosote bush. But first, he said, you must ask the plant for permission to use its leaves. And then, he said, you must pray to the Great Spirit, offering appreciation for his kindness in sending such a wonderful plant. And there was one more thing, the Tohono O'odham said:

"It's also better if you find one special tree to use most of the time. In this way you get to know each other and become friends."

■ VISITING RESERVATIONS

Outsiders are welcome on all of Arizona's 20 reservations, although with different degrees of enthusiasm. Sale and sometimes possession of alcohol is in most places prohibited. Hunting, fishing, and camping require tribal permits. In some areas, such as the Navajos' Monument Valley, hiking is outlawed. Where anything is forbidden, signs will be abundant.

Photography and videotaping also are unwelcome in many situations. Hopi villages and ceremonies may not be photographed, sketched, nor their sounds recorded. Visitors to the Yaqui village of Guadalupe will see many signs outside people's homes asking that their outdoor shrines not be photographed. Navajos, however, do a thriving business with photographers, charging a dollar or two for a pose. Even photographing some hogans calls for a "donation."

Since Congress passed the Indian Gaming Regulatory Act in 1988, parting tourists from their money in gaming halls has become a major industry on many reservations. Games include poker, keno, bingo, and slots. Some of the reservations have visitor centers, usually with an arts and crafts shop in it. Nearly all the reservations have trading posts in the larger towns. On the Navajo Reservation, hundreds of roadside stands selling jewelry and other crafts line the highways.

When driving across either the vast Navajo or Tohono O'odham reservations, take spare water and watch your fuel: Filling stations can be as much as 100 miles apart.

■ THE NAVAJOS

The Navajos are the most populous (165,650) tribal group in the United States. Their huge reservation (25,351 square miles) extends from Arizona into New Mexico and Utah. This high desert land, though hardly suited for supporting a large number of people, includes Arizona's most spectacular prehistoric ruins and many of its most dramatic land forms, including Canyon de Chelly and Monument Valley. Ethnically, the Navajos are related to the Apache: both came from the same Athapaskan stock that migrated from western Canada and Alaska to the Southwest sometime between A.D. 1400 and 1500.

Covering most of Arizona's northeast quadrant, the Navajo Reservation features more than 15 National Monuments, tribal parks, and historic sites. Like the Hopi Reservation it surrounds,, the Navajo Nation occupies American soil but feels like another country. Following are some of the places most worth seeing:

Window Rock, located on AZ 264 just west of the Arizona–New Mexico border, is the capital of the Navajo Nation. As such, it is home not only to tribal government, but also to the **Tribal Arts and Crafts Center** and the **Navajo Tribal Museum**. Both offer examples of fine Navajo rugs and demonstrations of how they are made. If possible, visit Window Rock in early September for the **Navajo Nation Fair**. The tribe's biggest annual event, the five-day fair attracts more than 100,000 people. It includes an all-Indian rodeo with more than 900 participants from across North America; an inter-tribal powwow; a parade, arts and crafts exhibits; agriculture and livestock displays; and all the Indian fry bread you can eat.

Hubbell Trading Post National Historic Site, 20 miles west of Window Rock at Ganado, has been dealing in first-rate Navajo weavings since 1878. Rugs from Hubbell were known as Ganado-style rugs, typically black, white, and gray designs on a red background. Warning: Good Navajo rugs don't come cheap.

Canyon de Chelly, just east of Chinle off US 191 is glorious to behold and is still farmed in the summertime by the Navajo. Wide and sandy at the entrance, it curves back into several side canyons, where, along creek beds lined with cottonwoods are a few old fashioned Navajo hogans, some newer ones, and small plots of farmland. Above them rise 1,000-foot red-brown walls. Occupied first by the mysterious Anasazi almost 2,000 years ago, then by the Hopi, and by the Navajo at the time the Spanish arrived in Arizona, the canyon bears thousands cliff paintings by all three groups. Access to the site is controlled by the Navajo. Jeep tours led by Navajo

NAVAJO RUGS

The designs used in Navajo rugs were largely developed towards the end of the 19th century when traders encouraged the Indians to produce blankets to sell to tourists arriving on the railroad. Consequently, certain designs have come to be associated with the trading posts that supplied them. Following is a brief outline of some of the more distinct examples of these traditional designs.

CHINLE
Named after the town of Chinle in Arizona. These patterns feature designs such as squash blossoms (pictured) within bands of plain color. (Woven by Evelyn Curley)

TWO GREY HILLS
Named after a village in New Mexico. Usually woven from very fine, natural, handspun wool in white, black, and brown colors with a dark border. (Woven by Maraline John)

GANADO

Named for the town where the Hubbell Trading Post is located. Almost always has a red background and dark border. Considered by many as the classic Navajo rug design because of its long history. (Woven by Evelyn Curley)

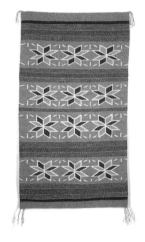

BURNTWATER

Named after an area south of Ganado. Features earth tones, a large variety of pastel colors, and complex border designs.
(Woven by Brenda Spencer)

CRYSTAL

Named after a trading post in New Mexico. Noted for the wavy lines within the bands produced by alternating colors of weft strands. This example features patterned squash blossoms similar to the Chinle. (Woven by Fannie Begay)

(all photos by George H. H. Huey)

guides are available from Thunderbird Lodge and are especially interesting, as the guides may tell you from their own experience about Navajo life in the canyon. The small fields along the stream are prized land passed down matrilineally. Almost indecipherable pathways lead down from the rim, along which Navajo families come with their goats or sheep in the summertime. *(Also see pages 72-74.)*

About 100 miles northwest of Canyon de Chelly in the vicinity of Kayenta is Monument Valley, with its majestic sandstone totems and towers. Along the road is an informal Navajo market where you can buy or admire exquisitely crafted silver jewelry and other Navajo crafts. Navajo guides also lead horseback trips into the area.

The ancient Anasazi ruins of Betatakin and Keet Seel at Navajo National Monument are described on page 92.

Only a few Navajos still live in a traditional eight-sided hogan (above), but their ceremonial use remains important. (left) A Navajo woman displays her jewelry.

■ APACHES

The Apaches are divided into a number of subtribal families—San Carlos, White Mountain, Tonto, etc.—and these inhabit several Arizona reservations. Despite their long and very prominent moments in Arizona history, they remain poorly understood by non-Indians; their blood-stained past has encouraged more imagination than it has straightforward scholarship.

Apache boys, in a photo likely dating from the 1880s. (Arizona Historical Society)

Arriving in the Southwest about A.D. 1400, they were hunter-gatherers who acquired horses from the Spanish in the 1700s. During the mid-1800s they were launching raiding parties against other tribes as far north as the Hopi mesas and as far south as Sonora, Mexico. Led by great warriors such as Cochise and Geronimo, they did not give up their lands and freedom to whites without some fierce fighting, and they were greatly feared by Spanish colonists in the 17th century and American pioneers in the 19th.

RIGHTS AND RIFLES

*T*o Americans generally, the aborigine is a nonentity except when he is on
... *T* the war-path. The moment he concludes to live at peace with the whites,
that moment all his troubles begin. Never was there a truer remark than that made
by [Gen. George] Crook [commander of the U.S. Army campaign against the
Apaches in 1871-72]: "The American Indian commands respect for his rights only
so long as he inspires terror for his rifle."

—John G. Bourke, *On the Border With Crook,* 1892

From the White Mountains to the Mogollon Rim in eastern and central Arizona
to the Chiricahua Mountains in the state's southeast corner, the U.S. Army
launched numerous campaigns against the Apache between 1870 and 1886, when
Geronimo finally surrendered.

The complete transformation of Apache society over the last 120 years is one of
the most fascinating but untold cultural stories in Arizona, for no other tribe has
changed as radically. As an *Arizona Highways* publication noted, the once-no-
madic Apaches now "excel as cowboys, ranchers, farmers, lumbermen, artisans,
[and] businesspeople." Little of that is found in their history.

About 200 miles northeast of Phoenix, the White Mountain Apaches own and
operate **Sunrise Ski Resort,** Arizona's largest ski area with more than 65 runs on
three mountains. But skiing isn't all the White Mountain Apache Reservation has
to offer. From spring through fall, this piney high country is a haven for camping,
fishing, and boating. Tribal permits are required for most recreational activities on
the reservation. Near Whiteriver, the **Apache Cultural Center** displays Apache artifacts and crafts and details the military campaigns launched against the tribe
from nearby Fort Apache in the 1870s; *(520) 338-4625.*

Adjoining the White Mountain Apache Reservation to the south is the **San
Carlos Apache Reservation,** which stretches from alpine meadows at its northern
reaches down through grasslands and into the desert at its southern end. This
reservation's most popular spot is man-made San Carlos Lake: 23 miles long, two
miles wide, and chock full of bass. Fishing permits and supplies are available at
San Carlos Lake Marina; *117 miles east of Phoenix and two miles north of Coolidge
Dam; (520) 475-2756.*

■ YAVAPAIS

The Yavapais are scattered about three reservations: Fort McDowell, Prescott, and Camp Verde. Originally a Yuman-speaking people culturally related to the Havasupais and Hualapais, Yavapai history became entwined with Apache in the 1860s as the two fought the white man together in the Verde Valley. In 1870, however, the starving Yavapais surrendered to the U.S. Army and began working as scouts for the white men. This gave the army a decided edge, and by 1873 the defeated Apache and Yavapai were herded onto reservations together. Today pure Yavapai blood has virtually disappeared, and much of their culture essentially has merged with the Apache.

■ HUALAPAIS AND HAVASUPAIS

The Hualapais and Havasupais are the people of the Grand Canyon. The Hualapai, whose name derives from a Yuman word meaning "pine-tree people," live on 1,551 square miles of forest and high plateau land abutting the canyon's south rim. The Havasupais ("People of the blue-green water") number only about 600, and are the most isolated of any Arizona tribe: Edward Abbey once noted that the Havasupais were an unusually wise people, having rejected a Bureau of Indian Affairs (BIA) scheme to blast a million-dollar road into the village to funnel in tourists. To reach their one village, Supai, drive 60 miles north of Arizona State Highway 66 through the Hualapai Reservation, park at Hualapai Hilltop and either walk or ride a mule eight miles farther into Havasu Canyon, a tributary of the Grand Canyon. Travel is by foot or horseback only in this canyon—and Supai is the only town in the United States that receives its mail by pack train.

At the bottom of this Eden-like spot are the village and store, and the 24-room Havasupai Lodge, as well as the Havasupai Tribal Arts Museum, which has displays of tribal history and local crafts. A trail leads to Havasupai campground and a series of magnificent waterfalls that plunge from 75 to almost 200 feet down cliffs of Redwall limestone into the turquoise pools of Havasu Creek.

Though tourism is important to the Havasupai, they still farm the canyon floor in summer and hunt game and collect wild plants atop Coconino Plateau in winter. *Reservations must be made in advance; campground is (520) 448-2121; lodge is (520) 448-2111.*

■ HOPIS

The Hopis, defying meteorological odds and conventional horticultural wisdom, have successfully raised corn, squash, and melons on the arid mesas of northeastern Arizona for at least 800 years. Not surprisingly, many of their sacred ceremonies center around the need for rain. Most astonishing is the snake dance, in which Hopi priests carry live snakes—including rattlesnakes—in their mouths. Since they live underground, the snakes are viewed as the logical intercessors to the gods, which in Hopi theology inhabit the Underworld. Hopi arts, along with their rituals, are highly developed: their contemporary pottery and kachina dolls are the most refined of all the Native American arts in Arizona today.

The Hopi villages are fascinating to visit, particularly Walpi, the "sky village" appearing to bud right out of the top of a mesa; and Old Oraibi, the oldest continuously inhabited town in the U.S. (since A.D. 1150).

The Hopi Reservation is completely surrounded by the Navajo Nation, an uneasy living arrangement born of ancient rivalries and U.S. government interference. The 10,000 people who make up the Hopi nation are culturally related to the Pueblo people of New Mexico and their rituals and art reflect those ties. Contemporary Hopi pottery and kachina dolls are refined works of art.

Hopi life, religion, and society are organized around an all-encompassing belief system called *Hopivotskwani,* the Hopi Path of Life. According to legend, it

ANCIENT AND MODERN TRADITIONS

Not so many years ago, a team of archaeologists excavating a Sinagua burial site near Flagstaff were astonished to discover the remains of an ancient Sinagua shaman interred with a dozen wooden wands carved and painted to resemble hoofs and hands. The find paled, however, in the light of what happened next. A modern Hopi, taken to view the remains, could not only identify the uses of the millennium-old paraphernalia, but also tell from them which clan the magician had belonged to.

For archaeologists, the incident was more proof of the long-suspected Sinagua-Anasazi-Hopi linkages. But it also illuminated something else: the phenomenal endurance of Hopi tradition and culture.

Hopi potter Marilyn Sakewa of Polacca decorates her pots with paint made from wild spinach and applies it with a yucca spine brush. (Kerrick James)

began when the first ancestors of the Hopi emerged from the spirit underworld to wander until they arrived at the arid mesas that would become their home. The Bear Clan, so called because they found a dead bear during their pilgrimage, settled at Shungopovi, in northeastern Arizona. As other groups arrived, they were given land to farm and accepted into Hopi society once they could demonstrate their acceptance of Hopivotskwani.

The concept of the Hopi Path is extremely difficult for an outsider to grasp, but it has to do with the presence of the spirit world in virtually everything. Every plant and animal has a spirit; every summer thunderstorm is generated in the spirit universe—those storms being critical to Hopi farming. Every winter solstice marks the beginning of ceremonial kachina dancing, which continues until mid-July. The kachinas, which appear to outsiders to be men dressed in elaborate and astounding costumes, are in Hopi belief the spirits of departed ancestors. They sing songs of admonition and perfected life, and they take the Hopis' prayers for rain, health, and fertility back to the spirit world.

❖

For hundreds of years the Hopis have lived on three mesas that rise above a wide valley. A road runs through the valley, where a scattering of schools, tourism; some of their villages do not welcome visitors, and those that do generally ask outsiders to register at the local community office.

First Mesa. A narrow, gravel road leads up to First Mesa from the more modern town of Polacca. On top, the view is sweeping. Some sections of the stone and adobe houses may predate the arrival of Columbus by 300 years. Of the three small, interconnected villages on top, the first is **Hano,** a Tewa settlement, formed in 1696 by Tewa Indians from the Rio Grande region who had fled from the Spanish. The Hopi let them live here on the condition they guard access to the mesa top. Amazingly, the Tewa have maintained their own customs and language despite centuries of Hopi influence. The most famous Hopi reservation pottery family, the Nampeyo, is from the Hano settlement. The first of these potters, known simply as Nampeyo, was born here about 1860. Her designs were influenced by prehistoric pottery found by her husband, Lesou, at a nearby archeological dig in 1895. Their descendants carry on the tradition they began, using clay taken from an ancient and proprietary Hopi source, and painting designs with a yucca spine brush.

Adjacent to Hano is the village of **Sichomovi,** where visitors will find **First Mesa Visitor Center at Ponsi Hall.** It is necessary to park here and register for a guided walking tour. At tiny **Walpi,** ancient houses and old defenses jut out from the rocky cliffs, forming a dramatic contrast of stone against the surrounding expanse of sky. *Take AZ 264 west of US 191 through the Navajo Reservation and past Keams Canyon. Visitor center telephone is (520) 737-2262.*

Second Mesa. Of the three mesas, Second Mesa is the most amenable to visitors. Below the mesa on the western edge, a complex of buildings, including a restaurant and motel, connect with the **Hopi Cultural Center.** The center's museum has fascinating exhibits of Hopi history culture. A second cafe, Nova-ki, is also located here. The mesa's three villages are **Shipaulovi, Mishongnovi, and Shunopavi.** *AZ 264 and AZ 87 join below Second Mesa. Cultural center, (520) 734-2401.*

Third Mesa. One mile south of AZ 264, at the eastern base of Third Mesa, stands the village **Kykotsmovi,** which means "Mound of Ruined Houses." **The Office of Public Relations** is here, along with the **Kykotsmovi Village Store**—stocked with groceries—and a few arts and crafts stores.

Two miles west of Kykotsmovi, **Old Oraibi** is perched on the edge of Third Mesa. Inhabited since a.d. 1150, this small village is considered by many to be the oldest continually inhabited community in the United States. (Ácoma also vies for the title). In 1900, the population neared 800, but six years later a widely publicized dissension caused many to leave. To settle a dispute between two chiefs, You-ke-oma and Tawa-quap-tewa, the two village leaders staged a "push-of-war" contest where the two groups stood on either side of a line cut into a mesa. They pushed each other until one group lost. You-ke-oma and his faction left to establish **Hotevilla**, about four miles away. Both villages welcome visitors and are known for their basketry and other crafts. The residents of **Bacavi,** situated across the highway, are also descendants of Oraibi's former inhabitants.

■ TOHONO O'ODHAM

The Tohono O'odham are the quintessential desert people: They believe, no doubt correctly, that their culture will abide in the arid heart of the Sonoran Desert long after we have squandered what we understand of its usable resources and gone on. Before the encroachment of Anglo culture, the O'odham successfully grew corn, squash, and beans on the dry ground and harvested the native saguaro fruit for dessert. Until they opened the Desert Diamond Casino in Sells in 1993, the O'odham had done little to generate tourism. They are not in the least hostile to outsiders, but neither are they as outgoing as, say, the Navajo and Apache. With the casino now generating 60 percent of the tribe's annual revenues, the O'odhams' attitude toward non-natives may be changing.

The **Pimas,** closely related to the O'odham, live with the **Maricopas** on the Gila River Reservation just south of Phoenix. If you can visit this reservation—America's second largest, with 2.8 million acres and more than 8,000 people—in mid-winter, you might be able to see their all-Indian Rodeo and Fair; *take exit 175 off I-10 south of Phoenix; (520) 383-2221.*

■ SMALLER TRIBES

The remaining Arizona tribes are much less well-known than those described earlier.

The **Kaibab Paiutes** and **Chemehuevis**, two descendants of the Southern Paiutes of the Great Basin, have very few members today. The Kaibab Paiutes inhabit the 188-square-mile Kaibab reservation on the Utah border. The Chemehuevis, who saw their farmlands become Lake Havasu when Parker Dam backed up the Colorado River in 1938, moved downstream to the Colorado River Reservation.

The **Mohaves**, a tribe of Yuman speakers, straddle the Colorado on the Fort Mohave Reservation just south of Bullhead City.

Still farther downstream, near the Mexican border, are the related **Cocopahs** and **Quechan** (Yuman) people. Both small tribes depend heavily on agriculture.

The **Yaquis**, 19th-century refugees from Mexican persecution, inhabit tiny reservations just southwest of Tucson and the incorporated Phoenix suburb of Guadalupe. The U.S. Government officially designated them an American tribe only in 1978; since then they have adopted a tribal constitution and transcribed their language into written form. Though small—about 5,300 members in Arizona— they seem more determined than ever to preserve their heritage.

Few if any **Zuni** Indians reside in Arizona, but the official state map shows a tiny Zuni reservation a few miles northwest of St. Johns, near the New Mexico border. This 17-square-mile "reservation" is in Zuni belief the ceiling of heaven, and it was given to the tribe as part of a complicated land swap in 1985.

Once every four years, immediately after the summer solstice, the Zunis make a 45-mile pilgrimage from their New Mexico reservation to this Arizona annex. They follow the Zuni River to a spring where they bathe, then proceed on to Kolhuwalawa, a dry Arizona lake bed that spreads over their underground spiritual afterworld. There they conduct ceremonies that are believed to date back at least a thousand years.

There are no roads or travelers' facilities on this tiny reservation, but visitors can drive to Zuni Pueblo on the Zuni reservation in New Mexico. This pueblo was one of Coronado's fabled Seven Cities of Cibola. *From St. Johns, head northeast on Arizona State Route 61, continuing 10 miles into New Mexico.*

MAKING ARIZONA

CHARLES DEBRILLE POSTON LIKED TO CALL HIMSELF the "Father of Arizona." Spiritually if not literally, he appears to have been exactly that. Were he alive today, however, he would find that the grown-up state little resembles the strange community he created at the old Spanish presidio of Tubac.

Poston was toiling as an obscure law clerk in gold-rush California when he read about the Gadsden Purchase in 1853. He must have sniffed opportunity, because he quickly organized a party of fellow adventurers and set out for the silver-veined hills of southern Arizona. His company moved into the ghost fort of Tubac, began rebuilding it, and commenced lucrative mining operations in the Santa Rita mountains nearby. Before long, Mexican miners and unmarried women drifted up from Mexico, and Poston installed himself as the town's *alcalde*. The Spanish word literally translates as "mayor," but Poston was more like a potentate. He ran the mines, performed marriages and granted divorces, baptized children and dispensed justice. Still, he appears to have been no dictator, but a Utopian and a precursor of modern libertarians.

"We had no law but love and no occupation but labor," Poston wrote, "no government, no taxes, no public debt, no politics. It was a community in a perfect state of nature."

This was true in still other ways, in Poston's mind. All the women in Tubac had come from Sonora, which, Poston wrote, "has always been famous for the beauty and gracefulness of its señoritas . . . . They are exceedingly dainty in their underclothing, wear the finest linen when they can afford it, and spend half their lives over the washing machine."

If the barest tint of condescension seems to color Poston's admiration, well, he was not to be the last Anglo pioneer who held such contradictions. In any event, his Utopia was short-lived. In 1861 Apaches reduced Tubac to rubble, and Poston fled for his life, later observing bitterly that "The Government of the United States abandoned the first settlers of Arizona to the merciless Apaches."

Still, Poston never ceased to dream—another quirk of character that would appear in so many pioneers and developers that followed him. He successfully lobbied Washington in 1863 to have Arizona separated from the Territory of New Mexico. He founded serious historical societies in Tucson and Phoenix. He proposed irrigation projects. Then he made a pilgrimage to Asia and became a

Zoroastrian, returned to Arizona and tried in vain to establish a sun-worshiping sect in the land he loved. He died impoverished in Phoenix in 1902.

It was not long after Poston's experiment at Tubac that larger waves of Anglo settlers came rolling in. They were mostly of three types: the cattle ranchers, the agrarian Mormons spilling down from Utah, and the miners. While few of these had such exotic ideas as Poston, they were, like him, following their dreams and questing in some form for personal freedom. They all faced the same headaches: a shortage of water, a surplus of Apaches.

■ THE APACHE WARS, 1871-86

No ethnic tribe on the planet has bounced so far and so often from utter vilification to romantic glorification as have the Apaches. A researcher from some other world flying in to comb through the voluminous histories, novels and movies about the Apaches would learn, for example, that they were "blood-drunk and beast-hot . . . fetid-breathed and shrieking . . . lecherous and without honor or mercy . . . the Apaches hate life and they are the enemy of all mankind." (All this from the 1950s novels of James Warner Bellah.) And then he would hear agent Tom Jeffords in a contemporary novel, *Blood Brother*, explaining that among the Apaches "there is no private hoarding, no cheating. Whatever they have is divided equally. . . . There's no caste system, and no aristocrats and no commoners. . . . I wonder by what standards we have arrogated to ourselves the right to call Indians savages?"

There is universal agreement on one fact regarding the 19th-century Apaches: they were incredible individual fighters. "There were 23 different Apache groups in Arizona, and there was no communication among them," explained historian David Faust, curator of the Fort Lowell Park Museum in Tucson. "Everybody was fighting his own war, essentially. If they had waged a coordinated war, they probably would have been able to hold out into the 20th century."

In purely objective terms, the Apaches were undeniably aggressors. When they emigrated into the Southwest, probably in the 16th century, they found much of the territory already occupied by farmers such as the Hopi and Pima. To survive, they raided when necessary. But the advent of truly bloody, vengeance-driven war came only after Spaniards and Anglos arrived.

The Camp Grant Massacre set the savage tone for the war with Anglo Arizona. In April of 1871, a motley posse of Anglos, Mexican-Americans and Papagos organized in Tucson rode the 60 miles northeast to Camp Grant, where a cluster of Arivaipa Apaches were living under an informal treaty with the U.S. Army. The Tucsonans, led by former mayor William S. Oury, suspected the Arivaipas of the incessant hit-and-run raids plaguing southern Arizona ranchers and supply wagons—which may indeed have been an accurate suspicion. But when the posse attacked at dawn on April 30, they found hardly any Apache men in the camp; most were out hunting. No matter: the raiders had come to exterminate Apaches. They killed between 85 and 100—the number is still disputed—and all but a handful of them were women and children.

"The attack was so swift and fierce," Oury later boasted, "that within half an hour the whole work was ended and not an adult Indian left to tell the tale."

The massacre focused national attention on the "Indian problem" in Arizona, although the consequences hardly did the Apaches any good. The raiders were tried for murder in Tucson and acquitted. Then President Ulysses S. Grant launched a carrot-and-bayonet effort to coax the Apaches into peace treaties and reservations, or, if they refused, to wage full-scale war against them. Gen. George Crook, a brilliant military strategist who thoroughly understood his enemy, directed the campaign of 1872-73 and came close to quelling the "problem" in those two years.

A network of 16 army forts laced through Arizona, providing a base for Crook's troops. The Apaches never attacked the forts directly—that would have been suicidal—but ambushed the troops in small scouting parties well away from the forts. The army employed friendly or "tame" Apaches as scouts to lead them through unfamiliar terrain in pursuit of the enemy. Neither side practiced much charity. If the Apaches captured a soldier alive, they would execute him either by lashing him to a convenient tree or cactus and perforating his torso with arrows; or by suspending him head down over a slow fire. Crook ordered his troops to make "every effort to avoid the killing of women and children," but women and children sometimes accompanied the warriors into caves or canyons from which the Apaches staged a last-ditch defense—and then the army bullets were hardly selective.

Nor did the atrocities end with surrender. In 1873, the Verde Valley Apaches and Yavapais surrendered to Crook at Fort Verde. The U.S. Government promised them an 800-square-mile reservation stretching 10 miles on either side of the river for a distance of 40 miles. This land would be theirs, they were promised, "for as long as the rivers run, the grass grows, and the hills endure." But this temperate, fertile valley was worth more to Territorial settlers than the honor of keeping the promise. After only two years, 1,476 Indians literally were herded 180 miles southeast to the arid San Carlos reservation. As described by Yavapai scout Rim-Ma-Ke-Na, in an unpublished history of the Yavapai-Apache tribes:

> They drive them like cattles [sic], they have no pity. Some have to be left and die. Those that can't go any farther. Even when it's rainy day and floody they have to drive them in the flood. And many are drowned. And that was one of the saddest thing that I ever saw.

Even with most of the Apaches installed on reservations, sporadic fighting and raiding erupted. The Chiricahua Apaches, led by Geronimo, held out in the mountains of southeastern Arizona until they also surrendered to Crook in 1886. They were then shipped by train to a prison camp in Florida.

Geronimo himself provided a pathetic epilogue to the Apache wars in the years following his detention. He reinvented himself as an exotic celebrity, making the rounds of fairs and conventions, selling autographs, buttons off his clothes, and other trinkets to amuse white Americans. There is an extant photo of him taken at the St. Louis World's Fair in 1904. He is wearing an ill-fitting wool coat, short hair and a stoic yet vacant gaze, and he is selling bows and arrows—a caricature Indian now, lurching gracelessly between two worlds. In that picture he appears as a prescient metaphor for much that would happen to Native Americans in the 20th century.

Geronimo (right) and his warriors were as well armed as the U.S. Army, and they knew the land much better, 1886. (Arizona Historical Society)

In the 1980s an Apache man set up shop in a teepee on the west outskirts of Tucson, charging people a dollar each to take his picture. He claimed to be Geronimo's grandson.

■ GRAZING, FARMING, AND MINING

The cattlemen, who established their herds in the high desert grasslands of the southeast and the temperate meadows of north-central Arizona, contributed an enduring romance to the frontier. They also created its first modern environmental disaster: not many of those grasslands survived. In 1870, an estimated 5,000 cattle grazed Arizona; by 1891 there were 1.5 million. The fragile land could not support them. In 1892 and '93 a devastating drought appeared—as it periodically does in the arid Southwest. The range was already overgrazed and overtrampled, and something between 50 and 75 percent of the animals died. When the rains finally returned, thousands of square miles, gnawed bare by the starving cows, was exposed to erosion. Raw desert replaced many of the grasslands, and ranching dwindled to a minor role in the state's future.

The Mormons proved to be better custodians of the land, but their welcome was checkered. Mormon expeditions into Arizona had begun as early as 1846, when the Mormon Battalion, a force of 500 pseudo-military volunteers under the command of Captain Philip St. George Cooke, punched a wagon trail through the uncharted land to California. This was no missionary or colonialist adventure; Cooke saw no good use for Arizona. It was, he wrote, ". . . a wilderness where nothing but savages and wild beasts are found, or deserts where, for lack of water, there is no living creature."

This land of "wild beasts" and, alternately, "no living creature" proved compelling enough to later Mormons who began spilling down from Utah in the 1870s. They came for three reasons: to colonize new farmlands, to try to convert Indians—specifically the Hopis—and to find refuges isolated enough to discourage the U.S. Government from harassing the polygamists among them. They founded settlements along the Little Colorado River in east-central Arizona, where they were harassed instead by floods, and established several more communities in the desert farther south, including Lehi (now the Phoenix suburb of Mesa), Thatcher and St. David.

Despite unforgiving and unfamiliar environmental conditions, Mormons in Arizona, as elsewhere, became successful farmers. A correspondent of the *Prescott*

Miner, writing in 1878, probably pointed out the reason: "The work done by these people is simply astounding," he wrote. "The alacrity and vim with which they go at it is decidedly in favor of co-operation or communism." Still, polygamy was as unwelcome in Arizona as it was elsewhere. The Territorial Legislature of 1885 disenfranchised polygamists, and Mormon skirmishes with gentile neighbors —ranchers, mainly—were not uncommon. The church ended sanctioned polygamy in 1890, although a handful of wildcat fundamentalists continue the practice in deepest northern Arizona even today. The more significant legacy of Mormons in Arizona, however, is this: the public schools in virtually every community they established remain among the state's best.

Mining formed the third territorial boom, and it reshaped the state's physical and political landscape in a far more profound way than anything else. The treasure buried in Arizona's mountains attracted a different breed of dreamer than the range or farmlands, because it offered the lure of quick and dramatic wealth.

Arizona's gold rush, a short-lived phenomenon, began in 1857 when an itinerant Texan named Jack Snively swished a pan through the Gila River and saw some residue glinting in the desert sun. Gila City, the town hastily assembled on the site, was a metaphor for the rush itself. After a year it had a teeming population of 1,200 prospectors, gamblers, prostitutes and assorted other merchants. In another two years the gold began to dwindle. In 1862 the Gila River, as if in moral outrage, went on a rampage and wiped out what was left of the town. When journalist J. Ross Browne passed through in 1864, he noted with finely tuned sarcasm that "the promising Metropolis of Arizona consisted of three chimneys and a coyote." Much the same fate befell other mining camps.

The silver boom followed gold, and it was not much more durable. The most famous lode was discovered in 1877 by a wandering miner named Ed Schieffelin, who had traveled with a U.S. Cavalry troop from California to establish Arizona's new Fort Huachuca. This was hostile land, controlled by the Chiricahua Apaches. At first Schieffelin tried to do his prospecting in the company of scouting parties dispatched from the fort, but he soon realized he would have to follow his own instincts in search of ore. As he left the safety of the fort alone, someone warned him, "All you'll ever find out there will be your tombstone."

Schieffelin lived to have the last laugh, and it was one energized by considerable wealth. He indeed found silver ore, and wryly named his first stake "Tombstone." In 10 years, the hills around the boom town that adopted that name yielded $19 million worth of silver. In 1886, however, the mines flooded and even Tombstone

The town of Bisbee as it looks today. (Kerrick James)

—which truly had been a metropolis, the largest town in the territory—collapsed into the role of historic artifact.

It was copper that finally etched Arizona onto the global mineralogical map. The copper boom also forged a permanent change in Arizona's character, one that persists today: copper transformed the territory from a frontier to an economic colony, a place largely owned and controlled by outsiders.

Copper mining had little in common with the small-scale, nickel-and-dime operations of men like Poston and Schieffelin. Anywhere between 20 and 100 pounds of ore has to be processed to yield a pound of copper, and a mine has to produce hundreds of tons a copper a day to pay off. This requires gigantic investments in land, equipment, personnel and science. Since no individual in Arizona Territory had such deep pockets, the boom was financed by corporations from back East. And while they brought considerable prosperity to Arizona, they also extracted a painful social price.

Jerome, Clifton, Globe, Bisbee—these copper-mining capitals of turn-of-the-19th-century Arizona appear quaintly picturesque today, with their neighborhoods of pint-sized Victorian homes snaking up and down precipitous hillsides

Copper miners thousands of feet below Bisbee, c. 1910. (Bisbee Mining & Historical Museum)

Fewer than 300 Victorian-era buildings remain in the mountainside mining town of Jerome, but slowly entrepreneurs are restoring them.

and gulches. In the middle of a Bisbee intersection stands a smashing socialist-realist-era copper statue of a miner stripped to the waist, bristling with muscle and wearing an expression of world-dominating confidence. The inscription reads: "Dedicated to those virile men—the copper miners." Viewing artifacts such as these from the safe distance of the 1990s, it is easy to romanticize the copper boom. In truth, it was an ugly business.

The miners worked in stopes, or pits hundreds of feet underground, drilling holes for dynamite and blasting the ore into rubble to be carted to the surface. There might be water up to their ankles, the temperature would be well over 100 degrees, and the humid air would be fouled by the stench of carbon dioxide and human excrement. Until well into the 20th century, safety records were not encouraging; in 1913, according to Phelps Dodge records, a laborer in the Copper Queen operation at Bisbee could expect to have a "lost-time" accident once every 474 shifts. There were many ways to die: quickly, in fires or cave-ins or untimely explosions, or slowly, from silicosis caused by breathing the fine quartz dust produced by the drilling. An article in the *Tombstone Epitaph*, even if written in the florid style of the era, describes in graphic terms the death of one Copper Queen smelter worker:

Joe Bailey of Bisbee is dead. . . . While pursuing his daily vocation, un-
mindful that death lurked nigh, a pot containing one ton of molten slag
came detached from the crane that was conveying it, and fell to the
ground below, a distance of twelve or fifteen feet, lighting squarely upon
the man. There were no cries of pain, no shrieks of anguish, no pleading
for mercy or assistance. The spirit of Joe Bailey had taken its flight.

Above ground, the miners and their families—those lucky ones who had families—lived in company towns built and owned by the mine operators. On the surface the companies seemed benevolently paternalistic; they provided baseball
fields, hospitals, schools, housing at below-market rent and plenty of credit. A retired Phelps Dodge geologist in Bisbee recently recalled that the company even
gave $50 "Christmas bonuses" to all the ministers in town. But all this was also
calculated to insure obedience to the company. "They used the carrot more than
the stick," said mining historian James W. Byrkit, "but the fear of losing these
things was always present in the background."

The event that illustrates the political muscle that the mine companies came to
have was the bizarre Bisbee Deportation of 1917. To this day it remains controversial in Bisbee; some long-time residents don't even like outsiders asking questions
about it. On June 27, 1917, a radical labor union, the Industrial Workers of the
World (IWW, or "Wobblies") called a strike. Although fewer than 400 were card-
carrying Wobblies, about half of Bisbee's 4,700 miners walked out. Mine management responded with a public relations blitz painting the IWW as German
sympathizers sabotaging the Allies' wartime copper supplies.

At 6:30 on the morning of July 17, Cochise County Sheriff Harry Wheeler and
a colossal posse of 2,000 "loyal Americans" fanned through Bisbee and arrested an
equal number of strikers in their homes. The vigilantes marched the captives
under armed guard two miles to the suburb of Warren. Those who agreed to return to work were freed; the other 1,186 were crammed into 23 boxcars and rail-
roaded to a camp at Columbus, New Mexico. Few ever returned to Bisbee, and
union power in Arizona was emasculated.

Thus the script for offstage control of Arizona was forged in copper. As a territory and then an adolescent state after 1912, Arizona never found the means to
sort out its own destiny. This remains the story today. Most of Arizona's banks
(and the desolate remains of its S&Ls) are owned out of state. Many of the most
ambitious development projects are planned and financed out of state. This is the
result of unchained growth: there is money waiting to be made here. The story of
Phoenix explains how.

RAILROAD TO THE CHRISTIAN WORLD

When the railroad arrived in Tucson on March 20, 1880, the city's very proud Mayor Leatherwood was unable to contain his excitement. After dispatching a number of celebratory drinks and a greater number of telegrams to dignitaries all over the United States, he and his cronies felt compelled to telegraph Pope Leo XII himself the following message:

> To His Holiness, the Pope of Rome, Italy
> The mayor of Tucson begs the honor of reminding Your Holiness that this ancient and honorable pueblo was founded by the Spaniards under the sanction of the Church more than three centuries ago, and to inform Your Holiness that a railroad from San Francisco, California, now connects us with the entire Christian World.
>
> —R. N. Leatherwood, Mayor

Before the message was wired, a few more temperate locals got wind of Leatherwood's potentially embarrassing idea. They raced to the telegrapher's office and begged the fellow not to send it. After some palm-greasing, the telegrapher complied. But perhaps because he didn't want to spoil Tucson's party, he wrote his own "response" to the boastful city fathers. The note was delivered to Leatherwood, and before looking it over, he read it aloud to the gathered Tucsonians:

> His Holiness the Pope acknowledges with appreciation receipt of your telegram informing him that the ancient city of Tucson at last has been connected by rail with the outside world and sends his benediction, but for his own satisfaction would ask, where the hell is Tucson?
>
> —"Antonelli"

ARIZONA POLITICS

Many an outsider who ventures to write about Arizona politics is visited by a ghostly spasm that causes the fingers to type the words ". . . frontier mentality . . ." Normally they appear not far from the beginning of the commentary, and if the writer is in good form, the reader will be treated to supporting anecdotage: Free-for-all gun laws that have allowed 50,000 Arizonans (so far) to sign up for permits to carry concealed weapons. Former Gov. Evan Mecham's education lobbyist who in 1987 proclaimed that "if a student wants to say the world is flat, the teacher doesn't have the right to try to prove otherwise." Current Gov. Fife Symington, who after declaring backruptcy and being indited on several counts of financial fraud, enthusiastically announced that he'd run for re-election in 1998.

Part of the explanation is simply that knaves and crackpots sometimes stumble into public service here, as they do in every other state. But there's also something deeper. Arizonans are fundamentally ornery, willing to defy conventional widom and spurn political correctness. We have a tenacious distrust of governing bodies and a ready resolve to take matters into our own hands (witness the state legislator who in 1997 tried to have the federal Endangered Species Act declared null and void in Arizona). The political wind generally blows hard from the right, but it is also rowdy and unpredictable.

President William Taft was among the first to notice this. Troubled by the populist tilt of Arizona's proposed constitution, with its provisions for voter initiative, referendum and recall, he refused to approve statehood until recall for judges was removed. (Taft, incidentally, had been a judge.) Once inducted into the Union, the first legislature of the new state immediately placed judicial recall on the ballot, and Arizona voters ordered it right back in.

From statehood in 1912 to the early 1950s, Arizona was essentially a one-party state, and that party was Democratic. It was more populist than liberal, however, as most citizens seemed to distrust big government as well as big business. The dramatic shift toward a two-party state, and then the dominance of the GOP, began in 1950 with the election of a Republican governor, Howard Pyle. By the end of that decade, registered Democrats still outnumbered Republicans by 68 to 32 percent—yet Republicans were consistently sweeping Democrats out of offices at every level. One explanation, among many advanced by historians, was that conservatives were registering as Democrats in order to have a voice in the dominant party's primaries, then voting for Republicans in the general elections.

Air conditioning was the prime reason for the rightward swing of Arizona. With the Valley of the Sun newly rendered fit for human habitation, metropolitan Phoenix rapidly attracted major industries and swarms of retirees. Between 1950 and 1960, Phoenix's population ballooned from 106,818 to 439,170, and more were streaming in from the Republican Midwest than from the Democratic South. The Phoenix newspapers, *The Arizona Republic* and the *Phoenix Gazette*, became relentless boosters of economic growth and conservative causes. As the state's most influential news media, they certainly helped build the GOP's power.

Tucson, which since 1950 has languished in Phoenix's economic shadow, has remained the state's Democratic stronghold. But even Tucson is slowly turning more conservative. Phoenix today has emerged as Republican and progressive; Tucson remains Democratic but more wary of taxing and spending than Phoenix.

Confused? So is the political theater of Arizona today. Or perhaps "contentious" is the better description.

We are at least true to our history. Through voter initiative, liberal Arizonans enacted women's suffrage in 1912, and conservatives inflicted Prohibition two years later. We gave ourselves the death penalty in 1914 and revoked it in 1916 and revived it in 1918. Today most of the issues are less profound than these but the list seems endless. Arizonans fight over everything. A county board of supervisors rezones a square mile of desert for a housing development, and opponents fan out through the shopping malls waving petitions to force a referendum.

Most remarkable of all is that Arizonans emerge from this turbulent atmosphere to achieve national political prominence that is out of all proportion to the state's population. In fewer than 30 years, three Arizonans have made a serious run at the presidency: Sen. Barry Goldwater (1964), Sen. Morris Udall (1976), and former Gov. Bruce Babbitt (1988). Two Arizonans now sit on the U.S. Supreme Court: William Rehnquist and Sandra Day O'Connor. Ex-governor Bruce Babbitt is Secretary of the Interior, a job previously held by another native son, Stewart Udall. Carl Hayden, who was first elected to Congress in 1912 and retired as Senate president pro tem in 1969, served Congress longer than any other American in history. There are numerous theories to explain all this, but the most logical is that of a former congressman from Tucson, James F. McNulty: "I suppose any 'frontier' state probably encourages the more ambitious," he says. "New growth is where things happen."

In other words, it's the frontier mentality.

■ ARIZONA TIMELINE ■

300 B.C. Hohokam begin irrigating land to grow corn in the Gila River Valley.

200 B.C. Mogollon become the first Southwestern culture to make pottery.

A.D. 200 After hunting and gathering on the Colorado Plateau for several centuries, the Anasazi begin farming.

1094 Last volcanic eruption in Arizona, at Sunset Crater.

1539 Friar Marcos de Niza and African slave Estevanico cross the southeastern part of state, where they note "stone cities" (pueblos) and claim territory for Spain.

1540 Drawn by fables of the Seven Cities of Cibola, Spanish adventurers arrive in Arizona under the leadership of Francisco Vásquez de Coronado.

1604 Juan de Oñate travels west from the Rio Grande across Arizona with Capt. Marcos Farfan, and later lays claim to parts of Arizona, Colorado, Nevada, New Mexico, Texas, Oklahoma, and Kansas for Spanish Crown—and himself.

1629 Franciscans begin establishing missions among Hopi villages in northeastern Arizona, but their conversions anger many Hopi shamen.

1680 Pueblo Revolt wipes out many Franciscan missions in Arizona, New Mexico, and western Texas, discouraging Spanish settlement in the region.

1687 Eusebio Francisco Kino, an Italian Jesuit educated in Austria, arrives in what is today the Southwest and northern Mexico. During the next 24 years the admired priest establishes 29 missions, travels 75,000 miles within Arizona, and teaches farming and ranching techniques to Native Americans.

1751 Anger at the Spanish for taking their most fertile land and rivalry between priests and Indian leaders prompt Pima and Papago (Tohono O'odham) Indians to revolt. Europeans are completely driven out of Arizona for a year.

1752 After blaming Jesuit missionaries for Indian conflicts, Spanish return to Arizona and establish a presidio at Tubac.

1767 King Charles III expels the increasingly powerful Society of Jesus from the Americas. All over Arizona Territory, Jesuits are arrested and expelled.

1774 Franciscan missionary Francisco Tomas Garces embarks on series of westward journeys from mission at Tubac. He names the Colorado River, becomes the first white man to enter the Grand Canyon from the west, and on July 4, 1776, notes in his journal several meetings with Hopi Indians.

1821   Mexico throws off Spanish rule, takes control of Arizona, New Mexico, and Texas.

1836-48   Texas Revolution and Mexican War turn most of Arizona over to U.S.

1853   James Gadsden, ambassador to Mexico, facilitates purchase of southern third of Arizona for the United States.

1857   Jack Snively finds gold in the Gila River and a three-year gold rush ensues.

1869   John Wesley Powell leads first American expedition through Grand Canyon.

1871   Camp Grant Massacre: posse of Anglos, Mexicans, and Papagos kills between 85 and 100 Apaches, mostly women and children.

1877   Ed Schieffelin finds silver in hostile Apache land and wryly names his stake "Tombstone" after the U.S. Cavalry predicts the Indians will kill him.

1878   The great "pathfinder" John C. Frémont is appointed territorial governor.

1880   First issue of popular newspaper the *Tombstone Epitaph* is printed—in a tent.

1880   Large scale copper mining begins in Bisbee, and continues until 1975.

1881   Gunfight at O.K. Corral in Tombstone between the Hollidays, Earps, Clantons, and McLowrys. In 30 seconds of gunfire, there are three deaths.

1912   Arizona admitted to the Union as the last of the 48 coterminous states.

1924   First Arizona Indian votes under provision of Congressional act granting citizenship to non-reservation Indians.

1930   President Coolidge dedicates Coolidge Dam, highest multiple-dome dam.

1930   Flagstaff's Lowell Observatory announces discovery of the planet Pluto.

1948   Arizona Supreme Court allows reservation Indians to vote in primaries—after 20 years of being disqualified from voting as "wards of the state."

1964   Arizona's longtime Republican politician Barry Goldwater is defeated by Lyndon Baines Johnson in presidential election.

1991   Central Arizona Project completed, delivering water from the Colorado River uphill to Phoenix. Tucson tastes it, doesn't like it, and shuts it off.

PHOENIX
VALLEY OF THE SUN

THOUGH PHOENIX HAS BEEN a city that typically defies the desert rather than allowing itself to be defined by it, weather determines the pace of life. The sun shines an average of 300 days per year, and for year-round residents this is a mixed blessing. November through April, the Valley of the Sun (a nickname for Phoenix and its brood of suburbs) enjoys some of the best weather in the country. Residents—seldom clad in more than a light jacket—drive convertibles with the tops down, eat outside at lunchtime, and devote most of their free time to outdoor pursuits—from golf to hiking the rugged desert mountains and canyons nearby. May through October, however, it's a different story. With temperatures in the 100-degree range almost daily during this period, people stick to their air-conditioned homes, cars, and offices. Foot traffic is light except in cooled shopping malls. Standard attire is a light T-shirt, shorts, sandals, and sunglasses. By mid-summer, those who have adapted to the heat may linger under a shade tree or possibly drink iced tea at an outdoor cafe that has a "misting system"—literally water mist that wafts down upon grateful patrons from overhead pipes. But most people would rather be neck deep in a swimming pool.

It used to be that Phoenicians joked and complained perpetually about two things: the summer heat and the city's dud of a downtown. As recently as 1990, on weekday evenings and most weekends, you could shoot a cannon down its empty streets. Though Phoenix was on its way to becoming America's seventh-largest city, art and theatrical venues were mostly small and mediocre, and except for a struggling symphony orchestra and a few hotel bars and restaurants near the convention center, there was no nightlife to speak of. Downtown shopping was nonexistent. Today, all of that has changed. Thanks to a $1 billion "quality-of-life" bond issue voters passed in 1988—the largest publicly funded culture and recreation effort ever undertaken by an American city—downtown Phoenix has been reborn. In an area now teeming with foot traffic 18 hours a day, seven days a week, there are a half-dozen new or refurbished museums and theaters, two new stadiums that are home to three sports teams, and inviting shopping areas and restaurants. To longtime locals, the new downtown seems like a mirage.

❖

In a way, what has happened to downtown is a realization of the big dreams of the community's founders, who envisioned Phoenix not as a dusty town that would fit into the desert, but rather as a flourishing oasis that might be wrought from it. Early on, agriculture was its *raison d'etre*, and when in 1911 Roosevelt Dam walled off the Salt River 60 miles to the east, the combined watersheds of the Salt and Verde rivers became a 13,000-square-mile catchment—an area larger than Belgium—to make Phoenix verdant.

A network of irrigation canals expanded across the valley, serving not only cash crops but also a lush urban landscape. Praising a new housing development in 1920, *The Arizona Republic* noted that the "umbrella of elm and ash trees are set so close together along these drives that the sun's rays barely penetrate the dense forest." Such developments forged the pattern for the next 70 years. Golf courses are now the Valley's most ubiquitous landscape. Suburban Fountain Hills boasts one of the world's highest fountains, a man-made geyser shooting water 560 feet high. (This is more than three times the height of Yellowstone's Old Faithful.) So many modern subdivisions were being built around man-made lakes that the Legislature finally outlawed the practice in the 1980s. In such a setting the desert seems as distant as another planet. But Phoenix's attitude toward the desert has its roots deep in its history. Bradford Luckingham, author of *Phoenix: The History of a Southwestern Metropolis*, explains that the American East, not the emerging West, was the early settlement's model. Pilgrims to territorial Phoenix found beauty in the desert not as it was, but in its potential to be an idealized version of the lands they had left behind: no snow, no industrial grime.

Once Roosevelt Dam guaranteed Phoenix a reliable flow of water, idealism and optimism seemed as pervasive as the year-round sunshine. Something first had to be done about Phoenix summers, however. Evaporative air conditioning (disaffectionately known as "swamp cooling" to Arizonans today) had been invented in 1908 by one Oscar Palmer at his father's Phoenix sheet metal shop, but amazingly, it was more than two decades before it became commercially available. Into the 1930s, Phoenicians routinely slept outdoors in summer, on their roofs, porches, or in screened backyard bedrooms. (The cleverest survivors planted the legs of their outdoor cots in pails of water to dissuade scorpions from crawling into bed with them.) Even after the advent of evaporative cooling, however, the July-August "monsoon" season remained nearly unbearable: during these humid days and

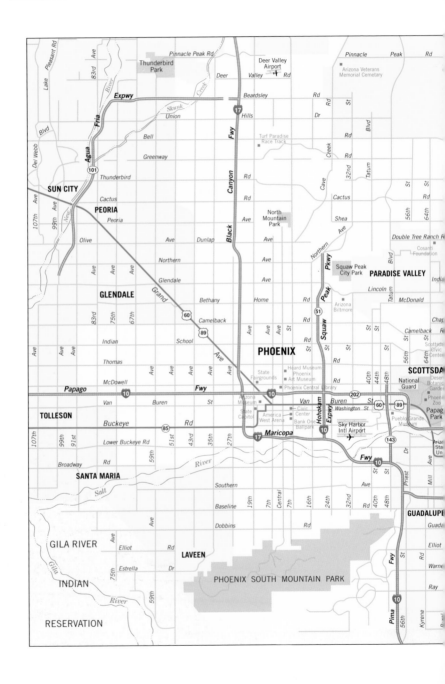

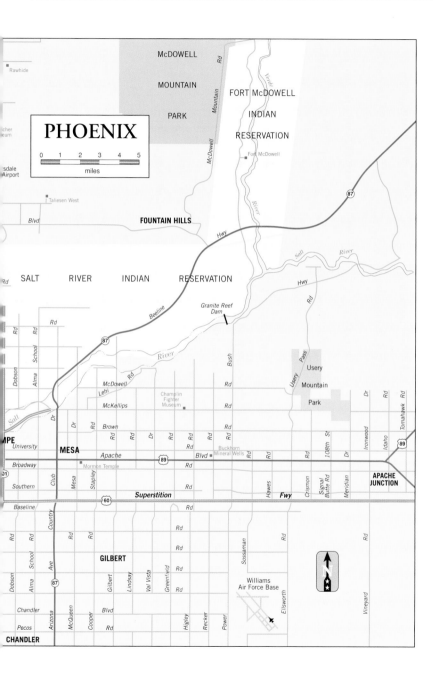

PHOENIX

0   1   2   3   4   5
miles

McDOWELL

MOUNTAIN

PARK

FORT McDOWELL

INDIAN

RESERVATION

Fort McDowell

Rawhide

icher
eum

sdale
Airport

Taliesen West

Blvd

FOUNTAIN HILLS

Hwy

87

Rd

SALT   RIVER   INDIAN   RESERVATION

Salt   River

Hwy

Rd

Beeline

Granite Reef
Dam

River

87

Rd

Rd

School

Alma

Dobson

Rd

Rd

Bush

Rd

Rd

Rd

Usery

Pass

Usery
Mountain

Park

Dr

Rd

Rd

Tomahawk Rd

McDowell

Lehi

McKellips

Champlin
Fighter
Museum

Salt

Dr

Dr

Rd

Brown

Rd

Dr

Rd

Rd

Rd

Rd

Rd

Rd

Rd

108th St

Ironwood

Idaho

89

MPE
University

MESA

Apache

89

Blvd

Buckhorn
Mineral Wells

Rd

Rd

Rd

Dr

APACHE
JUNCTION

Broadway

Mormon Temple

Rd

Crismon

Signal
Butte Rd

Meridian

Club

Mesa

Stapley

01

Southern

Hawes

Fwy

Rd

Superstition

60

Baseline

Rd

Country

Rd

School

Rd

Rd

Rd

Rd

Rd

Rd

GILBERT

Sossaman

Rd

Rd

Dobson

Alma

Ave

87

Gilbert

Lindsay

Val Vista

Greenfield

Rd

Williams
Air Force Base

Ellsworth

Vineyard

Chandler

Arizona

McQueen

Cooper

Blvd

Higley

Recker

Power

Pecos

Rd

CHANDLER

nights swamp cooling is about as refreshing as the breath of a panting dog. It was refrigerated air conditioning, in the 1950s, that finally primed Phoenix for its greatest boom. Without it, the Valley of the Sun would still be an agricultural center and winter resort.

Between 1945 and 1960, more than 300 new industries moved to the Valley, most notable among them Motorola. Phoenix successfully pitched its then-clean air, a climate that would never disrupt a manufacturer's operations or transportation, its lifestyle of leisure, and probably most significant of all, Arizona's right-to-work law, passed over the bitter objections of the labor unions in 1946.

During these great boom years, though, Phoenix's character was frequently called into question—a process that continued even into the 1980s. Down in intellectually priggish Tucson, people groused that there was nothing going on in Phoenix except the making of money and the playing of golf. The bigger city seemed like a gawky adolescent whose growth hormones had gone berserk, but whose cultural development was stalled at potty training. Except for the Heard Museum, Phoenix had no nationally recognized cultural resources, no pro sports until the 1970s, and no tangible urban atmosphere.

The engine that drives the Phoenix boom today is the city's raw youth. For practical purposes, Phoenix as an urban entity is barely 50 years old, which means that only energy and determination matter, not bloodlines or connections.

"There's a competitive spirit here that's almost Darwinian," explained Michael Lacey, editor of the liberal and aggressive *New Times* weekly. "People come out here, they create their own histories, they create own reputations. It's not based on who your family is. Sure, Phoenix is pretty conservative, politically and morally. But entrepreneurially, things are still up for grabs here."

There is trouble in entrepreneurial paradise, however. Intoxicated by the boom, Phoenix never got around to effectively planning its growth or managing its resources. Consequently, air pollution is bad enough in winter that Valley motorists have to use EPA-mandated oxygenated gasoline. Even at that, on most mornings a phlegmatic yellow-brown cloud hangs over the Valley like an inverted bowl.

Building on most of the metropolitan area's numerous mountains and buttes has never been effectively controlled. Pretentious houses encrust the slopes of landmarks such as Camelback Mountain, and developers still gouge roadways for eventual subdivisions across ridgelines and into canyons.

Water demand is outstripping the capacity of the Salt and Verde watersheds to

continued on page 150

PHOENIX ATTRACTIONS

Arizona Center

This open-air shopping mall is a wonderfully inviting place to hang out: You can picnic in the spectacular three-acre terraced garden, get fast food at the upstairs food court, or take your time at one of the center's three sit-down restaurants. There are one-of-a-kind boutiques, vending carts in the courtyard, some chain stores, but no big department stores. Includes a 24-theater cinema complex; within walking distance of almost every major downtown attraction. *Located north of Van Buren between Third and Fifth streets.*

Heritage and Science Park

A block away from the Arizona Center, this square block encompasses three important Phoenix institutions, all connected by a tree-lined walkway that runs from Monroe Street south to Washington. **Heritage Square** features more than a half-dozen restored turn-of-the-19th-century homes, some of which house museums and are open for tours. **Phoenix Museum of History** shows what life was like in early Phoenix. Some examples: "jail" was a rock with a chain attached, oyster parlors were a major fad, and townsfolk left clothes hanging in trees at the edge of town so Native Americans entering Phoenix could comply with an ordinance requiring all people to be fully dressed while in town. Adjacent **Arizona Science Center** is a massive complex that includes a planetarium, an Iwerks theater, and a waterplay exhibit. *Heritage Square, Monroe and Seventh St.; (602) 262-5071. Phoenix Museum of History, 105 N. Fifth St., (602) 253-2734. Arizona Science Center, 600 E. Washington, (602) 716-2000.*

America West Arena and Bank One Ballpark

America West Arena, a 19,000-seat coliseum opened in 1992, is home to the NBA's Phoenix Suns and the NHL's Phoenix Coyotes. Bank One Ballpark, a retractable-roof stadium with air conditioning, will be home to major league baseball's Arizona Diamondbacks starting in 1998. Between the Suns, Coyotes, and Diamondbacks, downtown Phoenix is guaranteed more than 160 days of sporting events each year. Suns and Coyotes games are often sellouts from November through spring. Both the arena and the ballpark are just south of the Heritage and Science Park along Jefferson Street. *America West Arena, Jefferson St. between First and Third streets. Bank One Ballpark, Jefferson between Fourth and Seventh streets.*

Central Library

An architectural delight worth visiting even if you don't need reading material; adjacent to the Margaret T. Hance Deck Park, which has a playground. *Library: 1221 N. Central; (602) 262-4636.*

Phoenix Civic Plaza

Open space with a fountain, surrounded by the convention center, Symphony Hall, and the excellent Herberger Theater Center. *Bounded by Second and Fifth streets and Monroe and Washington.*

Heard Museum

North of downtown just off Central Avenue lies perhaps the best cultural attraction in the city: the world-class Heard Museum. The collection contains more than 75,000 artifacts and artworks representing both prehistoric and modern Native American cultures. Excellent changing exhibits and often times demonstrations of Native American artisans and craftspeople at work. *22 E. Monte Vista Rd.; (602) 252-8840.*

Phoenix Art Museum

Recently expanded and renovated, the museum hosts an annual Cowboy Artists of America sale in October; Western art collectors come in droves and the event grosses about $1 million. *1625 N. Central Ave.; (602) 257-1222.*

Interactive displays in the Arizona Science Center. (Kerrick James)

Orpheum Theater

Early 1997 brought the reopening of the historic Orpheum Theater, Phoenix's first air-conditioned movie house now restored as an elegant playhouse. *203 W. Adams; for tickets (602) 252-9678; for tours (602) 262-7272 .*

Desert Botanical Garden

Located in east Phoenix, off Galvin Parkway, the garden is a tribute to desert flora that boasts 10,000 different plants, including half the world's cactus species. At Christmastime, visitors come at night and walk paths lit by the glow of thousands of luminarias (white paper sacks with sand in the bottom and a lighted candle at the center). During spring, many of the desert plants bloom in glorious colors. Exhibits explain historic uses of plants in the Sonoran Desert. There's also a demonstration garden of water-saving desert landscaping. *1201 N. Galvin Pkwy. in Papago Park; (602) 941-1217.*

Phoenix Zoo

Located next door to the Botanical Garden, the zoo is home to more than a thousand animals in habitats that closely resemble their natural settings. Environments include a tropical rainforest, grasslands, mountains, temperate woodlands, and of course, the desert. *455 N. Galvin Pkwy. in Papago Park; (602) 273-7771.*

Biltmore Fashion Park

This upscale outdoor shopping area features a flower-lined promenade, an excellent bookstore, and some very good restaurants. *Located in north Phoenix at the northeast corner of 24th St. and Camelback Rd.*

Squaw Peak and Camelback Mountain

Miles apart, these two landmark desert peaks are too rugged to be swallowed up by the urban sprawl that surrounds them. Each provides a strenuous workout and panoramic views. Bring a water bottle and wear hiking books.

The Squaw Peak summit trail, which rises 1,200 feet in 1.2 miles, is a hikers' highway, especially in winter. At the top, however, you find yourself on the edge of a wilderness preserve that stretches for several miles within the city. The peak is nine miles north of downtown. *Take the Squaw Peak Dr. turnoff north from Lincoln Dr. near 20th St.*

At 2,704 feet, Camelback Mountain is the highest peak in the area. The summit trail from Echo Canyon climbs 1,260 feet in just over one mile. Along it are large boulders, paloverde trees, and saguaro cactuses. *Accessible via Echo Canyon, off McDonald Dr. just east of Tatum Blvd. on the eastern edge of Phoenix.*

supply it, so the metropolitan area is now counting on the Central Arizona Project, which channels water from the Colorado River uphill to Phoenix and Tucson. This may not be enough to ensure either city's survival: The Colorado River, already dammed and diverted and drained to within an inch of its life, may not have enough water in it to meet CAP projections. The experts are divided.

Contemporary Phoenix, however, is behaving very much like a city with a future. Having pumped new life into its downtown, civic leaders seem to have gained a confidence and an optimism they previously lacked. Now that they have fixed downtown, perhaps they can solve other problems, as well.

■ VALLEY OF THE SUN

About 15 suburbs huddle around Phoenix; the exact number is slightly vague because some towns that qualify geographically as suburbs are not at all related culturally to the mother city. For example, the little town of **Guadalupe**, squeezed between Tempe and Phoenix's South Mountain Park, is a Yaqui Indian settlement, founded in 1904 as a refugee camp. The Yaquis, indigenous to Mexico, were around that time being conscripted into forced labor by Mexican President Porfirio Diaz, and thousands gained sanctuary in Arizona. Another sanctuary on the opposite corner of the valley is **Sun City**, manufactured in 1965 as one of the first retirement villages in the nation. Sun City's population is now about 38,000, its statutes still prohibit home ownership by anyone younger than 55, and 80 percent of its registered voters are Republican. It has its own professional symphony orchestra. **Mesa**, as Arizona's third-largest city, seems almost too big to be called a suburb. Founded by Mormons, and 15 miles east of Phoenix, it's a place where people raise families.

SCOTTSDALE

Scottsdale is wealth, resorts, art galleries, and the most progressive community in the state with regard to preserving its natural beauty. Population: 180,000 and growing. Founded as a farm village in 1888 by Winfield Scott, an army chaplain, for the following 60 years it was determinedly bucolic. A 1913 headline in the *Arizona Gazette*—this was classic Arizona boosterism—described it thus: "Scottsdale, [a] lovely oasis where olives and fruit vie with cotton and alfalfa in paying tribute to soil of great richness." The boosters eventually attracted enough attention to the "lovely oasis" that agriculture shrank into eclipse. Frank Lloyd Wright came in 1937 to build his winter home at the foot of the McDowell Mountains. A stream of artists followed. Dude ranches sprang up, eventually to be followed by world-class resorts. Eleanor Roosevelt, among others, came to shop. By the late 1960s, Scottsdale had international fame as a resort and art center.

Students of urban development appreciate Scottsdale for other reasons. Because land in Arizona historically was cheap, and seemingly unlimited, towns and cities typically would ooze into the horizons along spines of strip-zoned commercial development. Garish signs and billboards would line the strip, bleating for attention and generating visual cacophony. Scottsdale was the first Arizona city to attack this blight, enacting a restrictive sign ordinance in 1969. It worked: drive today along Scottsdale Road, the most important artery, and there is visual tranquility unequalled on any other main street in the state.

Scottsdale used to promote itself as "the West's most Western Town." Today, the only remnants of the frontier are the very expensive Western paintings in the galleries clustered along **Fifth Avenue.** There is contemporary art in the galleries, too, and **Scottsdale Center for the Arts,** which features changing art exhibits in its lobby gallery as well as an impressive performing arts series in its 800-seat theater. *Off Second Street at Scottsdale Civic Center Mall; (602) 994-ARTS.*

Scottsdale's numerous destination resorts seem engaged in competition to see which can devise the most exotic water gardens. Undaunted by criticism from downstate, Scottsdale still celebrates its origins as a "lovely oasis."

Civic Center Mall, with its grassy knolls, shade trees, fountains, and flower gardens plays host to numerous events, particularly in late winter and early spring, when temperatures are near-perfect. There is a Festival of the Arts in March, a renowned Culinary Festival in April, and free outdoor concerts every Sunday afternoon until the weather gets unbearably hot. *For information call (602) 994-ARTS.*

Another place to appreciate fine art is **Fleischer Museum,** located in north Scottsdale near the Princess Resort. A small but exquisite space, the Fleischer showcases paintings representative of American Impressionism. The museums's permanent collection includes more than 200 paintings from the California impressionist school. *17207 N. Perimeter Drive; (602) 585-3108.*

Set in to the foothills of the McDowell Mountains in northeast Scottsdale is **Taliesin West,** founded in 1937 as the winter home of Frank Lloyd Wright and his school of architecture. The low-slung Taliesin West buildings—built of stone and redwood beams—exemplify Wright's philosophy that structures should fit into their natural settings and "grow from the inside out." *(See pages 194-195.)* Associates and students at Taliesin West continue to follow in Wright's footsteps. Tours are available. *13201 N. 108th St. at Cactus Road—from Shea Boulevard turn left on Frank Lloyd Wright Boulevard and follow signs; (602) 860-8810.*

TEMPE

Tempe has **Arizona State University,** the state's largest with more than 45,000 students on its main campus, and a great downtown. Tempe started life as a ferry landing on the Salt River in 1871. Its original name was Hayden's Ferry, but a later visitor thought the landscape, punctuated with hulking gray-red buttes and groves of mesquite, reminded him of the Vale of Tempe in Greece.

Tempe's future character was ordained in 1885, when the Territorial Legislature voted to build the state's normal school, or teachers' college, in the town. That future, however, was a very long time in gestation. Tucson and graduates of its University of Arizona lobbied successfully for decades to keep the little Tempe college poor and obscure. Finally in 1958, while the legislature still cowered, a statewide

The Nelson Fine Arts Center at Arizona State University in Tempe (above). The skyline of Phoenix as seen from Camelback Mountain (opposite). (both photos by Kerrick James)

referendum changed the name of the college to Arizona State University. Academic respectability and parity with the old university to the south was then inevitable, given the Valley's political muscle, but it still took another 20 years.

Thanks to the university, Tempe has a more animated night life and more entertainment options than the other Valley suburbs. ASU hosts one of college football's major bowl games, the Fiesta Bowl, and the school's **University Art Museum** is known for its collection of American, Latin American, contemporary, print, and craft art; *Nelson Fine Arts Center, Mill Ave. and 10th St.; (602) 965-2787.*

Tempe's compact downtown has more life in it than all the other suburbs combined—the result of a rare urban renewal success story. On Mill Avenue, the main street sidewalks were widened, a forest of ficus trees was planted, and three blocks of handsome turn-of-the-19th-century commercial buildings were restored. Now the city is preparing to turn the Salt River and its flood plain, which cuts off downtown on the north, into a five-mile linear park that is to include wildlife refuges, bike paths, water sports and even "urban fishing."

OUTDOOR PURSUITS

Phoenix's several mountain ranges are not as high as those surrounding Tucson, but they offer entertaining hiking and great views. Besides the aforementioned **Squaw Peak** and **Camelback Mountain** trails *(page 149)*, South Mountain's much easier **Hidden Valley Trail** is recommended.

A traditional warm-weather pastime is **tubing the Salt**, meaning floating down the gentle Salt River east of Phoenix in an inner tube. Boating and jet skiing also are popular on the chain of lakes created by the dams on the Salt; **Roosevelt Lake**, 50 miles east of Phoenix, is the largest.

Golf is unquestionably the Valley's most popular winter sport. The good news in terms of water conservation is that the newer courses are mostly desert layouts that tend to minimize water usage. The bad news is that it can cost a fortune to play golf in the Valley during winter, and courses are often crowded. Summertime brings bargain greens fees and wide-open play. There are literally scores of courses in the Valley, from small municipal links to championship layouts designed by the likes of Jack Nicklaus and Pete Dye. *For a listing of courses, call the Arizona Golf Association, (602) 994-3035; or visit the* Arizona Republic *Web site: http://www.azcentral.com and click on "Arizona Golf."*

T U C S O N

THERE IS SOMETHING SPECIAL, EVEN MYSTICAL, in the desert light of Tucson. Lynn Taber-Borcherdt, an artist who moved here from Chicago, explained: "In the early works here, I began painting sharp, overexaggerated shadows. You would know what time of day it was in the painting by the shadows. Then I started noticing that sometimes when the sun was setting, and I would be on the other side of a cholla, I could see it glowing. So then I moved into making the objects in the painting glow, or almost pulsate, with light. Now my new thing is to let different colors of light bathe my paintings—the amber of twilight, the blue-green cast of moonlight on the mountainside. I'm fascinated with luminosity and iridescence. If I hadn't come to Tucson, none of this would have found its way into my work. My paintings in Chicago were dark, dark, dark, dark, dark."

Taber-Borcherdt's observation reaffirms an old Tucson aphorism: you get paid in sunshine. It's true enough in economic terms—Tucson is a chronically low-wage city, but there are always plenty of people willing to stick around and take the low-wage jobs, supplementing their paychecks, in a sense, with the psychological rewards of living in a place with a (mostly) benign climate and astounding natural beauty. But the light—constantly changing, toying with the forms and textures of the mountain slopes—is a source of inspiration all by itself.

Nature has not created many more spectacular natural settings for a city. Metropolitan Tucson's 780,000 people sprawl across a desert basin defined by four mountain ranges, each lying in a cardinal direction from the city's midpoint and each exuding a distinctive character. The 9,157-foot Santa Catalinas on the north are heroic and craggy, a late Beethoven sonata of gneiss and granite. The Rincons, to the east, appear smooth and rounded, as if they had been buffed. The twin peaks of the Santa Ritas, to the south, often wear caps of snow; the summit of Mount Wrightson towers to 9,453 feet. The small Tucson Mountains close off the western horizon like randomly sized sawteeth. Phoenix's much smaller mountains seem to poke up in the middle of the urban area, like geological afterthoughts. Tucson is contained by its mountains.

The city, sorry to report, has not lived up to its stage setting. Strip-zoned arteries six, eight, ten miles long, choked with billboards and speculative shopping centers, carry rivers of traffic between the mountains. There is little distinguished public architecture. In writing about his hometown for the *Arizona Republic* in

1997, reporter Kenneth LeFave admitted: "At first glance, Tucson is one of the ugliest cities on Earth. . . . Tucson from the highway looks like a truck stop."

Tucson's character, however, is not illustrated in its architecture. Its story is more complex than that.

The seminal event in Tucson's history as an American town was a rainstorm a couple of hundred miles away. This was in 1885, and Tucson had dispatched its delegate C. C. Stephens to the Territorial Legislature in Prescott with instructions to bring home some political pork. Stephens' stagecoach got stuck in the mud, and by the time he arrived, the legislature had parceled out the coveted insane asylum to Phoenix and the teacher's college to Tempe, leaving only the university for Tucson. In the crude frontier town this was so widely regarded as the booby prize that when Stephens came home to explain it at a public meeting, he was pelted with eggs, rotten vegetables, and a dead cat.

The University of Arizona opened for business in 1891 with one building, 36 students, and six professors. Its curricula tilted heavily in the direction of mining and agriculture, the two sciences that had immediate application in 19th-century Arizona. At this point there was still no high school in the territory, so the professors had to teach prerequisites as well as college courses. With such a modest

Sonoran-style adobe buildings still lined Tucson's Stone Avenue in the 1880s.
(Arizona Historical Society)

beginning, it was a decade or two before Tucson forgave poor C. C. Stephens and began to feel the influence of its frontier university. *(See pages 97–101 for more on the history of Tucson.)*

The University of Arizona today has 35,000 students, a massive research establishment, and, of course, a major intercollegiate sports juggernaut. In 1997, UA's Wildcats basketball team inspired riots around town when it won the coveted NCAA championship. The university shapes the city's character as pervasively as the mountains have shaped its geography. Compared to Phoenix, Tucson is more liberal, more cosmopolitan, more intellectual, and more conceited—and less wealthy. The university is the city's largest employer, and the spine of its economy. When Tucson is mentioned in the national news, it is usually because of the university. The process of dendrochronology—tree-ring dating—was developed on its campus, as was the newer science of garbology—the study of contemporary human cultures by analyzing what they throw away. The university's facilities have attracted everything from a scrap of the Shroud of Turin (for testing) to a new postseason college football game, the Weiser Lock Copper Bowl.

Tucson also distances itself from Phoenix by its attitude toward the Sonoran Desert. Phoenix repudiates the desert; Tucson embraces it. There is relatively little

Tucson today. (Kerrick James)

agriculture in Tucson's history, no irrigation, and no river comparable to the Salt. Tucson's "rivers" are its network of arroyos, dry most days out of the year, but periodically tearing through town on a muddy, rain-swollen rampage. Even when dry, however, these arroyos nourish what biologists call a xeroriparian habitat, a word marrying Greek and Latin roots for "dry" and "riverbank." These are linear forests of mesquite and palo verde trees and bird habitats, and they have the effect of extending tendrils of the lushest imaginable desert through the urban landscape. Reminded so frequently of the desert they live in, Tucsonans tend to be more respectful of it.

Grass lawns—a preposterous waste of water in this climate—still grow in the older central part of the city, but in many newer subdivisions grass isn't even allowed. Most Tucsonans, in fact, have learned to *hate* grass.

The truth is, Tucson will never be much like Phoenix, and the most important reason is that its people are, and always have been, more individualistic, more contentious, unwilling to agree on any single vision for the city. It seems as though most Tucsonans have not, for the most part, moved here in order to build a great city, but to be left alone and pursue personal dreams. They fight incessantly, and mostly they fight *against* things, such as freeways and rezonings of virgin desert land, rather than *for* things. There are more environmentalists per square mile in Tucson than anywhere else in Arizona, yet there is little support for quality-of-life urban projects. Nothing remotely like Phoenix's billion-dollar bond issue has been proposed in Tucson, and it would not pass if it were.

"I think people have moved here to get away from things: cold weather, families, commitments," former Arizona Theatre Company Director Gary Gisselman once said. He tried to schedule plays that would encourage people to think about community, but there is no evidence so far that this has borne fruit.

But is this metropolis of 780,000 determined individualists an unproductive place? Decidedly not. The sanctuary movement to defy the U.S. Government and protect Central American refugees from deportation was born in Tucson. Biosphere II, a controversial experiment in which eight "bionauts" spent two years in a sealed ecosystem, is just outside Tucson. And there is Lynn Taber-Borcherdt, who described the other effect Tucson has had on her art:

"The other thing that happened is harder to describe. The soul of my work changed. It had something to do with the quiet, the peace, the serenity, listening to the crickets, watching the hawks soar. I read a lot, thought a lot—things like 'who are we?' I turned inward, and that found its way into my paintings.

Baroque architecture in Arizona. *Follow I-10 east to I-19 south, then take exit 92 to the mission; (520) 294-2624 (see above).*

University of Arizona
A lovely campus in central Tucson with many attractions open to the public: Flandrau Planetarium, the University Museum of Art, the Center for Creative Photography and the Arizona State Museum are the most interesting. *Visitor center is at University Blvd. and Cherry; (520) 621-5130.*

Arizona-Sonora Desert Museum
A marvelous zoo, arboretum, and natural history museum with Sonoran animals and plants in their natural settings. *Take Speedway Blvd. west across Gates Pass to Kinney Rd. 2021 N. Kinney in Tucson Mountain Park (520) 883-2702 (see page 38).*

Saguaro National Park
The Sonoran Desert's most fascinating and famous cactus forest. *East and west of Tucson on either side of I-10; (520) 733-5100 (see page 39).*

Mount Lemmon Highway, Santa Catalina Mountains
A beautiful two-lane road through spectacular mountains on the city's northern edge *(see page 55).* Closer to Tucson, Sabino Canyon's 4.2 mile Phone Line Trail offers fine views *(see page 75).*

Pima Air and Space Museum
A great collection of 130 historic aircraft, the most dramatic attraction of which is an SR-71 Blackbird—the fastest jet ever built. *Take I-10 east to 6000 E. Valencia Rd. exit. Turn left and continue two miles. (520) 574-9658.*

Titan II Missile Museum
An hour-long guided tour (involving many steps) to view a disarmed ICBM in its underground silo, among other sites. *20 miles southeast of Tucson off I-19. Take Duval Mine Rd. exit and head west; (520) 6245-7736.*

Biosphere II
A three-acre airtight structure designed to research an ecosystem's ability to recycle air, water, and nutrients in order to sustain plant and animal life. *5 miles northeast of jct. SR 79 and SR 77 to Biosphere II Rd.; (602) 825-6200.*

SR-71 Blackbird at the Pima Air and Space Museum. (Kerrick James)

ARIZONA TOWNS

ARIZONA HAS TWO MAJOR CITIES and a more varied scattering of small towns than any other state. We have desert towns, mountain towns, Native American towns, Hispanic towns, mining towns, company towns, farm towns, cow towns, border towns, retirement towns, tourist towns, and ghost towns. What follows is not an all-inclusive, objective statewide stroll through them, but some personal notes on the more engaging ones.

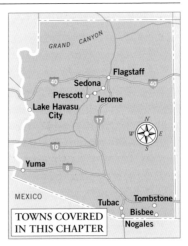

TOWNS COVERED IN THIS CHAPTER

■ SOUTHEASTERN ARIZONA TOWNS

BISBEE

"Bisbee—the city of foul odors and sickening smells," bitched the *Tucson Citizen* at the turn of the 19th century. Brewery Gulch, one of its main streets, was an open sewer, "covered with a slime several inches deep and about four feet wide." Gambling and prostitution were endemic, and beds in the rooming houses were booked in shifts. The classical image of the early Bisbee copper miner is that of a man who spent eight hours underground in the mine, the next eight hours boozing and wenching, and the next eight hours sleeping it off. Certainly not everyone's lifestyle conformed to this scenario, but enough did to solidify Bisbee's status as the quintessential Western mining town.

Serious copper mining began in these hills and gulches six miles north of the Mexican border in 1880. By 1900, Bisbee was the largest, most prosperous settlement in Arizona Territory. It was crude but at the same time remarkably cosmopolitan. The copper mines had attracted immigrants from Germany, Serbia, Italy, Ireland, Mexico, even Russia. Each ethnic group clustered in its own "town" or neighborhood. Some longtime Bisbee folk recall the charm of it all—the Germans making wine, the Serbs raising goats (their neighborhood was called "Goat Grove"), the Irish raising hell. Underground, in the mines, these people depended on each other for their lives, so they got along well. Above ground, cosmopolitan Bisbee was tense with ethnic rivalries. "You never went to the show by yourself; you always took someone with you," said Les Williams, a retired miner. "Each 'town' had its own gang. We stole burros from each other, we'd play baseball with each other, then we'd fight after the games."

One group never entered Bisbee's churning ethnic stew: an unwritten law held that no "Chinaman" could stay in town overnight. Behind this lay a morbid reason. In early Bisbee, widows of men killed in mine accidents sometimes would eke out a living by taking in laundry, and the white citizenry feared competition from the Chinese.

The mining era ended in Bisbee in 1975. It had been the town's sole industry, and the economic shock waves were enormous. Houses tumbled onto the market for as little as $800, and that attracted a wave of artists, bohemians, and assorted dropouts. Bisbee's "hippie era," as older townspeople disdainfully called it, lasted about a decade. Eventually one of the "hippies" turned 30, opened a restaurant and became mayor; he now runs a bed and breakfast.

Today the town still has some bohemians, many serious artists, wonderful Italianate Victorian architecture, no industry, and an utterly seductive, delightful spirit. Bisbee is Aspen turned inside-out, kicked into a time warp and trapped in a happy reverse universe devoid of traffic lights, designer labels or pretentious boutiques. Bisbee is a town where one can walk the narrow, decaying, mountainside streets in the evening and hear someone practicing Bach fugues on a piano in questionable tune, or browse in the afternoon in galleries with Tarahumara artifacts or locally made contemporary pottery on display. Bisbee, more than any other town in Arizona, is a place in which to re-invent oneself; the presence of more than 6,500 people doing just that makes it the most fascinating small town to visit in Arizona.

Visiting Bisbee: Most visitors to Bisbee—located on US 80, 94 miles southeast of Tucson—will enjoy tours of the underground **Copper Queen Mine.** Its four levels comprise 147 miles of passageways—guided by retired miners themselves, as well as a 13-mile bus tour around the enormous **Lavender Open Pit Mine;** for tours, call (520) 432-2071. Bisbee also hosts an impressive number of annual events. The town's steep hills make April's La Vuelta de Bisbee one of the world's most harrowing professional bicycle races. Spring's Wine at the Mine festival is more a colossal community block party than a serious wine tasting (no one actually spits out the wine). Visitors to Bisbee at any time should bring a camera; the colors, textures, and historic buildings of the town are a photographer's dream.

TOMBSTONE

No newspaper ever wore a more memorable masthead than the famous *Tombstone Epitaph*. Tombstone, in its silver-boom prime of the early 1880s, was the West's most notoriously violent town. While its history has been embellished by Hollywood as well as popular historians, it was undeniably a place in which men lived fast and died in trivial quarrels. The killing was common enough that the *Epitaph* ran its accounts of the everyday grim-reaping under a standing headline: "Death's Doings." Lawlessness was abundant enough that in 1882 it even attracted the notice of President Chester Arthur, who threatened to send in the army. Hearing that, the *Epitaph*, in the finest tradition of Arizona boosterism, ran an editorial ridiculing Arthur and insisting that "We were never in a more peaceable community than Tombstone and law and order is absolute." In the three months preceding that editorial, the Epitaph had chronicled eight killings.

It was a uniquely colorful town, a melange of adventurers, drunks, whores, rustlers, honest working stiffs, and wealthy sophisticates. The silver mines were throwing off enough money that Tombstone built ambitious show halls and imported vaudeville and serious theater. At one point there were 110 liquor licenses in town, but Tombstone also boasted, according to historian John Myers, "the best food between New Orleans and San Francisco." The 1887 Thanksgiving menu from the Maison Doree Restaurant listed these entrees:

> Papillote
> Paté Financiere
> Saddle of Lamb à la Milanese
> [And, lest anyone forget where he was . . .]
> Buffalo Tongue

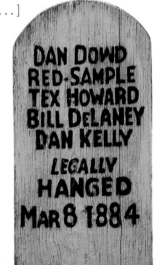

But Tombstone has secured enduring fame not for its culture, but for all that flying lead. The shootout at the OK Corral in 1881 remains the most notorious gunfight of all time.

The complicated prologue to the shootout was essentially a struggle for political spoils in

Tombstone was one tough town, as the tombstones at Boot Hill explain.

newly created Cochise County. On one side were Sheriff Johnny Behan and the Clanton clan, ranchers who moonlighted as cattle rustlers and harbored stagecoach robbers. The (relatively) good guys were U.S. Marshal Wyatt Earp, his brothers Virgil and Morgan, and the infamous alcoholic gunfighter "Doc" Holliday. On the afternoon of October 26, the Earps and Holliday strode purposefully into the vacant lot at Fremont and 3rd Street, where five young members of the Clanton gang were rumored to be looking for a fight. According to later testimony by Ike Clanton, Wyatt Earp shoved his pistol into Clanton's belly and growled, "You son of a bitch, you can have a fight." Clanton turned white and fled, pistols and shotguns began blazing, and in about 30 seconds—Wyatt Earp's estimate— three of the Clanton men lay dying and Virgil and Morgan Earp had been seriously wounded.

The story doesn't end there, and the aftermath tells much about the nature of life and justice in frontier Tombstone. The Earps and Holliday faced a hearing on murder charges, and were cleared. Two months later, a midnight marksman tried to take out Virgil Earp, but succeeded only in crippling his left arm for life. Three months after that, an assassin did kill Morgan Earp. Wyatt, operating well outside the law on the trail of vengeance, gunned down three of the men he suspected of killing his brother, then left Cochise County for good.

Visiting Tombstone: Located on US 80, 70 miles southeast of Tucson, Tombstone is a tourist town, making a living from its historic infamy. The restored **Crystal Palace Saloon**, among others, is open for business. **Helldorado Days** every October includes a parade, gunfight reenactments, and in several recent years, visits by Edward Earp, cousin of Wyatt. **Allen Street,** once lined with bars, casinos, and cathouses, has been beautifully restored; it has served as a set for Japanese crews

Architecturally, the Cochise County Courthouse exuded order and dignity—qualities hard to find anywhere else in Tombstone. (Arizona Historical Society)

filming samurai Westerns. The original **Cochise County Courthouse**, built in 1882, is now a state historic park. It is the most sophisticated piece of Victorian neoclassical architecture in the state—an anomaly to ponder while listening to the reenacted gunfights echoing in the street two blocks away.

TUBAC

This lovely unincorporated village in the lee of the Santa Rita Mountains is the oldest non-Indian settlement in Arizona, a place redolent with history. Several times in its first 150 years of existence it was a locus of the conflict between European and Native American civilization in the New World.

Tubac was established as a *visita*, or chapel served by an itinerant priest, around 1726—that, at any rate, is the date of the first recorded baptisms by one Fr. Agustín de Campos. The next generation was a time of increasing tension in the upper Pima Indian lands (the *Pimería Alta*), however, with not only more Jesuit missionaries but also Spanish silver miners flooding in. The European attitude was summed up in the term *gente de razon*—"people of reason"—which the Spanish used in census documents to describe themselves, as opposed to the unenlightened (even if freshly baptized) native *bárbaros*. In 1751, the Pimas revolted, killing two priests and more than 100 ranchers and miners, and burning churches—including the one at Tubac. The following year the Spanish established the presidio of Tubac, their first permanent military presence in Arizona.

The fifty soldiers stationed with their families at Tubac succeeded in quieting the Pimas, but the Apaches proved to be the presidio's doom. In 1774 Tubac's commander, Juan Bautista de Anza, made his famous expedition to open a route to California and established the settlement that would become San Francisco. Two years later the Tubac garrison was moved to Tucson where it could more effectively protect the route. Thus disarmed, Tubac was repeatedly raided, abandoned and resettled. Journalist J. Ross Browne, who passed through Tubac in 1864, described it in the most pathetic terms: ". . . harassed on both sides by Apaches and Mexicans and without hope of future protection, the inhabitants of Tubac for the last time have abandoned the town, and thus it has remained ever since, a melancholy spectacle of ruin and desolation."

Eventually Tubac did rise again, phoenix-like; the grasslands of the surrounding Santa Cruz Valley seemed ideal for ranching. Then in 1948, a nationally known artist named Dale Nichols established an art school in Tubac, and even though it lasted only a year, it placed Tubac on the map as an art center.

Charming, slow-paced, and unpretentious, Tubac has some 50 galleries and boutiques and a state historical park with exhibits on the settlement's long history. Prices for art are substantially lower than in Arizona's other major art centers, Scottsdale and Sedona. One gallery owner, however, sounded an alarm: while the number of galleries in Tubac is growing, the number of working artists is dwindling. "The cost of housing is climbing out of their reach," he said.

Visiting Tubac: Approximately 45 miles south of Tucscon, Tubac attracts visitors to its many galleries and annual festivals such as the Cinco de Mayo (May 5) fiesta and the **Tubac Festival of the Arts** in February. Many shops close for the summer. Four miles south, the ruin of the 1822 mission of **San José de Tumacácori**, now a national historic park, is open every day.

Jesus with the crown of thorns at San Xavier del Bac.

Lonely graves lie behind the mission of Tumacácori.

■ CENTRAL ARIZONA TOWNS

PRESCOTT

"Norman Rockwell America," the *Los Angeles Times* once called it. "For those of us who grew up in bland, instant slurbs, Prescott is a glimpse of a childhood we might have chosen instead, had anyone thought to ask," pined the *Tucson Citizen.*

Prescott, a small city of 31,000 people is indeed a picturesque place, and its collection of prim Victorian homes—more of them, by far, than anywhere else in Arizona—inevitably triggers these wistful lines from visiting writers. Add a near-perfect mile-high climate with four distinct seasons, none of them harsh, and Prescott seems like everyone's choice for an ideal place to live. Of course there is a catch: no industry. It's tough to earn a living in Prescott. That hasn't stopped people from trying, though, and through the 1990s the city has experienced steady population growth.

The town was founded, curiously, as a consequence of the Civil War. President Lincoln had designated Arizona a territory in 1863 and dispatched his appointed governor, John G. Goodwin, to set up a government. En route Goodwin heard that there was a nucleus of Confederate sympathizers at Tucson, the presupposed capital. The gubernatorial party went instead to Fort Whipple, an army post in northern Arizona, and in 1864 wisely founded the capital of Prescott on politically virgin ground.

Prescott lost the capital to Tucson just three years later (eventually it migrated yet again to Phoenix), but nearby gold mining and ranching delivered a boom to the town anyway. It became as legendary for drinking as Tombstone for gunfighting; by the early 1900s there were about 40 saloons lining Montezuma Street, still known today as "Whiskey Row." In *Roadside History of Arizona*, Arizona historian Marshall Trimble swears that, "The macho custom of thirsty cowboys in off the range was to start their binge, or 'whizzer' as they called it, at the Kentucky Bar and take a drink in every bar all the way to the Depot House, thirty-nine saloons away." Forty drinks!

There remain a few token historic bars on Whiskey Row, and on Saturday nights they sound boisterous enough to convince passersby that at least a sliver of the tradition endures.

Visiting Prescott: Lying about 100 miles north of Phoenix, Prescott is home to the excellent **Sharlot Hall Museum** which sprawls through several historic buildings and details the history of Prescott and Arizona Territory. The surrounding **Prescott National Forest** is laced with delightful mountain hiking trails; ask for a map at the Forest Service office in town. No other Arizona town of its size seems to have as many festivals and annual events as Prescott. A sampling: Bluegrass Festival (June); Territorial Days (crafts, entertainment, and historic home tours— June), Frontier Days and World's Oldest Rodeo (July). Horse racing season at Prescott Downs is from late May to late August.

To understand the enduring charm of Prescott, simply walk the Victorian neighborhoods that stretch about six blocks in each direction from downtown. In these neighborhoods, domestic life still spills from house out to street; people lounge on their cool porches, greeting strangers as well as neighbors. On a winter evening, as a light snow slowly blankets the town, families walk downtown under umbrellas to stroll and throw snowballs in the park surrounding the county courthouse. Norman Rockwell, indeed.

SEDONA

"There are only two places in the world I want to live," Max Ernst, the German-born surrealist painter who emigrated to Arizona in the 1940s, told his friends. "Paris and Sedona."

Ernst built a house in the lee of the red rocks of Sedona; he was one of many thousands who have been enchanted by the place. Another typical Sedona story was that of the New York stockbroker who flew in on a visit in 1973, fell instantly in love with the rocks, and bought a house the next day. Impulsive? "No," he said. "Impulsive would be the same day." The famed jazz drummer Louis Bellson, who once appeared at the Jazz on the Rocks festival, looked up at the great red buttes towering 500 to 2,000 feet over the town and spoke for his wife, the legendary Pearl Bailey, who was ill at home. "If Pearly was here," Bellson said, "She would say, 'God lives here.'"

Maybe God does: the landscape certainly is supernal.

Bell Rock, Courthouse Butte, Capitol Butte, Bear Mountain—these erosion-sculpted rocks seem almost to be alive. They change color and character almost hourly. In a gray, woolly fog they seem to float, eerily, like velvet ghosts. Under a midmorning sun they can be a pale and cool violet, then as the day burns on they shift into the red and orange regions of the spectrum. After sunset, when the fire colors have burned out, the rocks turn the color of rust (which is what they are, on the surface) against a violet sky, and all their crevasses and canyons blacken into impenetrable, ominous mystery. It is the perfect stage set for a production of Wagner's *Götterdämmerung*—"Twilight of the Gods"—in a production staged by the gods themselves.

The town of Sedona has a short but intriguing history. It was founded in 1902 by a young Missouri couple, Carl and Sedona Schnebly. Beginning in the 1960s it became an art colony, and in the 1970s it exploded with retirees. In the early 1980s Page Bryant, a psychic, claimed to have divined four metaphysical vortices in the red rocks around it, and Sedona also became a New Age mecca. In 1987 the Harmonic Convergence drew at least 5,000 people to town, a few of whom willingly paid $75 for tickets to go sit on Bell Rock at the moment that it was supposed to depart for the galaxy of Andromeda. For the most part, however, the

Sculptor and rancher Marguerite Brunswig Staude commissioned Sedona's Chapel of the Holy Cross in 1953; she called it "a spiritual fortress so charged with God that it spurs man's spirit godward!" (Kerrick James)

(opposite) Oak Creek and Cathedral Rock, two of Sedona's loveliest attractions. (Kerrick James)

New Age crowd in Sedona has proven to be quiet, unobtrusive, and simply searching for ways to heal the earth and its inhabitants.

Art remains Sedona's prime industry. Out of a population of 9,200 there are an estimated 300 professional artists in town, about 50 galleries and an annual outdoor sculpture exhibition on the banks of Oak Creek. In some inexplicable way, the Red Rocks are involved in all this. Touring the galleries, the visitor will notice that although there is a plentiful variety of art, there is seldom anything combative, confrontational, or unyieldingly baffling. Jim Ratliff, owner of one of Sedona's prime contemporary galleries, said it isn't simple conservatism. There is an energy in red rock country, he explained; he doesn't know what it is, but he believes it is real, and that somehow it fuels the creative process.

"But it can only be used in a positive way," he said. "If someone tries to use that energy to create something negative, they don't stay around. They have to go somewhere else. The red rocks spit them right out of here."

Visiting Sedona: Sedona is about 120 miles north of Phoenix, via I-17 and AZ 179. In town an essential stop is **Tlaquepaque**, a fetching collection of art galleries and boutiques built in the fashion of an eighteenth-century Spanish village. The Red Rocks must be explored at close hand, of course, and the best way is on foot. An excellent trail map, entitled *Experience Sedona*, is available at local bookstores and boutiques. There are hot-air balloon concessions and consultants who arrange weddings among the hot rocks. Jazz aficionados who think their music is naturally a creature of the night, properly played only in smoky nightclubs, invariably are converted by Sedona's **Jazz on the Rocks** festival. It's a day-long September lawn party featuring stars as bright as Diane Schuur and the Count Basie Orchestra, and it has become Arizona's premier music festival. Tickets always sell out; order early.

JEROME

Indians were mining Mingus Mountain for its copper when the Spanish arrived in the area over 300 years ago, but the first American town was not founded here until 1876. For the next 60 years the town was assaulted by floods, fires, and epidemics, but the wealth buried under it in Mingus Mountain kept it booming. At its peak, Jerome was home to 15,000 people, and the mountain—honeycombed with more than 100 miles of mine shafts—was subject to continuous blasting. Finally the tormented mountain responded. After a season of abnormally wet weather, a piece of the mountain collapsed in a colossal mud slide that swept away hundreds of structures. A quaint fraction of Jerome, some 300 buildings, still hugs the mountainside. Today, Jerome numbers only a few hundred citizens, but they are a colorful lot.

Visiting Jerome: Jerome is located between Prescott and Flagstaff on US alt 89 (AZ 89A). Just outside of town off highway stands the former home of mining magnate James S. Douglas, now converted into a state historical park and museum. **Jerome State Historic Park,** (520) 634-5381. The rest of the town's homes, many of them abandoned and deteriorating, others restored and well-kept, are a jumble of cottages and Victorian-style houses clinging to the steep slopes of Cleopatra Hill. The free-wheeling spirit of Jerome's old mining days prevails, and tourists now visit the former jailhouse, a brothel-turned-restaurant, and an array of funky shops, art galleries, and cafes.

FLAGSTAFF

Except for the winter and spring winds, which can be ferocious, this town of 56,000, 148 miles north of Phoenix, enjoys the best location in the state. It curls around the southern foot of 12,643-foot Humphreys Peak, the highest point in Arizona. In winter, people flock to Flagstaff to ski; in summer the perspiring lemmings swarm up from Phoenix and Tucson to escape the heat. So many geologic and prehistoric attractions cluster around Flagstaff that one suspects the town was founded as a tourist magnet (it wasn't). The ruins of Walnut Canyon and Wupatki lie respectively 11 and 25 miles away. Oak Creek Canyon creases into the plateau 10 miles south; the Grand Canyon is 80 miles north. Sunset Crater, looking like the mother volcano to a brood of baby cones, is 15 miles out of town; Meteor Crater, the best preserved crater on the planet, is 45 miles east.

Flagstaff will regret this spectacular setting only if a new or reactivated volcano someday appears on its horizon. It could happen; Sunset Crater last erupted in A.D. 1065—a few moments ago in geologic time.

Like so many other Arizona settlements, Flagstaff hasn't made the best of its lovely physical setting. The main commercial arteries through town, Milton and Santa Fe (the old Route 66), are jammed with signs and billboards clamoring for attention. Off these streets, however, Flag's green, forested neighborhoods and cool, pine-scented air make it seem like a wonderfully enticing place.

Flagstaff's first permanent resident was a rancher and prospector named

Jerome has become a magnet for artists and art galleries. (Kerrick James)

Thomas F. McMillan, who homesteaded a ranch in 1876. When the railroad arrived in 1881, both cattle and timber industries boomed. Tourists and astronomers followed. In 1894, Percival Lowell and his wife founded and personally supervised construction of the hat-shaped Lowell Observatory on a mesa just west of town. Lowell planned to map Mars; he theorized that its recently discovered patchwork of lines was a canal system to carry water from its polar icecaps to the arid red deserts. Lowell died in 1916 unable to prove that the Martian lines were in fact canals, but he correctly predicted the existence of a ninth planet from observing the minute wobble of Uranus. In 1930, Clyde W. Tombaugh discovered that planet, Pluto, with the Lowell scope.

Flagstaff's most important institution today is the Northern Arizona University, which has an enrollment of 22,000 students. **Flagstaff Festival of the Arts** consumes most of July and early August, offering classical music, art films, dance, and professional theater. The prime attraction is an excellent festival orchestra whose players are drawn from symphony orchestras that are dormant during the summer—something that Flagstaff decidedly is not.

Visiting Flagstaff: A high priority should be to see two nearby ancient Indian ruins. To reach the Sinagua ruins of **Walnut Canyon** take exit 204 from I-40 seven miles east of Flagstaff, and travel south three miles to the visitor center. **Wupatki National Monument** is located 14 miles east of the US 89 turnoff between Flagstaff and Cameron. *(Also see* "THE FIRST ARIZONANS" *beginning on page 78).* The **Museum of Northern Arizona** also demands a visit; its changing exhibitions cover the entire natural history and human settlement of the Colorado Plateau. The museum is three miles northwest of downtown on US 180

Guided tours of **Lowell Observatory** are conducted weekdays at 1:30 P.M. One mile from downtown, west on Santa Fe Avenue and up the road to Mars Hill. **Arizona Snowbowl** on the San Francisco Peaks offers Arizona's highest-elevation skiing, with runs dropping from 11,200 feet.

■ DESERT TOWNS ON THE COLORADO RIVER

LAKE HAVASU CITY

On its face, this appeared a truly absurd scene: a gaggle of sun-baked British tourists aboard an imitation sternwheeler named the *Dixie Belle*, sailing past a fake

The London Bridge in Lake Havasu City. (Kerrick James)

British village under the London Bridge on a man-made lake in the Mojave Desert.

The one American aboard wondered aloud whether any of the Britons found this just a touch silly. Three replies:

Julia Smyth: "A lot of people felt upset when London Bridge left London. It'd be the same if someone took your Golden Gate, wouldn't it? But all of us who've seen it here have found it quite lovely."

George Griffith: "It's wonderful; it's as if you've taken us back in time. When we go into a shop in England now we're bombarded with such horrible music. Here it's very quiet and pleasant."

Peter Penrose: "It's fantastic what you Americans can do. Where you don't have any history, you just make it."

In Penrose's few words is the story of Lake Havasu and the small, young city of 37,600 on its eastern shore. Until 1938, the year Parker Dam was completed downstream, there was no lake here—just the ruddy Colorado slinking its way through the parched Mojave Desert. The town dribbled into existence a couple of decades later. Its famous attraction, the London Bridge, went up in 1971. When the bridge arrived as a kit of 33,000 tons of Dartmoor and Aberdeen granite stones, there was nothing for it to span, so a channel was dredged at the edge of the lake, thereby manufacturing an island.

The town and the bridge were the brainchildren of California magnate Robert McCulloch, who moved his factory to Lake Havasu in 1964. According to local legend, McCulloch and his partner, C.V. Wood Jr., were watching television one evening when Johnny Carson noted that the obsolete London Bridge, built in 1824, was for sale. McCulloch turned to Wood and said, "Let's buy it." They did, for $2.4 million.

McCulloch's purchase drew international ridicule at the time—Britons in particular were incensed—but it turned out to be a remarkably canny purchase. It became the second biggest tourist draw in Arizona (after the Grand Canyon) and brought a constellation of supporting attractions, from an English heraldry shop to speedboat regattas. McCulloch died in 1977, and 10 years later his chainsaw factory, which at its peak had employed 1,800, moved to Tucson. Without tourism, Lake Havasu City would have vanished as quickly as a puddle in the Mojave Desert. McCulloch's flight of whimsy, the London Bridge, saved the town from the flight of McCulloch's factory.

Visiting Lake Havasu City: Fishing enthusiasts face a dilemma here. The best months for fishing the lake's bass, crappie, catfish, and bluegill are May through September, but these are truly hot times in the Mojave Desert. Lake Havasu City's average May daily high is 95.3 F ; July is 108.6 F; September is 102.5 F. Early mornings on the lake are reasonably cool, of course, but what does one do the rest of the day?

The rest of the year at Lake Havasu is very pleasant (January's average high is 67.3 F) for anyone not frustrated by the uninterested fish. Winter boating is a popular pastime, and the major local festival is **London Bridge Days** (with a British theme, of course), held in October. The **London Bridge** itself is more than a curio (or Arizona's heaviest antique, as some wags have called it). Look closely for the many pock marks on its stones; these are the mementos of Nazi fighters strafing the bridge. Lake Havesu City is reached via AZ 95, 206 miles west of Phoenix.

YUMA

Poor Yuma. Possibly no small city on the continent has suffered such consistently bad press for so long a time.

J. Ross Browne wrote of Yuma in 1864: "Everything dries: wagons dry; men dry; chickens dry; there is no juice left in anything living or dead by the close of summer. . . . Chickens hatched at this season, old Fort Yumers say, come out of the shell ready cooked; bacon is eaten with a spoon; and butter must stand for an hour in the sun before the flies become dry enough for use. . . ."

In 1882, Charles H. Phelps wrote a travelogue in verse that must surely rank among the nastiest poems ever published about a town. An excerpt:

> Through all ages baleful moons
> Glared upon thy whited dunes;
> And malignant, wrathful suns
> Fiercely drank thy streamless runs. . . .

It continues today, with hapless Yuma still suffering from missiles of hostile wit lobbed from afar. Phoenix's satirical cartoonist, Bob Boze Bell, once drew a two-page spread in the *New Times* weekly, proposing some fresh civic slogans to the Chamber of Commerce: "Join the YUMAn race—out of town" Or: "You don't live in Yuma, YUMArinate." The Chamber has responded, gamely enough, with

brochures that begin by asking: "Where's Your Sense of Yuma?"

Yuma came into existence because of the California gold rush. To reach California and its promise of wealth, prospectors somehow had to cross the Colorado River—a much more formidable barrier than it is today, with five states now sucking water out of it. A U.S. Army report in 1846 estimated it was 600 feet wide at its narrowest. By 1850, both Indian and Anglo entrepreneurs were operating ferry services, and, as happened at so many other points of commingling, friction ensued. The army established Fort Yuma on the California side of the river (although it was under the Arizona command) and subdued the eponymous Yuma tribe. The wagon traffic increased, and a civilian settlement, originally christened Colorado City, began to grow across the river from the fort.

It is not difficult to understand why Yuma had public relations woes. In territorial days it was the hottest and driest place Anglos had yet attempted to settle in Arizona, and with San Diego 170 miles off over one treeless horizon and Tucson 220 in the opposite direction, it was easily the most remote as well. In 1876, it

Modern petroglyphs at Chloride by R. Purcell.

(opposite) A kayaker, paddling down the Colorado River south of Hoover Dam, stops to explore Emerald Cave. (Kerrick James)

Culture in territorial Yuma: the Philharmonic Band, 1895. (Arizona Historical Society)

won its second industry, the Territorial Prison, which was essentially carved into a bluff overlooking the river. Eventually inmates from around the country were shipped here; they termed it, without humor or affection, the "Hell Hole." Think about it: nine-by-eight-foot cells, with two tiers of three bunks each, one bucket for a latrine (emptied once a day), and 120-degree summer temperatures. By the time it closed in 1909, 3,069 convicts had slowly simmered through their sentences there, and only 26 of them—fewer than one per year—ever successfully escaped.

Modern Yuma, a city of about 60,000, has managed to make an asset of this improbable climate. About 40,000 snowbirds, most from the Northwest and Canada, descend on the Yuma area every winter. Questioned by *Arizona Highways* on why they chose Yuma over Phoenix or Tucson, most cited the small-city friendliness and relaxed pace. The extreme rarity of freezes in this very low desert basin makes it an ideal location for citrus farming. In fact, if Arizona had huddled all its agriculture along the Colorado River instead of trying to force the central deserts to bloom, the state would not have as serious a water problem as it does today.

Pearl Hart (with guitar) was one of Yuma Territorial Prison's celebrated inmates; she did hard time from 1899 to 1902 for robbing a mail stage. (Arizona Historical Society)

Visiting Yuma: The **Territorial Prison**, now a state historical park, is a captivating attraction—an illustration of how the low Sonoran Desert environment could formally function as punishment. As one Arizona Historical Society employee said, this prison is "the bleakest place in Arizona." *Information: (520) 783-4771.*

Several companies offer intriguing boat trips up the Colorado River, wide and shallow in the Yuma area, to visit prehistoric petroglyph sites. (Avoid in summer.)

SPRING TRAINING

For the most concentrated dose of Cactus Fever, in March take a hotel room in Scottsdale, a suburb of Phoenix. Preferably, find a hotel (like the Day's Inn) that also houses the players of one of the eight or so major league teams that base their training operations in the Phoenix area. Then again, it isn't really necessary; after all, you're pretty close to most of the action just being in Scottsdale.

Within a few blocks of the major hotels on Scottsdale Road is newly renovated Scottsdale Stadium, where the San Francisco Giants play their games. A 20-minute drive will pass at least two other ball parks, one of which is sure to have a game. The Oakland Athletics play in Phoenix at Phoenix Municipal Stadium and the Anaheim Angels are close by at Tempe Diablo Stadium. It's a good idea to order your tickets before you even go to Arizona; spring baseball has become awfully fashionable these past few years.

Several other baseball stadiums lie within 45 minutes of Scottsdale. The town of Chandler is the spring home of the Milwaukee Brewers, and Mesa is home to the Chicago Cubs. The Seattle Mariners have a spanking new home in Peoria, which is also home to the San Diego Padres. Two hours down Interstate 10 is Tucson, where the Colorado Rockies hold forth at Hi Corbett Field, and the Arizona Diamondbacks commence spring play in 1998.

In addition to the regularly scheduled major league games, you should consider other, potentially more intimate baseball experiences. You can call the team offices to learn when the "B" games are scheduled. Usually they are played in the mornings at smaller facilities that allow real contact with the younger players. (As a rule, you won't find too many front line players at these games.) You can also search out training fields where teams teach technique and hold minor league scrimmages (try Indian School Road in Scottsdale, or near Tempe Diablo Stadium).

After the game, or for dinner, try the Pink Pony on Scottsdale Road, traditional stomping ground of real baseball people but now more of a hot-spot for visitors and fans. The steaks are good and the bar is hopping. Not too far away is Don and Charley's, which is "home" to Cubs and Giants and their fans. The waitresses are often wives or girlfriends of players, and they can talk baseball knowledgeably.

Outside of Scottsdale, there is good food and lots of baseball life at Avanti, in Phoenix. Be sure to make reservations at these places, as they're crowded all spring.

When you come, expect the weather to be good and hot. Bring your swimsuit, sun block, and extra-dark shades. Plan on renting a car (a pink Cadillac convertible is the automobile of choice), because Phoenix is laid out like Los Angeles and public transportation is inconvenient.

—Gene Seltzer

Spring training baseball at Scottsdale Stadium. (Kerrick James)

VISITING MEXICO

"Sonora is where civilization ends and *carne asada* begins," wrote the Mexican philosopher José Vasconcelos. Sonora is the Mexican state adjoining Arizona. Carne asada (literally "roasted beef," although it is normally grilled) is one of its great attractions—along with sensational seafood, not-yet-spoiled beaches, folk-baroque Spanish missions and, once away from the border, warm and hospitable people.

Tourists in Southern Arizona invariably visit **Nogales**, the industrial Mexican border city 60 miles (96 km) south of Tucson. Generally they travel nowhere else in Sonora. This is a mistake.

Nogales ("Walnuts" in translation) is neither historic, charming, nor quaint. It is a teeming chemical reaction between an affluent nation and the edge of the Third World. The tragedy is that the *norteamericano* who becomes acquainted with Mexico through Nogales (or any other border city) not only will misunderstand the country, but also may leave with unwarranted prejudices. A few years ago, shopping in Nogales was trying to negotiate the best price for a painting of Jesus or Elvis on black velvet. In the last few years, many shops have gone upscale, offering impressive Mexican folk art, crafts, and imports. Their sheer variety is almost entertainment enough; in one small shop shoppers may find: leather duffel bags, fake Toltec icons, margarita glasses, statues of St. Francis of Assisi, and double basses. Bargain prices, for the most part, are history. Most of the tourist shops are along the first three blocks of Calle Obregón, up to its intersection with Calle Aguirre. Obregón continues south for about five miles, however, with shops mainly serving Mexican clientele. These are interesting, too.

A different experience awaits the visitor in Sonora's interior. There is little developed tourism in the state, so visitors see Mexican society as it really is—the unrestrained passion of the crowd at a semi-pro *beisbol* game; the old itinerant tool sharpener who plods through the residential streets of Hermosillo, the capital, playing melodies on his panpipes. Sonorans are outgoing and curious about foreigners, and it's easy to strike up conversations in the streets (providing you speak some Spanish—few Sonorans, other than those who work in the tourist shops and hotels, have studied English).

Rocky Point and **Guaymas**, two shrimping towns on the Gulf of California, offer superb seafood in unpretentious restaurants at prices that are at most half what one would pay on the coasts of California or Texas. **San Carlos**, adjacent to Guaymas, also has excellent restaurants and seaside resorts. San Carlos, however, is mostly a colony of U.S. expatriates and weekend condo dwellers, and exudes little of the character of a Mexican town.

Far off any beaten track is the quiet village of **Tubutama**, which is worth visiting just to see the folk-baroque mission church of **San Pedro y San Pablo de Tubutama**, built in 1788. Its facade is an architectural carnival of spirals, quatrefoils, sculpted seashells, and flowers, and even a pair of angels with the bodies of children and the faces of old men, floating heavenward and carrying what appear to be chickens. It is naive and ambitious at once, and it radiates a sensation of perfect innocence and purity. There are no hotels or even restaurants in Tubutama.

Alamos is a seductively beautiful Spanish colonial town that grew out of the wealth generated by the nearby Sierra Madre silver mines in the 1700s. Scores of restored mansions line its narrow, tunnel-like streets, their rhythmic Romanesque colonnades forming a kind of visual music that serenades the stroller. The central plaza and courtyards of the mansions are awash in bougainvillea, jasmine, and the poplar trees (*alamos*) that gave the town its name. Most of the mansions have been restored by Americans, a few as hotels and restaurants. Alamos is no more typical of Sonora today than is Nogales, its cultural opposite, but it is lovely.

U.S. citizens need no passport or visa for visits to Mexican border towns unless the stay exceeds 72 hours. Visits to the interior, if you're driving, require a visa and *turista* permit for the car, an "automotive importation" fee, and a blizzard of bureaucracy.

Should one even try driving? There are other difficulties. First, most U.S. auto insurance companies do not insure policyholders driving into the interior of Mexico; supplemental insurance must be bought from a company specializing in it (see the Yellow Pages in Tucson or Nogales). Major U.S. auto rental companies do not allow their cars to be taken into Mexico, although a handful of local firms do. Supplies of unleaded gasoline (*sin plomo*) are no longer a problem, although road maintenance definitely is. As for the issue of road safety, it depends on the individual's level of comfort in coping with unfamiliar situations. Mexican traffic may appear anarchic to *norteamericanos*, but at least everything happens in slow motion. In my experience, it is easier than driving in Europe.

For those not wanting to drive in Sonora, there is an inexpensive train linking Nogales, Hermosillo, Guaymas, and Ciudad Obregon. Tickets may be purchased through Arizona travel agencies specializing in Mexican travel or at the Nogales,

Sonora, train station. There also are some organized tours that travel by bus. The best-known are the delightful three-day Kino Mission Tours conducted every fall and spring by the non-profit **Southwest Mission Research Center** in Tucson; call (520) 621-6278. This tour visits the historic mission churches at **San Ignacio, Tubutama, Oquitoa, Pitiquito, and Caborca.** The missions are wonderful and these small towns, all but untouched by tourism, represent the real Mexico.

The silver city of Alamos in Sonora, Mexico. (Kerrick James)

A   R   T   S

TELEVISION AND MARKETING, claims conventional wisdom, have almost finished transforming the United States into one homogenized, continental village. From Seattle to Miami our skylines cut similar profiles, our symphony orchestras play the same music and shudder through identical financial crises, and artists everywhere pursue the same bankable trends.

This guidebook dissents. The arts in Arizona are and always will be unique because they are driven by engines that are uniquely our own: our history, which still lies close to the surface. Our simmering stew of three distinct human cultures. Our landscapes. Our light. These are cultural and environmental imperatives that always will influence art—for the better, usually.

The sculpture of Prescott artists Rebecca Davis and Roger Asay is one example. They make intellectually challenging art out of the everyday stuff of the Arizona environment: pebbles, boulders, saplings, trees. It isn't just avant-garde kitsch. On the south shore of the little lake in Tucson's Reid Park, Davis and Asay have planted five pecan trees—trees stripped of all leaves, bark, and small branches, sanded smooth, painted five different tones of red and, finally, turned upside down. They are as sensuous, in their own curious way, as Renoir's sun-dappled nudes. "We inverted them," Asay explained, "to take them out of context so people don't just dismiss them as bare trees. What we hope is that people will begin to see the trees differently, and more intently." People do.

In 1989, New Mexico architect Antoine Predock attempted an astoundingly deep and intellectually thorny abstraction of both Arizona's culture and landscape in his design for a single building: the Nelson Fine Arts Center at Arizona State University in Tempe *(see page 154)*. Its complex profile, a ramble of colliding boxes, triangles, terraces, and plazas, resembles at once a Hopi pueblo and a desert mountain range. Its color, a washed-out gray-purple stucco, was borrowed from a rock the architect found on a nearby hill. The building's story line, as Predock has explained it to baffled visitors, is a cultural cross-section of the site: the gurgling pools in its underground lobby recall the canals of the vanished Hohokam, while a flat panel jutting into the sky suggests an endangered artifact of the modern West, the drive-in movie screen. It is a mystical and magnificent building, and *The New York Times* architecture critic, Paul Goldberger, was exactly on target when he wrote that it illustrates "how it is possible for a piece of architecture to be deeply ingrained in the architectural traditions of a place, yet unlike anything we have seen before."

Traditions of a place. This is what is to be most cherished in the arts of Arizona.

■ ARCHITECTURE

Arizona is the only state in which the oldest functioning architecture is also the best. This is a prodigious tribute to the unknown designer of San Xavier del Bac, but also a raincloud over the résumés of all the architects since. This mission was built 200 years ago, probably by itinerant Spanish craftsmen and bewildered native laborers, in an Apache-beseiged outpost a thousand miles from any building of comparable ambition. And yet architects even today seem helpless to do much except sigh in envy, bow in humility, and muddle on making lesser buildings.

San Xavier was intended, wrote the captain of the Spanish presidio at Tucson in 1804, "to attract by its loveliness the unconverted [Indians] beyond the frontier." Ironically, this was both naivete and arrogance on the founding Jesuits' part; the Tohono O'odham people's concept of God was and still is rooted in nature, not at the altar of a transplanted Spanish baroque church.

But the builders spared no expense on their magic show. The church is built in the traditional cruciform plan, crowned with two belfries and a bravura dome, and decorated with a portal of such architectural sizzle that the eye hardly knows where to alight. This portal has everything—spires, scrolls, seashell motifs, eggs, arches, saints, even a cartoon: a cat and a rodent crouch on opposing scrolls just below the parapet, glaring at each other in eternal standoff. And after this the interior is no letdown, strutting a cavalcade of statuary, murals, and a stunning reredos that echoes the organization of the portal. In his three-volume survey of American buildings, architectural historian G. E. Kidder Smith called the interior "hair-raising." His late colleague Reyner Banham went even farther: San Xavier del Bac, he flatly proclaimed, "is the most beautiful man-made object in America Deserta." This mission is off I-19 just south of Tucson.

From the coming of the railroad in 1880 to 1900, Arizonans were infatuated with Victorian architecture; it was a symbolic way of proclaiming the frontier civilized (and Americanized). In a quick 20 years it seemed to the residents that they were civilized enough, and the time arrived to declare cultural independence from those effete Eastern shores. The result was the Mission Revival of 1900-1915, and the still more romantic Spanish Colonial Revival of 1915-1930. These two movements left Arizona with some of its loveliest buildings. San Xavier, though, was not their inspiration; California was. These "Spanish" styles were encouraged by West Coast promoters eager to capitalize on the romantic mythology of the *conquistadores*. Like Californians, Arizona newcomers were not particularly interested in participating in Hispanic culture, but they loved wrapping themselves in its imagery.

In the 1930s came another reversal. Phoenix and Tucson, finally edging toward the country's economic mainstream, felt they had to begin looking like real cities instead of pink Iberian fantasylands. Color, ornament, and romance became high crimes, and from then until the 1970s most architecture in Arizona echoed the modernist credo of "less is more" in vogue everywhere else. Modernism left Arizona with many of its least ingratiating buildings. Finally, then, yet another re-thinking—and yet another Hispanic revival. This one, still in progress, has no formal name, although one hostile critic has proposed "Taco Deco." It is simpler and cheaper than its predecessors, and repetitive to the point of cliché, but it also is an effort—if not quite a noble one—to perpetuate an architecture with a sense of place.

Since 1970, a growing minority of Arizona architects have tried to establish a different tradition: buildings that reside in harmony with the land. Their inspiration, if not their style, stems from the ideas of Frank Lloyd Wright *(see page 194)*. These buildings may take their colors, their forms, even their moods from the land. Along with Predock's Nelson Fine Arts Center, one of the best examples is The Boulders Resort in Scottsdale. A sculptural, free-form main building embraces a little "mountain"—a grumpy 200-foot-high pile of feldspar and granite boulders. It has the grace of a coolly contemporary ballet on a Fred Flintstone stage set. Guest "casitas" are strewn around the jumbled, rocky landscape with no attempt to impose order where it would not naturally exist. As successful as the building is, the philosophy of designer Bob Bacon should, in the long run, be even more appreciated. When asked what he would have designed for this site had the assignment been a cathedral instead of a resort, Bacon replied, "Nothing."

The connoisseur of architecture should see numerous other Arizona buildings, most of them around the two metropolitan areas.

In Tucson: the 1927 Spanish Colonial Revival **Pima County Courthouse,**

continued on page 196

MODERN ARIZONA ARCHITECTURE

From Frank Lloyd Wright's famous school Taliesin West to Antoine Predrock's Nelson Fine Arts Center, Arizona has inspired creative design and some of the best of modern architecture. The following are examples of a new tradition in Arizona architecture where the buildings are designed to blend in with their desert surroundings.

TALIESIN WEST
Location: 12621 Frank Lloyd
   Wright Blvd., Scottsdale
Function: school of architecture
Architect: Frank Lloyd Wright
Year Built: 1937–1938

LOEW'S VENTANA CANYON RESORT
Location: 7000 N. Resort Dr.,
   Tucson
Function: resort
Architect: Frizzell, Hill, and
   Moorehouse (San Francisco)
Year Built: 1983

ARIZONA BILTMORE

Location: 24th St. and Missouri Ave., Phoenix
Function: resort
Architect: Albert Chase McArthur
Year Built: 1929

BOULDERS

Location: 34631 N. Tom Darlington, Carefree
Function: resort
Architect: Bob Bacon
Year Built: 1984

NELSON FINE ARTS CENTER

Location: Arizona State University, Tempe
Function: Houses the University Art Museum, a theater, dance studios, and classrooms
Architect: Antoine Predock
Year Built: 1989

FRANK LLOYD WRIGHT

On a warm October Sunday morning in 1987, some 250 disciples of organic archi-tecture from around the world gathered on a Scottsdale hillside to celebrate, remi-nisce, and listen to words of inspiration. The occasion was the fiftieth anniversary of Frank Lloyd Wright's creation of Taliesin West, and the atmosphere was more like a religious service than a gathering of architects.

The prelude was a suite for violin and piano composed by Wright's third wife, Olgi-vanna—confident, big-boned music with a whiff of Rachmaninoff about it. The ser-mon was a recording of Frank Lloyd Wright speaking on the spiritual value of education. The missionary report previewed a touring exhibition on the architect's life and work, about to go on the road in search of new converts. "We feel this exhibition has the possibility of changing the architecture of America by the twenty-first centu-ry," said the managing trustee of the Taliesin Fellowship, "and possibly the world."

Wright died in Phoenix in 1959, a few miles away from his beloved Taliesin West. His had been the longest, most creative and most controversial career of any architect in modern American history. What followed his death, however, had no precedent except in the ranks of religious prophets and political leaders. Wright, even today, lives on among his former associates and apprentices as the guiding spirit, the one fountain of Truth in architecture. The commune-like Taliesin fellowship continues as ever, spending its summers in Wisconsin and winters in Scottsdale. The Frank Lloyd Wright School of Architecture still instructs its students in a curriculum more like a medieval apprenticeship than a modern university education. Most oddly of all, the design vocabulary of the Taliesin architects has not changed since Wright's death. They talk of preserving only the *spirit* of Wright's philosophy of organic architecture, but in practice they also perpetuate his exuberant geometry, his contrapuntal mass-ing, his repetitive ornamentation—all the elements that together make up the thing Wright claimed to despise so virulently: style.

Wright designed roughly 50 buildings for Arizona, about one-third of which were built (some, like Phoenix's First Christian Church, were finished posthumously by Taliesin Associated Architects). Among them are both masterpieces and flights of silly fantasy. They have not had widespread influence on architecture in Arizona (except that practiced at Taliesin), which is unfortunate. Wright early on developed a philos-ophy of desert architecture that took its inspiration from the spare, angular land-scape, and at its best, it was and is beautifully harmonious.

"I suggest that the dotted line is the line for the desert; not the hard line nor the knife edge," he wrote in 1940. He had studied the desert's thorn forest—cholla, saguaro, ocotillo—and noticed how the needles of these plants broke up and filtered the harsh sunlight spraying through them. Obviously, a building couldn't literally wear a skin of needles, but an architect could articulate and shade and texture wall surfaces for the same effect. A high, straight, flat wall surface would reflect light and appear as a foreign presence imposed on the landscape, but a broken one—a "dotted line"—would settle gracefully into it. In this respect Taliesin West is the masterpiece; perhaps no other Wright building, architect Pietro Belluschi once said, so perfectly gathers in "the mood of the land."

Wright, however, blithely violated his own philosophy whenever he felt like it. There is little "mood of the land" in Gammage Center, his 1959 auditorium at Arizona State University. Originally designed as an opera house for Baghdad, it looks like a great pink wedding cake festooned with hoops and baubles that appear to have been inspired by the tales of Scheherezade, or that may simply have floated down from Mars. Its acoustics, however, are stunning. Wright's Arizona Capitol, which he designed in one morning in 1957, still generates debate—even though it was never built. It was a geometry student's nightmare, a gigantic, lacy gridlock of triangles and hexagons and heaven-storming spires. Reviewing a show of Wright drawings in 1990, *The Arizona Republic's* art critic Richard Nilsen declared flatly that Wright was a crackpot and that this project was a perfect "capitol for the planet Mongo." But it was perfectly in tune with the baroque sci-fi aesthetic of the 1950s, and had it been built, in two or three generations it would have gracefully aged into one of Arizona's architectural treasures, a rival to San Xavier del Bac.

Wright was both genius and hypocrite, visionary and gadfly. In deifying him, the disciples at Taliesin have done him no favor. His buildings speak better for him.

Taliesin West offers tours daily. From Scottsdale Road take Shea Boulevard 4.6 miles east to Frank Lloyd Wright Boulevard. Turn left and follow the signs; (602) 860-8810. **Gammage Center** at Mill Avenue and Apache Boulevard in Tempe can be viewed from outside, but normally is locked except for scheduled concerts. **First Christian Church**, 6500 N. 7th Avenue in Phoenix, welcomes visitors from 8:30 to 5 on weekdays. Check in the church office. The **Arizona Biltmore**, 24th Street and Missouri in Phoenix, actually was designed by Albert Chase McArthur; Wright's contribution as "consultant" was smaller than is popularly believed. The rest of Wright's Arizona buildings are private homes, and are not open to the public.

Church and Congress streets; the historic west end of the **University of Arizona** campus, Park Avenue and University; and **Loews Ventana Canyon Resort**, 7000 N. Resort Drive. The latter, designed in 1984, drew considerable inspiration from Wright's unbuilt San Marcos-in-the-Desert hotel of 1928.

In Phoenix: the **Luhrs Tower** (1929), 45 W. Jefferson, a successful marriage of Art Deco and Spanish Colonial Revival—and to this day, the best of Phoenix's several dozen high-rises. **Brophy Prep** (1928), 4701 N. Central Avenue, is the most lyrical Spanish Colonial Revival building in the state. **Tempe City Hall** (1971), 31 E. Fifth Street, Tempe, is a personal favorite, although many still condemn it as architectural conceit: an inverted pyramid of glass and steel bursts up from street level, shading a lovely subterranean courtyard. The one work of Paolo Soleri worth visiting is **Cosanti**, 6433 Doubletree Road, Paradise Valley, an intimate village of earth-cast organic forms. Soleri's much better-known **Arcosanti**, 70 miles (112 km) north of Phoenix, is uninteresting as architecture; as a social experiment it has more to do with totalitarianism than harmonious living with the Earth. Essentially, Soleri would have us all live in concrete beehives.

Four miles south of Tubac, see the mission of **San José de Tumacácori**. In Sedona, the 1956 **Chapel of the Holy Cross**, wedged between a pair of ruddy buttes, is the provocative retort to Wrightian organic architecture, an impassive, defiant creation that appears more powerful than the mountains around it. Take AZ 179 three miles south of Sedona to Chapel Road, turn left and proceed one mile. Finally, the 1905 **El Tovar Hotel** at the Grand Canyon's South Rim is a truly amazing accomplishment: a sprawling wooden pile of styles from the Victorian Gothic to Richardsonian Romanesque that still manages, somehow, to seem elegant, and that does no dishonor to the great spectacle at its back.

■ THE VISUAL ARTS

Virtually all artists who come to Arizona from somewhere else are changed by the environment here. It is not only that new subjects materialize on their canvases; that would be expected. But a fresh temperament, a different attitude, perhaps even a new spirit may also pervade their work. Sometimes it is subtle; more often it is a dramatic change.

Howard Conant, a painter who for 10 years also headed the University of Arizona Department of Art, moved to Arizona from New York City in 1976. He was a geometric abstractionist, and his New York paintings often seemed to express tension and energy and violence, even when the subject had nothing at all to do with the city. They were jagged and searing. After five years of work in a quiet desert studio, his paintings were still as crisp as ever, but the fury had all evaporated. Gentle, rolling lines had replaced processions of severe, knifelike triangles. He even gave in and painted a sunset, albeit an abstract one.

"A sunset is just about the lowest thing a professional artist can do," he said. "Postcard artists do sunsets. Cowboy artists do sunsets. But I'd fallen so in love with the desert that I finally just decided, what the hell—I've got to do it. I succumbed."

Artists have been interpreting the Arizona environment since some anonymous Hohokam first scratched the likeness of a scorpion onto a boulder. Possibly he was expressing a vivid encounter with that environment—a nasty sting. In 1873, the famous painter Thomas Moran accompanied John Wesley Powell on the latter's third expedition into the Grand Canyon, and the following year completed what is still one of the grandest and most evocative paintings ever made of Arizona, *The Chasm of the Colorado.* On a single gigantic canvas (7 by 12 feet), Moran portrayed the canyon splashed with golden sunlight, splattered by a furious thunderstorm, and haunted by clouds of mist lurking in shadowy abysses—all at once. Moran wrote that the canyon was "by far the most awfully grand and impressive scene I have yet ever seen," and it may be that his imagination outpaced even the canyon's real-life grandness. The painting was hung in the U.S. Senate lobby, and viewers were electrified. From there it played a role in the transformation of Arizona. Inspired by the tremendous public reaction, the promotion-minded Santa Fe Railway a few years later began commissioning artists to come out and paint Southwestern subjects, particularly Arizona and New Mexico. Their work helped create the tourism boom and promote the settlement of these scenic and exotic lands.

Arizona's visual art separates into several basic categories. Landscapes are the most obvious, and among the most abundant, as a day's gallery browsing will show. Western art, less respectfully called "cowboy art," is another.

Western art is controversial in Arizona. The intelligentsia scorns it. Collectors are enchanted by it. The average person cannot afford it—not the capably executed works, at least. Paintings by Howard Terpning, among the most highly regarded of Arizona's living Western artists, have sold for as much as $312,500.

Yet art critics turn apoplectic virtually in unison when the subject of Western art arises. In Tucson's *City Magazine*, writer Karin Demorest concluded:

> [*The* Western Artist] is on a treadmill, telling the same story over and over again, stubbornly refusing to stray from the stock images of the genre —the cowboy, the Indian, the horse, the desert landscape, the mountains, the sunset. Furthermore, his preoccupation with authenticity and technique deprives him of real expressiveness and individuality. . . . Subject matter, authenticity and technical skill are the standards by which Western art is both made and judged, with little if any attention paid to composition, spatial quality or drawing. A piece is considered good, even great, if the subject looks utterly real: the number of feathers in the Indian's headdress correct, the spots on the Appaloosa just the right color, the stirrups flawlessly rendered. . . .

So why the popularity? The answer is as obvious a cliché as the classic cowboy-in-the-sunset painting: the themes in these scenes from a romanticized past are those cherished by the collectors themselves (who, according to Demorest, are almost exclusively white males, over 45): independence, heroism, nature in its raw form (and so awaiting a man's challenge), and nostalgia for a bygone era free of cynicism and ambiguity. Interestingly, women seldom appear on Western artists' canvases, except as idealized and therefore untouchable Indian squaws.

Native American art, and art portraying Native Americans, are two other prominent categories. Among the former are some well-known tribal specialties: Tohono O'odham wire baskets, Apache *ga'an* masks, and Navajo sand paintings and rugs. Most prized in Arizona, however, are Hopi kachina dolls.

Like so many other Native American art forms, kachina (pronounced "kat-SEE-na") dolls now serve both ceremonial and commercial roles in Hopi life. Some Hopis benefit: a top-drawer doll can sell for several thousand dollars. Others grieve: the most beautiful and intricate dolls no longer go to young Hopi girls, but to tourists and collectors. The positive note, however, is that because of their commercial success, the art of Hopi kachina carving has grown much more intricate and elegant over the last two or three generations.

Kachina dolls traditionally are carved from cottonwood roots by men as gifts for their female children. The dolls represent the living kachinas, masked

(opposite) A Hopi kachina doll. (Paul Chesley)

intercessors to the Hopi spirit world who help to guarantee such critical matters as rain. Many published sources say that the gifts are to educate the children in the Hopi way, but the more important reason is to insure their eventual fertility.

Nineteenth-century kachina dolls were rudimentary and statically posed, and the arms, legs, and fingers were simply implied by bulges extruded from the torso. Modern kachinas explode with energy and detail; they frequently are frozen in a dance pose, and their very distinct limbs ripple with musculature. On the most intricate dolls, even individual strands of hair and barbs of feathers are carved. At the risk of taking sides in a Hopi controversy, the view here is that this is one treasured Native American art that has benefitted from its commercialization.

Art portraying Native Americans, however, deserves the most respect when it is least commercial. Mass-marketed images of Indians, which have made more than a few Arizona artists wealthy, invariably reduce their subject to cliché: the noble savage, the stoic squaw, the innocent, saucer-faced infant. Some artists have been more honest. Among them is Barry Goldwater, later elected to the U.S. Senate, who took a celebrated series of photos of the Navajo people in the 1930s. Even today, the best art portraying Native Americans remains photographic: it is easier to tell the truth through a lens.

Viewing art: The principal art museums in Arizona are all noted in "PHOENIX," "TUCSON," AND "ARIZONA TOWNS." One generalization: the various university museums stay closer to the cutting

The historic Hubbell Trading Post stocks everything from Doritos to 19th-century Indian pottery to Navajo rugs. (Kerrick James)

edge and take more risks than the municipal museums. One special museum is the University of Arizona's **Center for Creative Photography**, one of the best photographic museums in the country. Its shows change periodically, and its archives house works of more than 1,400 photographers—including the complete *ouevre* of Ansel Adams, Edward Weston, W. Eugene Smith, and Richard Avedon. Their prints are normally stored away from public view, but visitors may make requests for private print-viewing sessions; *(520) 621-7968.*

Buying art: Scottsdale's **Fifth Avenue** galleries are the best-known in the state, and they serve the well-heeled traditionalist best. Tucson's **Congress Street** galleries mostly feature price tags a fraction of Scottsdale's and offer more adventure—though the quality varies wildly. **Sedona** has many excellent galleries but little provocative art; **Tubac's** shops also tend toward conservatism but are lower-priced.

CLASSIC SOUTHWEST JEWELRY

Trading posts such as Hubbell on the Navajo Reservation (preceding page) were important places for the trade and sale of Indian art all across the Southwest.

NAVAJO CONCHA BELTS

The idea for concha belts derived from disk-shaped hair ornaments sold to Plains Indians by white traders as early as 1750. Navajos linked hair ornaments to form decorative belts, impressing into the silver Mexican designs. Circa 1885.

ZUÑI BRACELET

The Zuñis have two reservations, one in New Mexico and a small one in Arizona. For centuries, Zuñis traded turquoise to Plains Indians for buffalo hides and to Mexican tribes for parrot plumes. Over the years the Zuñi have become famous for their extraordinary work in turquoise and silver as exemplified left in this huge, sunburst design cluster bracelet. Circa 1930.

COCHITI PUEBLO SILVER SQUASH BLOSSOM NECKLACE

Traditional squash blossom necklaces feature side pendants in the shape of a squash or pumpkin flower. In this necklace, the squash blossoms have been replaced with crosses; this particular design has a double-barred cross with a heartlike bottom, resembling the Catholic sacred heart and the Indian dragonfly that in many Pueblo cultures was the symbol for water.

(photos by Eduardo Fuss)

Bisbee is a good place to catch emerging artists' work on the cheap. **Jerome** defies categorization; it is the least predictable art center of all—a welcome characteristic for adventurous buyers. There are galleries specializing in Native Americana in every city, but the **Hubbell Trading Post**, a National Historic Site founded in 1876 at Ganado on the Navajo Reservation, is one worth a special trip: its selection of quality Navajo rugs is staggering *(see pages 114-115)*. For Western art collectors, October brings the Phoenix Art Museum's annual **Cowboy Artists of America** sale, a social event that always grosses more than $1 million in sales.

■ PERFORMING ARTS

Another cliché: Because Arizona is a young state, and because it has relatively little in the way of old wealth, its performing arts organizations are still struggling through their adolescence. Like many clichés, this one has a nucleus of truth in it. But it isn't the full story.

The oldest arts organization still performing is the Tucson Symphony Orchestra, which was founded in 1928—an accomplishment for what was then a town of about 30,000 souls. The Phoenix Symphony followed later, but it was the first arts organization in the state to take the plunge into "major" status, meaning full-time employment for its musicians. That decision was made in 1981, and the years since have, in truth, been difficult: chasmic deficits have plagued the orchestra, and emergency fund drives and staff layoffs have been necessary to keep it afloat. One of its peculiar curses is, strangely, Phoenix's attractive winter climate. Wealthy and cultured people are drawn by it to retire in Phoenix (or commute to winter homes here), and while they often *attend* the Phoenix Symphony, some of their *donations* still go back to the great old orchestras in their snowbound home towns— Minneapolis, Cleveland, Boston.

The highly acclaimed Arizona Theatre Company is even younger—it was founded in Tucson in 1967—and it also has faced tough financial times and emerged intact. It now functions as a statewide organization, still headquartered in Tucson, but staging six plays each season in both Tucson and Phoenix. The Arizona Opera Company, likewise based in Tucson but serving both cities, produces five operas per season. It lives scrupulously within its budget, a considerable achievement for any opera company, and one reason is its conservative "Top 40" repertoire of operas—Mozart, Rossini, Puccini & Co. In fairness, the Arizona

Opera probably can't afford many artistic risks at this awkward point in its life. It is too mature and established to take a wild, youthful plunge into the avant-garde, and yet not secure enough to produce, say, Krzysztof Penderecki's *Black Mask,* lose money on it, and not be hurt. Call it, if you must, adolescence.

Risks are being taken in abundance, however, by smaller groups and determined individuals. In Phoenix, Planet Earth Multi-Cultural Theatre stages alternative productionsy. In Tucson, the Theatre Congress stage is home to Dames Rocket Theatre Co., which produces topical plays dealing with women's views, history, and community; and to Upstairs Theatre Co., which stretches the limits of contemporary drama.

■ FOLK ART

Thanks to its profusion of cultures (once again), Arizona also is spectacularly rich in folk art—from cowboy poetry to Mexican murals to Tohono O'odham "chicken

A street mural in Tucson's Barrio Histórico is a good example of Arizona's folk art. (Kerrick James)

scratch," a musical style apparently transmitted to the tribe by the Jesuit and Franciscan missionaries long before Anglo settlement. (Certainly no other tribe plays a repertoire of polkas and two-steps on accordion, saxophone, drums and electric guitar.)

No broad survey of folk art is possible in this short treatment, but one curiosity unique to Arizona seems especially worth describing: the century-old tradition of Arizonans wryly poking fun at their own habitat in verse, gag, and cartoon image.

Most of this folk art, predictably, plays on the heat or the desert's general inhospitality. One reliable place to find it is in the *Arizona Republic* columnist Sam Lowe's annual Hot Weather Poetry contest. This quatrain was among 1996's published entries:

Phoenicians will deodorize,
This dripping sweat to stop.
And then we reach for handy wipes
And mop and mop and mop.

This poetic tradition dates back at least to 1879, when a ballad attributed to a pioneer Tucson bartender first circulated. A remarkably clever and well-paced tale, it begins with the Devil being given permission (presumably by God, though this detail is left unstated) to select a land as a special annex for Hell. It is, of course, Arizona—and Satan undertakes to improve on it:

. . . He filled the river with sand till it was almost dry,
And poisoned the land with alkali
And promised himself on its slimy brink
The control of all who from it should drink.
He saw there was one more improvement to make,
He imported the scorpion, tarantula and rattlesnake,
That all who might come to its country to dwell
Would be sure to think it was almost hell.
He fixed the heat at one hundred and seven
And banished forever the moisture from heaven . . .

The punchline, of course, is inevitable: when the Devil at last completes his "improvements":

... *F*or his own realm compares so well
He feels sure it surpasses Hell.

None of this is serious put-down: anyone who actually disliked this environment would not be moved to write wry and ironic verses about it. In truth, it is a form of braggadocio. Wrote James S. Griffith, Arizona's preeminent cultural anthropologist of folk art, "One of the points of the genre is that it takes a real tough character to put up with whatever country is being described." This seems to be no less true today, even given the palliative of air conditioning, than it was in 1879. Wimps dwell not in this land.

■ KITSCH

Arizona may well lead the nation in the production of kitsch, a distinction that need not cause us embarrassment. Kitsch is the natural consequence of having rich landscapes and cultures that invite reduction into sentimental or cartoonish

Cigar store cowboys and Indians have always been icons of Southwestern kitsch. (Kerrick James)

Where's the beef? Amado's longhorn architecture has recently been reborn as a restaurant.

images, along with a vibrant tourist industry that supplies customers with cash in hand. *Objets de kitsch* generate jobs and revenue today, and over two or three generations they undergo a quiet metamorphosis into important cultural artifacts—i.e., antiques. The only immediate problem is telling folk art and kitsch apart. The line is blurry.

Architectural kitsch abounds in Arizona. A fine example is the giant stucco teepee in the old mining town of Globe; it currently houses a bar. A better-known institution is Bedrock City, a Fred Flintstone theme park of free-form boulder-like buildings strategically placed at the intersection of US 180 and Arizona State Highway 64, the two main routes to the Grand Canyon's South Rim. More extravagant is the downtown Phoenix Mercado, a boutique fantasyland that marries Taco Deco to the recklessly festive pink, purple, yellow, and turquoise colors of postmodernism.

Arizona's animals and plants lead to endless production of kitsch. The scorpion and the saguaro seem especially inspirational. In 1971 the legislature proclaimed the bola the state tie of Arizona, and the quintessential bola (for tourists, that is) must have an authentic Arizona scorpion encased in a transparent plastic clasp. (Few Arizonans under retirement age would be caught dead in a bola of any sort today; as Arizona novelist Ray Ring explained, "The official necktie, the string bola, is so goofy most wives won't let their husbands appear in one.")

The saguaro, perhaps because of its anthropomorphic friendliness, pops up in boutiques everywhere. There are saguaros made of green-painted stovepipe, stuffed felt, soldered copper, blown glass, and glowing neon. The Arizona State Museum even has a miniature saguaro made by a Tohono O'odham artist out of scrap telephone wire. None of Arizona's cultures seem able to resist the siren of kitsch.

Other examples: there is a peculiar building in Amado whose very entrance is a gigantic cow skull and horns. Numerous Arizona towns and cities have "Old West" shopping villages with a steak house and assorted curio shops. (Pinnacle Peak steak house, with locations in north Scottsdale and in Tucson's Trail Dust Town, even has an especially kitschy ritual: any unsuspecting customer who wears a tie to dinner will be attacked by waitresses ringing cowbells and wielding scissors; they snip off the tie and staple it to the ceiling.) A recent development is chile kitsch: red peppers are turning up in stained glass windows, dangling from people's ears, and glowing on Christmas trees.

Any image, if replicated over and over, eventually ceases to be usable in fine art or even folk art. It parks in the province of kitsch and from there it will not budge. This is the one thing to regret about kitsch. It is all but impossible today for anyone to paint a saguaro in a sunset, a noble and honest Arizona image, and have it be taken seriously. Literal paintings of Indians have long been snubbed by everyone outside the Western art establishment; recently even highly stylized renderings have become suspect—those images of Navajo women in immense, flowing robes have badly overpopulated the galleries.

Arizona, however, seems inexhaustably rich in subject matter. If the saguaro is for now too hazardous for the serious artist to approach, there are a few dozen neglected species of cacti still out there, waiting.

ARIZONA DREAMS

IT IS A WARM WINTER DAY, and I am walking in a park in downtown Mesa listening to a developer talk penguins.

"You know how hot it is here in the summer," he says, unnecessarily. "So imagine the effect of watching 19 penguins frolicking in a fountain around an igloo. It would be absolute dynamite!"

He's serious, he swears; his plan is just on the back burner at the moment because the projected cost of the desert penguin habitat has bloated to about 10 times the original projection. I soberly record all this in my notebook, and a few weeks later report it as part of a special newspaper project commemorating the 75th anniversary of Arizona statehood.

The reason I didn't simply laugh and dismiss him as a crackpot is that his scheme nestled seamlessly into the continuum of Arizona's story.

From the Gadsden Purchase of 1853 to today, Arizona has always been a land for dreamers, "a blank slate on which they could etch their visions of the future," in the words of Arizona State Museum ethnohistorian Thomas E. Sheridan. If penguins and igloos in downtown Mesa seem preposterous, they are hardly more so than the necklace of lakes that now drapes through the heart of the Mojave Desert (complete with London Bridge), or the Victorian hotels in the mining towns, clasped desperately to the sides of mountains and gulches. We have remodeled the land to meet our needs and dreams, rather than accepting it on its own terms. Often we have done no good. Wrote Charles Bowden in *Blue Desert*, "Here the land always makes promises of aching beauty and the people always fail the land." A harsh judgment, but not one without the resonance of much truth in it.

The first miracle of technology that reconstructed the face of Arizona was the railroad. Until this, virtually all the architecture had been native—that is, built with the materials at hand. In the desert towns, that meant dirt, primarily—dirt mixed with water, poured into a form, and dried in the abundant sun to make adobe. The word descends from the Arabic *al-tub*, "the brick," which suggests its fundamental importance in arid lands everywhere. Adobe made perfect sense in the Arizona deserts. Its great thermal mass helped keep interiors cool through the torrid summer. Houses were built close together, which helped shade the spaces between them. Instead of front and back yards patterned after the rural English

model, they incorporated shady, enclosed Mediterranean courtyards. But once the railroads came, bringing building materials from back East, pioneer Arizonans couldn't wait to discard adobe in favor of Victorian architecture. Mud was symbolic of the Mexican past; gables and balustrades represented an affluent, expanding America—even though this architecture made little sense, environmentally or aesthetically, in the desert.

The hunger of the pioneers to make Arizona look like someplace else meant that it would never again have a unique and environmentally sensible built environment. When mirrored glass towers burst into vogue nationally in the 1970s, architects dutifully reproduced them in Phoenix. No one asked the obvious question: why bounce more sunlight around in a place that already has quite enough of it?

Water projects were the next phase in the makeover of Arizona. Mining and farming both require generous and reliable water supplies, which never existed naturally here. Arizona's rivers are trickles one season, torrents the next. It took a network of dams to control them: Roosevelt in 1911, Coolidge in 1929, Hoover in 1935. All were federal projects, as their names imply. Arizona didn't have the money to tame its own rivers, and at that time it didn't have the political influence to wrestle Washington into paying, either. These dams exist because there was money to be made in Arizona, and the people flocking here to make it needed the water.

Thus tricked into unnatural behavior, these rivers made Phoenix green and created the spectacle of vast recreational lakes—Powell, Mead, Havasu, Roosevelt—in treeless landscapes that enjoy 3 to 10 inches of rain in a year. Other water projects have changed the landscape in ways less obvious to the casual visitor. Driving south toward Tucson along I-10, one views tens of thousands of acres of farmland now lying fallow, choked with tumbleweeds. Thirsty Tucson has bought this farmland for the rights to slurp the aquifer underneath.

But the most important effect of all the water projects has been that they have made big cities possible. This has been both boon and curse. Without the cities, Arizona would have had little to contribute to the arts and sciences, it would hardly seem cosmopolitan, and it wouldn't offer either its residents or visitors the diversity it now does. At the same time, these cities are draining the water, fouling the air, and gnawing away the desert and mountains around them. This cannot go on forever.

(previous pages) Construction of Hoover Dam, in 1935 the world's largest, claimed the lives of 96 workers.

A perceptive visitor to Arizona may discern a messy contradiction in what we say about the land and what we do to it. For example, we rhapsodize endlessly over the sunsets and mountain views, but we don't prohibit billboards. Several other scenic states do, notably Vermont, Maine, Alaska, and Hawaii. In Sedona, arguably the town with the loveliest natural assets in all of Arizona, there is no public access to its sparkling little river—it's all private property barred by a phalanx of "No Trespassing" signs. No one thought of a riparian park until it was too late.

The contradiction can be explained, even if not easily forgiven. Arizona has grown up too fast for its own good. Our population was 750,000 in 1950; it was 4.5 million in 1996. Most Arizonans are newcomers; too few of us have the deeply bedded roots that would give us a better understanding of and stewardship for the land. Too many of us moved here pursuing private dreams, and with the notable exception of the pioneer Mormons, we have always been busier developing personal resources than communal ones. City councils find themselves under constant pressure to allow new housing developments and shopping centers (and widen the streets on the way), but there is not enough competing clamor for more parks and greenbelts. Development is enormously controversial in Arizona today, but for 50 years it has been happening so fast that proponents and opponents only lurch from one battle to the next, never finding the time to take a long, careful look at what we really want to do with the land.

There are some positive signs. In 1980 the legislature finally enacted a statewide groundwater code, which mandates that by the year 2025, Arizona wells may draw no more water out of their aquifers than is being replenished by nature. There is a growing positive environmental activism. The Nature Conservancy's Arizona chapter, for example, is buying up endangered land at an astounding rate. The Conservancy fielded a three-year, $3.98 million fund drive to protect 14 threatened riparian corridors along rivers and arroyos. It comes almost too late, however. According to the Conservancy, 90 percent of Arizona's prime riparian woodlands already are gone.

In his bicentennial history of Arizona, author Lawrence Clark Powell articulated our difficulties in a few perfectly chosen words. The state's most serious problem, he wrote, is "peculiarly Arizonan, that of a rising flood of people into a land naturally unsuited to large numbers of people." Yet this land's promises of aching beauty have always drawn people with their dreams, and in successive laminations of civilizations they always will. Ours will not be the last.

BACK ROADS OF ARIZONA

I EASE MY CAR OFF THE DESERTED FOREST ROAD by the Mogollon Rim and onto a carpet of straw-colored pine needles. This is very close to the place, as best as I can tell, where the Tonto Apaches introduced themselves to Gen. George Crook, the U.S. Army's top Indian fighter, one autumn afternoon in 1871. Crook and his men were blazing a trail and gaping at the scenery, just as tourists do today, when suddenly the crisp alpine air was clotted with arrows. The troops scrambled for cover. Most of the Apaches melted back into the woods, but two found themselves trapped right on the rim, a sheer escarpment overlooking another forest 2,000 feet below.

The soldiers closed in. The Apaches leaped over the edge, apparently choosing suicide over capture. Crook's men stared in horrified amazement. But when they peered over the rim to look for the corpses, what they saw were two very live Apaches spidering down the near-vertical wall. Crook fired, and an arm of one of the fugitives went limp, blood spurting from an artery. His pace never slowed.

I peer over the rim myself and try to imagine doing that with one arm—and suddenly I feel very much like Crook did. Because of encounters like this, he eventually developed a profound respect for the people he had been sent to Arizona to subdue. They understood this beautiful but treacherous land in ways that the incoming wave of white settlers never would. If I had not made the effort to get to the Mogollon Rim—and it took three attempts, because the gravel road is often blocked by snow—I never would have fully understood this chasmic difference between our culture and theirs. This is one of the compelling reasons for leaving Arizona's cities and freeways behind, and taking the back roads. There is no better way to get to know the state except to walk it.

This chapter outlines eight drives, all rich in scenery, history, and surprises—such as the world-class bookstore on a desert ranch 40 miles from the nearest city. All start from one of Arizona's three main urban areas: Phoenix, Tucson, or Flagstaff. Some are easy day trips; some will take two, three, or four days. Most of the roads on the suggested routes are paved, and all are accessible to two-wheel-drive passenger cars except in heavy rain or snow.

One's sense of adventure may occasionally be called upon. The last time I drove US 191 from Alpine to Clifton, I encountered exactly three other cars in 95 miles.

Snowfall on the red rocks near Sedona as seen from Schnebly Hill Road. (Kerrick James)

It's a great scenic highway, but not a great place for your fuel injection to take early retirement. Summer or winter, *always* carry emergency drinking water while driving in Arizona.

■ ANCIENT ARIZONA TRAIL

This trip begins and ends in Flagstaff. As outlined here, it would cover about 575 miles and take four full days. Along the way is a wealth of prehistoric ruins, petroglyphs, and the most improbable land forms in North America. Most of the drive is on the Navajo Reservation, offering opportunities to engage a distinct contemporary culture, as well. *Best times: April through October.*

DAY 1: From Flagstaff, drive seven miles east on I-40 to **Walnut Canyon National Monument**, a V-shaped furrow 385 feet deep, lined with Sinagua ruins halfway down the canyon walls. This is a perfect place to contemplate the question of whether Arizona's prehistoric cultures, in the throes of a population boom after A.D. 1100, faced the threat of war over limited resources. Walnut Canyon's settlements certainly *look* defensive; why else would they have been built in such preposterous locations? Tantalizingly, an archaeologist has found one "foreign" arrowhead in the rib cage of a Sinagua woman buried here—but just one.

Next stop is **Petrified Forest National Park**, 105 miles east on I-40. Petrified Forest's ruins aren't worth a long visit, but near the Puerco Ruin is one of the most prolific and astounding collections of Anasazi petroglyphs in existence. The Park Service doesn't point it out, so most visitors miss it. Walk south from the ruin to the edge of the mesa it's on and look among the rocks just below.

After Petrified Forest, turn north into the Navajo Reservation and visit the **Hubbell Trading Post**, in business since 1876, and now a National Historic Site. The days when you could buy an inexpensive Navajo rug are now as remote as the era of nickel Cokes, but the weaving is more lovely and imaginative than ever. The prehistoric and geologic wonders of **Canyon de Chelly**, another 36 miles north on US 191, have been described in some detail in the "FIRST ARIZONANS" and "CANYONS" chapters. Stay overnight, preferably in the historic Thunderbird Lodge.

DAY 2: Take the 18-mile South Rim Drive to Canyon de Chelly's Spider Rock Overlook early in the morning, then take either a half-day or full-day tour of the canyon floor and its Anasazi ruins with a (required) Navajo guide. Anyone who hasn't done this hasn't experienced even a fraction of the wonders of this canyon. Guides may be hired at the visitor center, or at Thunderbird Lodge (which arranges trips in six-wheel military surplus vehicles).

In late afternoon, hike the 2.5-mile round-trip trail to White House Ruin, the one trail on which visitors are allowed without guides. In the evening, drive 81 miles to Kayenta, where you will need reservations (there are few motels). Next morning, you'll visit the largest and most astonishing Anasazi ruins in Arizona.

DAY 3: The two ruins of **Navajo National Monument** are **Betatakin** and **Keet Seel,** both built in deep sheltering alcoves in the walls of Tsegi Canyon. Betatakin is a three-hour hike in and out, led by a park ranger, and limited to 60 people a day (first come, first served). Keet Seel is a 16-mile round trip best taken on horseback; the hike is a death march through soft, wet sand. Because of a budget squeeze, the Park Service opens Betatakin only from the middle of May to the end of September, and Keet Seel from Memorial Day through Labor Day.

Reservations for Keet Seel are essential and must be made one to two months in advance; call the Navajo National Monument at (520) 672-2366. If you take only the half-day Betatakin tour, return to Kayenta in the afternoon, then take US 163 19 miles north to **Monument Valley.** The 17-mile dirt road through the Navajo Tribal Park is rough but manageable. Plan to be on the mesa at the park entrance for sunset.

DAY 4: West on US 160, then south on US 89 to **Wupatki National Monument** and **Sunset Crater.** Skip the northernmost ruins, Lomaki and the Citadel, and go to the Wupatki ruin (behind the visitor center) and Wukoki. These ruins are labeled as Sinaguan, but their architecture has Anasazi written all over it. At the end of the Ancient Arizona Trail, you now know enough archaeology to be suspicious.

■ SCENIC SEDONA TRAIL

Everyone staying in Flagstaff visits Sedona, 28 miles to the south. There are two scenic ways to go, however, and a day trip offers an opportunity to experience both. *Best times: March through November.*

From the beginning of I-17 in Flagstaff, drive south 19 miles to Schnebly Hill

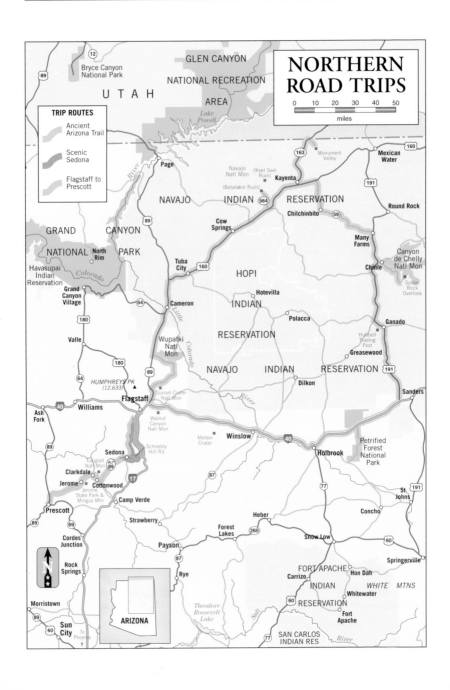

NORTHERN ROAD TRIPS

0 10 20 30 40 50
miles

GLEN CANYON

NATIONAL RECREATION

AREA

Lake
Powell

TRIP ROUTES

Ancient
Arizona Trail

Scenic
Sedona

Flagstaff to
Prescott

UTAH

Bryce Canyon
National Park

12

89

Page

Monument
Valley

Mexican
Water

160

163

Navajo
Natl Mon
(Keet Seel
Ruin)

Kayenta

191

NAVAJO

INDIAN

564

RESERVATION

Round Rock

(Betatakin Ruin)

Chilchinbito

59

89

Cow
Springs

Many
Farms

GRAND

CANYON

Canyon
de Chelly
Natl Mon

NATIONAL

North
Rim

PARK

Tuba
City

160

Chinle

Havasupai
Indian
Reservation

Colorado

HOPI

Spider
Rock
Overlook

Grand
Canyon
Village

64

Cameron

Hotevilla

INDIAN

180

Ganado

Polacca

Hubbell
Trading
Post

Valle

Wupatki
Natl
Mon

RESERVATION

Greasewood

180

89

Colorado

NAVAJO

INDIAN

RESERVATION

191

64

HUMPHREYS PK
(12,633)

Sunset Crater
Natl Mon

Dilkon

Sanders

Flagstaff

River

89

Ash
Fork

Williams

Walnut
Canyon
Natl Mon

Meteor
Crater

Winslow

40

Petrified
Forest
National
Park

89

Sedona

Schnebly
Hill Rd

40

Holbrook

Tuzigoot
Natl Mon

ALT
89

Clarkdale

Jerome

17

87

77

St
Johns

191

Cottonwood

Jerome
State Park &
Mingus Mtn

Camp Verde

Concho

60

Prescott

Heber

89

69

Strawberry

Forest
Lakes

260

Show Low

60

Cordes
Junction

Payson

87

Springerville

Rock
Springs

Rye

FORT APACHE

Hon Dah

WHITE   MTNS

Carrizo

Whitewater

Morristown

INDIAN

89

Theodore
Roosevelt
Lake

60

RESERVATION

Fort
Apache

Sun
City

60

Salt

ARIZONA

77

SAN CARLOS
INDIAN RES

River

To
Phoenix

N

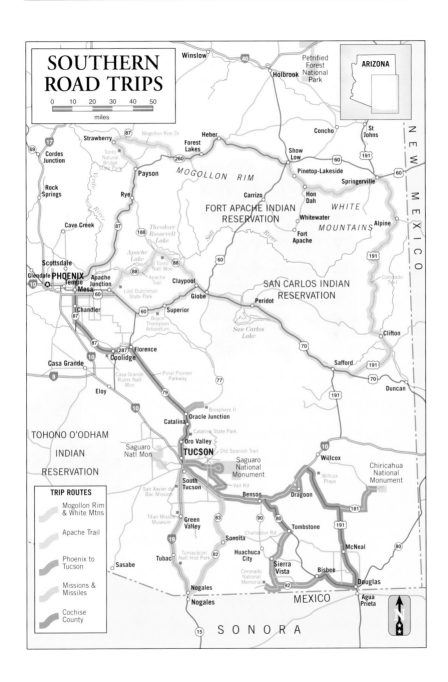

SOUTHERN ROAD TRIPS

0 10 20 30 40 50

miles

ARIZONA

Winslow
Holbrook
Petrified Forest National Park

N E W   M E X I C O

Strawberry
Mogollon Rim Dr
Heber
Forest Lakes
Concho
St Johns

Cordes Junction
Tonto Natural Bridge State Park
260
Payson
MOGOLLON RIM
Show Low
60
191
Pinetop-Lakeside
Springerville
60

Rock Springs
Rye
Carrizo
Hon Dah
WHITE
Cave Creek
Theodore Roosevelt Lake
188
FORT APACHE INDIAN RESERVATION
Whitewater
Fort Apache
MOUNTAINS
Alpine

Scottsdale
Apache Lake
Tonto Natl Mon
88
60
191
Glendale PHOENIX
10
Tempe Apache Junction
Mesa
88
Lost Dutchman State Park
Apache Trail
Claypool
Globe
SAN CARLOS INDIAN RESERVATION
Coronado Trail

Chandler
60
Superior
Peridot
87
60
Boyce Thompson Arboretum
San Carlos Lake
Clifton

Casa Grande
287 Florence
Coolidge
Casa Grande Ruins Natl Mon
Pinal Pioneer Parkway
70
Safford
191
70

Eloy
8
79
77
191
Duncan

10
Biosphere II
Oracle Junction
Catalina
Catalina State Park

TOHONO O'ODHAM
INDIAN
RESERVATION
Saguaro Natl Mon
Oro Valley
TUCSON
Old Spanish Trail
Saguaro National Monument
Willcox
Chiricahua National Monument

South Tucson
San Xavier del Bac Mission
Vail Rd
Benson
Willcox Playa
Dragoon

TRIP ROUTES

Mogollon Rim & White Mtns

Apache Trail

Phoenix to Tucson

Missions & Missiles

Cochise County

Titan Missile Museum
Green Valley
83
90
80
Tombstone
191
181
McNeal
80

19
Sonoita
Charleston Rd
Tubac
Tumacácori Natl Hist Park
82
Huachuca City
Sierra Vista
Bisbee
Sasabe
Coronado National Memorial
92
Douglas

Nogales
Nogales
MEXICO
Agua Prieta

15
S O N O R A

N

Road, then take this 15-mile graded dirt road into Sedona. Few people do, but their reward is a spectacular view into the gaping mouth of Oak Creek Canyon from 1,800 feet overhead. The mountain road "demands a driver's attention," as *Arizona Highways* author James E. Cook has written, but it normally isn't dangerous. A good friend advises, however: don't do it at night. After a day among Sedona's galleries and red rocks, take US 89a back to Flagstaff. For about 15 glorious miles, the road winds alongside the creek on Oak Creek Canyon's floor. En route, gape at the polychromatic sandstone and limestone strata on the canyon walls, and the erosion-sculpted gargoyles on the ridges. Special recommendation: it's almost impossible to get an overnight reservation at Garland's Oak Creek Lodge, eight miles north of Sedona on US 89a. The regulars book it a year in advance. Dinner reservations, however, are obtainable. The menu is fixed nightly, you'll be seated with strangers (who generally prove engaging), and you'll enjoy the best dinner between Phoenix and Denver. *(See "*PRACTICAL INFORMATION,*" page 251).*

■ FLAGSTAFF TO PRESCOTT, SCENIC ROUTE

This drive begins in Flagstaff and ends in Prescott, a distance of just 90 miles over the prescribed highways. With all the attractions and mountain switchbacks en route, this is a long one-day trip, although the actual driving time is just three hours. *Best times: March through November.*

Take US 89a 28 miles through Oak Creek Canyon to Sedona. Continue on 89a to **Tuzigoot National Monument,** a fascinating Sinagua pueblo ruin on a hill cresting 100 feet over the Verde River Valley. Like Walnut Canyon, this defensive citadel implies a distinct fear of invasion. Continue south on 89a to Jerome and Mingus Mountain. **Jerome** is a retired Victorian mining town now blossoming with boutiques and art galleries, funkier and cheaper than Sedona's. Continuing on over 7,743-foot Mingus Mountain, 89a offers rim-of-the-world views. Around the junction of US 89a and 89 five miles north of Prescott are the Granite Dells, a garden of Precambrian boulders weathered into improbable shapes. There's no state or national park at the Dells, but they're worth an exploratory stop.

■ MOGOLLON RIM/WHITE MOUNTAIN SCENIC DRIVE

Most visitors to Arizona, if they encounter the Mogollon Rim at all, see it from below: as a vast, green wall, planed flat on the top, butting against the sky 90 miles northeast of Phoenix. Looking up, it's an odd sight. Looking down, it is considerably more dramatic. Seeing it for the first time, a wide-eyed U.S. Army Capt. John C. Bourke wrote in 1891, "it is a strange upheaval, a strange freak of nature, a mountain canted up on one side."

The Coronado Trail, a.k.a. US 191, which various chambers of commerce would like to have us believe traces the route taken by Francisco Vásquez de Coronado in 1540, is the loneliest and loveliest mountain highway in Arizona. Elk, deer, raccoon, wild turkey, and even black bear can often be sighted from the car, and brief side excursions on gravel logging roads will take you to pristine streams and canyons that aren't seen by more than a few dozen people a year. This 582-mile round trip from Phoenix will take two full days to cover both lonely wonders. *Best times: April through October.*

DAY 1: Leaving Phoenix, head north on Arizona Highway 87 to Tonto Natural Bridge State Park. The 90-mile drive, which climbs gradually from the low Sonoran Desert to the 5,500-foot elevations of Tonto National Forest, skirts lovely mountain scenery. After a wet winter, the roadside parade of wildflowers in March and April is spectacular. **Tonto Natural Bridge,** a 400-foot limestone arch spanning a 150-foot-deep canyon, deserves a visit. From the natural bridge, continue up Highway 87 to the top of the rim. Just beyond milepost 281 is the Mogollon Rim Road (Forest Road 300), to the right. It's 42 miles of well-graded, lightly traveled, gravel road with vertiginous views over the rim, just to your right. Stop often to stare. Beware of logging trucks rumbling around blind curves, and the wind gusts which may whip you while you are peering over the rim. At day's end, stay either in Pinetop-Lakeside or Springerville. The former has more interesting choices in accommodations *(see pages 254-255)*; the latter is 56 miles on down the road, which will slice an hour's driving time off the next day's rather long route.

DAY 2: From Springerville, head south on US 191 to Clifton. This 123-mile drive will demand four to five hours even without stops, and you should stop frequently to enjoy the astounding mountain scenery and wildlife. Check weather forecasts before departing; a sign just south of Alpine warns: RT 191 NOT

MAINTAINED NIGHTS, WEEKENDS, OR DURING STORMS. Another adds: NEXT SERVICES 90 MILES.

The highest paved road in Arizona, US 191 crests at 9,092 feet at Hannagan Meadow. Between Hannagan Meadow and Clifton, US 191 resembles a 60-mile-long corkscrew mashed into the Ponderosa pine forest and lathered with asphalt. Its hairpin turns are as tight as Scrooge's Christmas budget; the 15- and 20-mph warnings are, for once, realistic. Several automotive magazines have cited it as one of the best serious-driving roads in America. Decide early on whether you intend to enjoy serious (i.e., quick) driving or the scenery; you cannot do both. Either way, watch out for wildlife crossing the highway. A few miles from the highway, excursions off US 191 to the **Blue River** or **Black River** are particularly rewarding, but the state highway map offers little help in navigating these dirt and gravel roads. Stop at the **Apache-Sitgreaves National Forest** office in Springerville or Alpine and buy a detailed forest map ($3). Rangers are happy to direct visitors to the prettiest scenery and offer advice on road conditions.

Twelve miles north of Clifton the highway exits the national forest and begins weaving down toward the desert. Six miles later is the **Morenci Mine,** the second largest open-pit copper mine in the world. Reactions of passersby range from awe at the astounding scale of the operation to revulsion at the indelible scarring of the now lifeless land. One mile farther, off the east side of the road, is an oddly poignant sight: a hillside cemetery, not moist and green and shady, but choked with prickly pear and cholla cacti. The graves, dating from 1900 to the 1930s, are marked with handmade wrought-iron memorials and lead-pipe crosses, works of folk art. They form a silent monument to the harshness and bleakness of these early miners' lives. Until 1937, Clifton's copper was all extracted from underground mines.

From Clifton, take US 70 west to Globe, then US 60 to the **Boyce Thompson Southwestern Arboretum** three miles west of Superior. The arboretum offers a fine nature trail through a virtual desert forest, and has a good variety of desert plants for sale. From the arboretum, continue on toward Phoenix, and at Apache Junction take Arizona Highway 360 (the Superstition Freeway) into the city—*not* the traffic-light-clotted US 60/89.

The alpine beauty of the Mogollon Rim offers a welcome respite from the desert.
(Kerrick James)

■ APACHE TRAIL

This one-day, 164-mile loop through the Sonoran Desert east of Phoenix today has nothing to do with Apaches—it doesn't even quite reach the San Carlos Indian Reservation. During the Apache wars, however, U.S. Army troops and Indian scouts combed the desert and mountains around here, trying to track down bands of Apache guerrillas. The loop passes the dramatic **Superstition Mountains,** three of the lakes devised by damming the Salt River in the early 1900s, a lovely **Salado Indian ruin,** and the **Boyce Thompson Arboretum.** Despite the short distance, it could be a long day. *Best times: October through April.*

From Phoenix, take Arizona Highway 360 (the Superstition Freeway) east and then Arizona Highway 88 to **Lost Dutchman State Park** at the base of the Superstitions. The park itself offers little except camper spaces, but its loop drive provides a gateway for day hikes into the Superstitions. Walk the **Siphon Draw Trail** at least a couple of miles into the mountains; the awesome brute thrust of the craggy walls at your side will make you feel altogether insignificant.

Past Tortilla Flat, the highway deteriorates into a gravel road on its way toward Roosevelt Dam. President Teddy Roosevelt, who came to dedicate the dam in 1911, called this road "one of the most spectacular, best-worth-seeing sights of the world." Roosevelt's eponymous structure, claimed to be the world's largest masonry arch dam, isn't a disappointing sight either, and the road provides a striking view of it. Roosevelt Lake, an improbable sprawl of water 17 miles long, is well stocked with fish, and, on weekends, party animals from Phoenix. Five miles southeast of the dam, still on Highway 88, stop at **Tonto National Monument,** the lone ruin of the prehistoric Salado people open to the public. The Salado furrow archaeologists' brows; they can't agree on who these people were or where they came from. The main cliffside pueblo of 16 (remaining) rooms was inhabited from about A.D. 1250 to 1450. See the Boyce Thompson Arboretum (described in the preceding drive) en route back to Phoenix.

■ PHOENIX TO TUCSON: SCENERY AND SCIENCE

The 110-mile commute between Arizona's two large cities normally takes just under two hours on Interstate 10, but nobody enjoys the desolate drive. A slightly

A Navajo horseman herds his sheep in Monument Valley.

longer route of 132 miles offers less traffic, more scenery, several bits of history, and a convenient opportunity to visit the controversial Biosphere II. *Best times: October through April.*

From Phoenix, take Arizona Highway 360 (the Superstition Freeway) east to Apache Junction, then Arizona Highway 79 south to Florence. This little desert town doesn't draw many tourists; it is best known for its several state and federal prisons (about 4,700 of Florence's population of 7,510 view the world through bars). However, there are a couple of reasons for non-felons to do time in the town. One is its architecture. Florence has several interesting Territorial adobe buildings, including one, the **Clark House,** that features Italianate Victorian detailing. (Unfortunately, it's nearly in ruins.) More extravagant is the second **Pinal County Courthouse,** a sprawling Victorian pile with a French Second Empire cupola. Built in 1891, it still serves as a three-dimensional billboard advertising a grand future for Florence that never materialized. The other is the **Pinal County Historical Society Museum,** the only museum in Arizona to maintain a room devoted to execution paraphernalia. In here are the actual nooses used in 25 hangings at the Arizona State Prison between 1920 and 1930, complete with mug shots of the men (and one woman) whose necks they embraced. There's also a chair from the gas chamber and other grisly tools of the executioner's trade. The museum is at 715 South Main Street.

A short nine-mile side trip from Florence is **Casa Grande Ruins National Monument,** the one remaining high-rise left from the prehistoric Hohokam civilization. This four-story mud building in the flatlands of the desert also has an attitude that is unmistakably defensive. Archaeologists theorize that it was used as a solar observatory to mark summer and winter solstices, and perhaps as housing for a Hohokam priesthood or managerial elite. Visitors theorize: yes, but they also must have needed to keep watch on, and keep out, some external threat.

Forty-two miles south from Florence on Arizona Highway 79, turn left on Arizona Highway 77 for a visit to **Biosphere II.** The sealed, three-acre terrarium, which sustained eight human bionauts for two years of experimental captivity in is five miles east of the highway junction. Serious science, monumental performance art, or tourist trap? Visitors will find evidence of all three at Biosphere II.

For this privately funded $150 million project, bionauts were locked into the near-airtight terrarium with 3,800 species of plants and animals. The immediate objective was to see if the eight humans could sustain themselves for two years with only the food and oxygen generated inside the container. In the long term, it seemed to be a feasibility study for colonizing Mars. Since its inauguration, Biosphere II came under fire from an increasingly skeptical press, but visitors seem to enjoy the tours.

In 1994, Biosphere II virtually exploded in a fury of staff resignations, firings, lawsuits, and arrests. Since then, however, Texas billionaire Ed Bass, the money behind the project, has forged ties with Columbia University, and the scientific community has begun to take it seriously. Bionauts are no longer sealed inside the terrarium; it's used for short-term ecological studies. It still has the trappings of a theme park, but there does seem to be science going on at the same time.

Return to Arizona Highway 79 and drive 27 miles south to Tucson. If enough daylight is left, stop at Catalina State Park, which offers a wonderful hiking trail—Romero Canyon—probing the north face of the Santa Catalina Mountains.

■ MISSIONS AND MISSILES

Visitors staying in Tucson routinely make the swift 60-mile drive down I-17 to the Mexican border city of Nogales. Here's how to make a very full day of it, and see much more than the tourist shops of Nogales' Calle Obregón. *Best times: any.*

The not-quite-twin bell towers of **San Xavier del Bac** pop into view to the west off I-17 soon after you leave Tucson. (The east tower was never crowned with a dome; the least exotic but most likely explanation is that the remote parish simply ran out of money.) The church is the most elaborate and lovely Spanish mission in what is now the United States, and no one should miss it.

Twelve miles south on I-17 is the **Titan Missile Museum**, an actual (though now disarmed) ICBM resting in its underground silo. Once it was programmed to target a Soviet city; the museum will not say which one. In a fascinating reversal of Cold War tensions, Russian visitors now tour it alongside Americans.

Another few minutes' drive south on I-17 finds the historic Spanish presidio of **Tubac**, now jammed with art galleries and boutiques. Practically next door is Arizona's other Spanish mission, **San José de Tumacácori,** now a national historical park. Just south along the access road from Tumacácori is a local monument to the olfactory sense: the retail store of the Santa Cruz Chili & Spice Co., the most seductively aromatic room in Arizona.

Nogales, Sonora, is the obvious stop for lunch. Tourists generally gravitate toward one of three restaurants, all under the same ownership: La Roca on Calle Elias and El Cid, and El Greco, both on Calle Obregón. All three offer seafood, steaks, and Mexican food; El Greco is at once the least expensive and the most pleasant. All three are only a few blocks across the border; park in one of the pay lots on the U.S. side and walk—you'll be happy you did.

The best route back to Tucson is not the same quick zip up I-17, but a leisurely 80- to 100-mile meander through what is becoming known as Arizona's wine country. From Nogales, drive north on Arizona Highway 82. These beautiful rolling grasslands, punctuated by groves of billowing oak trees wherever a depression collects extra rain, used to be prime rangeland. The recent discovery that the soil underneath is of the helpfully acidic *terra rossa* variety is now encouraging a

boomlet in grape cultivation and winemaking. Today, Arizona has 12 wineries, up from zero in 1980. **Sonoita Vineyards,** in the nearby village of **Elgin;** and **R.W. Webb Winery,** on the I-10 frontage road west of the Sonoita exit, offer tasting and tours; others certainly will follow. Arizona wine is not yet a match for California's, either in consistency or value. But it has come a long way in a very few years. Return to Tucson via Arizona Highway 83 and I-10—after no more than modest indulgence in some Arizona wines.

Wine grapes flourish in the acidic terra rossa *soil of southern Arizona. Above are a selection of Sonoita wines. (Kerrick James)*

■ COCHISE COUNTY

Cochise County is 6,400 square miles bristling with history and breaking hearts with its scenery. Birders worldwide know about Cochise County; the San Pedro riparian forest alone supports more than 350 species of migratory or breeding birds. The original county seat was Tombstone, the old West's most notorious town; the present county seat is Bisbee, modern Arizona's most entertaining town. On a lonely ranch out here is the Southwest's most engaging bookstore. Although the Cochise County line lies only 30 miles east of Tucson, a basic introduction to its scenery and civilization will cover some 425 miles in three days. *Best times: any.*

DAY 1: Don't take any of the obvious connections from Tucson to I-10. Drive east on Broadway to Old Spanish Trail and meander southeast: this is the scenic route, and it's worth the few extra minutes. **Old Spanish Trail** winds past **Saguaro National Park** and **Colossal Cave**, a Pima County park; and a private castle crowning a ridge half a mile southeast of the cave. At I-10, drive 23 miles east and take the US 80 exit to **Tombstone** *(see page 164)*. From Tombstone, veer southwest to **Coronado National Memorial,** a Huachuca Mountain preserve that probably was never even approached by Sr. Coronado, but perhaps appreciated in the distance as his band slogged along the San Pedro River 10 miles to the east. Take the snaking drive up the paved Memorial road to 6,575-foot **Montezuma Pass,** and you can see the obvious route the Spanish explorers would have taken through the valley below. In summer, you also will see squadrons of hummingbirds assaulting the plentiful flowers of the mountain yucca here, and possibly even the elusive coati—a raccoon relative that moves with the grace of a cat. Spend the night in Sierra Vista if you prefer predictable chain-motel comfort, or in **Bisbee** *(see page 162)* if you're open to steep, crumbling streets, bed-and-breakfasts in old rooming houses, and unsolicited entertainment. Last time I was just about to drift off to sleep in Bisbee, someone in Brewery Gulch began serenading the moon on a tenor sax. Bisbee is built on the sides of two intersecting gulches, so the wail echoed all over town. No matter, this was Bisbee, and nobody had anything important to do tomorrow anyway.

DAY 2: Rise early and drive to the **Chiricahua National Monument** on Arizona's eastern edge, the most dramatically sculpted mountain range in the state. Plan to spend half the day on one or more of the monument's many hiking trails.

En route to or from the Chiricahuas, stop in the border town of **Douglas** to see a drop-dead architectural masterpiece: the lobby of the 1907 **Gadsden Hotel,** an opulent, two-story marble neo-Renaissance wonderland. The architect was Henry Trost, who had fallen under the spell of Louis Sullivan in Chicago a dozen years earlier. Don't be discouraged by the rather plain exterior of the building; go inside. If you want to spend the night, rooms are inexpensive but hardly as stunning as the lobby. Otherwise, return to Bisbee.

DAY 3: Take US 191 north for a sneak visit to the **Willcox Playa,** that strange Pleistocene dry lake bed—which may become a vast, few-inch-deep wet lake with the rains of late summer. The playa is no state or national park; there are no posted instructions for going there. Look for the railroad tracks 3.5 miles south of I-10, turn left and follow the dirt road paralleling the tracks to the edge of the playa. En route back to Tucson, stop first at the **Amerind Foundation** in Dragoon. Dragoon is just an unincorporated clump of ranches, but Amerind is one of the Southwest's best museums of archaeology, founded in 1937 by a Connecticut businessman who became mesmerized by the remnants of prehistoric Arizona.

Fifteen miles west off I-10, even more improbably, is the **Singing Wind Bookstore,** which has enjoyed acclaim in the *Los Angeles Times,* the *Wall Street Journal,* and even the *Congressional Record.* It's the dream of ranchwoman Winn Bundy, who has more than 100,000 titles for sale, along with a wealth of free literary wisdom, in two rooms of her ranch house. The shop's emphasis is on books of the Southwest, but anything else that happens to interest Bundy or her fanatically loyal customers is here also. Take the Ocotillo exit at Benson, drive 2.3 miles north, look for the "Singing Wind Ranch" mailbox ventilated with bullet holes, turn right, and let yourself through the gate. For any pilgrimage through Arizona and the Southwest, this place is both the beginning and end.

PRACTICAL INFORMATION

■ AREA CODES

The area code for the Phoenix metropolitan area, including Tempe, Mesa and Scottsdale, is **602**. For the rest of the state, use **520**.

■ METRIC CONVERSIONS

1 foot = .305 meters
1 mile = 1.6 kilometers
Centigrade = Fahrenheit temp. minus 32, divided by 1.8

■ WHEN TO COME

Ideally, a prolonged visit to Arizona will be in the fall or spring; these seasons offer temperate weather in the deserts and high country at the same time. Cost-conscious travelers may want to schedule their visits in these seasonal windows that include both (usually) tolerable weather and off-season hotel/motel rates:

> Flagstaff and the high country: April–May and November
> Phoenix: April and October–December
> Tucson: April and October–December

If economy is not the most important consideration, simply see the high country May through October and the deserts November through March.

(following pages) The best photographs of Monument Valley usually are taken around sunrise and sunset.

TEMPS (F°)	AVG. JAN.	AVG. MARCH	AVG. JULY	AVG. SEPT.	AVG. NOV.	RECORD HIGH	LOW
Phoenix	65°	75°	105°	98°	75°	122°	16°
Tucson	64°	72°	98°	94°	73°	117°	16°
Flagstaff	42°	49°	82°	74°	51°	97°	-30°

PRECIPITATION (INCHES)	AVG. JAN.	AVG. MARCH	AVG. JULY	AVG. SEPT.	AVG. NOV.	ANNUAL AVG.
Phoenix	.75"	.80"	.74"	.60"	.57"	7.3"
Tucson	.86"	.71"	2.54"	1.34"	.59"	11.6"
Flagstaff	2.21"	2.30"	2.45"	1.54"	1.75"	21.0"

■ GETTING AROUND

Arizona's four largest airports with commercial service are: Tucson International, Phoenix Sky Harbor, Flagstaff Pulliam Airport, and Grand Canyon Airport. Fares to and from Phoenix are much cheaper than to the other cities; many Tucsonans drive the 110 miles to Sky Harbor to take advantage of round-trip fares to the East Coast that are at least $100 less. Sky Harbor has a convenient close-in location —it's 10 minutes to downtown—but the airport's layout, with no fewer than three separate terminals connected by shuttle buses, is a paradigm of inconvenience. Allow a few minutes extra when departing or making connections.

Both Phoenix and Tucson have extensive municipal bus services, but in these sprawling, low-density cities, mass transit simply is not practical for most users. Taxis are expensive because there are long distances to cover. For the visitor arriving by air, frankly, a rental car is the only realistic choice.

Speed limits on the interstates are 75 mph in rural areas and 55 in the cities. Radar enforcement is ubiquitous, but detectors are legal and in common use. With long distances to cover between settlements, Arizonans tend to drive fast. State law requires the use of seat belts.

The state highway map, published by *Arizona Highways,* is available at tourist information centers in every town, as well as at many bookstores. For extensive travel on the Navajo and Hopi reservations, a very detailed map called "Indian Country" is published by the Automobile Club of Southern California. *Arizona Highways* publishes a variety of lavishly illustrated and authoritative books to help guide the traveler around the state. They include *Travel Arizona, The Back Roads,* and three volumes titled *Outdoors in Arizona,* covering hiking, camping, and fishing and hunting. To order these books call *Arizona Highways* at (800) 543-5432.

EATING IN ARIZONA

Oh! If we could only live as the Mexicans live, how easy it would be!" pined Martha Summerhayes, a young Army bride who came to Arizona in 1874. "For they had their fire built between some stones piled up in their yard, a piece of sheet iron laid over the top: this was the cooking-stove . . . a kettle of frijoles (beans) was put over to boil. These were boiled slowly for some hours, then lard and salt were added, and they simmered down until they were deliciously fit to eat, and had a thick red gravy. . . ."

Ms. Summerhayes went on to rhapsodize about several other staples of the Mexican table in Arizona Territory, including chile colorado and chile verde (red and green chile beef stew, respectively), tortillas, and carne seca (sun-dried beef simmered with onions and peppers). Recipes for these dishes have endured virtually unchanged for more than a century, and Arizonans, both newcomers and natives, rhapsodize still. Mexican food is Arizona's culinary religion.

This is only proper. In fact, it should be in the state constitution. It perpetuates our historic roots. For gringos, it cracks open a door, at least, into Mexican culture. And of course it tastes wonderful. Forgive me if I turn moist-eyed and mystical, but there is something about Mexican cuisine that seems akin to the essence of life. Its forms are those of nature's geometry: the circle (tortilla), the cylinder (flauta), the arch (taco). Its flavors are likewise elemental: chile habanera evokes pure fire; a very fresh guacamole laced with lime and cilantro captures both the color and mood of springtime. Mexican food also can reflect the complexity of nature; it isn't merely hot. Huachinango a la Veracruzana is a perfect example. This is red snapper filet sautéed with onion, garlic, tomatoes, green olives, capers, and—if the chef is really cookin'—nutmeg. All these flavors form rival factions of piquancy that circle each other warily, struggle briefly for power on the taste buds, and finally embrace and trip down the tube dancing and singing in tight-woven harmonies. Snapper can be a dull fish, but not when prepared in a Veracruz pan.

Huachinango a la Veracruzana remains relatively rare on Mexican restaurant menus in Arizona. Most kitchens still cling to the frontier; this is a conservative religion.

The traditional Mexican restaurant meal here invariably begins with a basket of deep-fried tortilla chips (usually complimentary) and an accompanying salsa of chopped or puréed tomato, jalapeño chile, onion, and cilantro. Depending on how the restaurant perceives its clientele, this salsa may range from annoyingly mild to incendiary. The entrées typically consist of a wide choice of "combination plates" mixing tacos, enchiladas, tamales, flautas, burros, and chiles rellenos, accompanied by rice, beans and warm flour tortillas. Dessert is likely to be either sopapillas, fried bread puffs with honey; or flan, a creamy cinnamon-flavored custard. Nobody pretends that this is a heart-smart diet, but some restaurants at least have begun to substitute vegetable oils which are lower in saturated fat for the traditional lard. This has a slightly deleterious effect on the flavors of some dishes, but it seems like a sensible trade-off.

There are some other pleasing trends developing in Mexican dining around the state. One is the gradual appearance of regional cuisines other than the beefy ranch-style Sonoran that has prevailed since—well, since Arizona was part of Sonora. Mexican food is a far larger universe than most norteamericanos ever imagine, and this should come as no surprise: Mexico comprises tropics, deserts and more than 5,000 miles (8047 km) of seacoasts; and Aztecs, Mayas, Pimas, Spaniards, French, and Americans have all exerted their influence in different regions. Thus a pan de cazon, which is kind of a shark-and-bean sandwich from the Yucatán peninsula, has no family ties to birria, a savory goat pot roast from Guadalajara. Both, along with other regional specialties, gradually are becoming more widely available in Arizona. So is Sonoran coastal cooking, in which spicy shrimp replace shredded beef in tacos and enchiladas. Finally, there are several new shoots and permutations of Mexican cuisine that fall under no single culinary label, although "nouvelle Southwestern" covers some of it. This cooking weds Mexican ingredients to the latest French techniques, often to smashing effect but occasionally to bizarre ends. I have tried Anaheim chiles stuffed with lobster and brie and fried with beer batter, which were stunning, and Mexican sea bass swimming in blueberry sauce, a very unstable marriage of ingredients. Generally, the new cuisine is much more expensive than the old.

Innovation and a wide variety of ethnic dining have come fairly late to Arizona. There are at least a couple of reasons. Our two principal cities were not large until recently, and except for Mexican-Americans, they had no concentrated ethnic enclaves. The influence of the frontier may have had a lingering effect, too: a mean land demands a mean cuisine. Emblematic of territorial Arizona was cowboy stew, or, as more colorfully labeled in Louise DeWald's Arizona Highways Heritage Cookbook, "Son-of-a-Bitch Stew." Ingredients: all the meat and most of the internal organs of a freshly butchered calf, slowly boiled for five hours. Warns the classic recipe, "Never add spices or vegetables to a Son-of-a-Bitch; spoils the true flavor of the ingredients."

By the late 1970s the last remnants of the s.o.b. culinary philosophy finally were swept aside by new waves of immigrants and an increasingly alert tourist industry. The growing-up process has been astoundingly rapid: today you can eat as well in Arizona as in California. A Tucson bistro serves wine-steamed mussels year-around for happy hour; a Phoenix cafe introduces cuisine from El Salvador to Valley residents. A trattoria in Patagonia, pop. 874, serves pasta that draws customers from all over Arizona. There is not yet a distinctive "Arizona cuisine" except for traditional Sonoran, but this simply reflects the character of our land: a young, volatile, attractive haven for a great stew of immigrants. A London-born Indian who along with his three brothers has built a successful trio of Punjabi restaurants in Flagstaff, Tempe, and Tucson explained it simply: "Arizona looked like an interesting change for us."

Tucson's citizens love to dine out. El Charro, the city's oldest Mexican restaurant, is popular with tourists. (Kerrick James)

CHILE SCORCH SCALE

Chiles enhance taste, are intriguing to look at, and can scorch the unsuspecting. How is chile heat measured? In 1911 a Mr. Scoville gave us a guide to chile heat by testing a range of chiles on some non-chile eaters (how they later fared is unrecorded). Some common chiles and their heat levels are recorded below.

CHILE	SCOVILLE HEAT UNITS	RATING
Mild Bell	0	0
R-Naky, Mexi-Bell	100-500	1
NuMex Big Jim	500-1000	2
Pasilla, Española	1000-1500	3
Sandia, Cascabel	1500-2500	4
Jalapeño, Mirasol	2500-5000	5
Serrano	5000-15,000	6
Cayenne, Tabasco de Arbol	15,000-30,000	7
Aji, Piquin	30,000-50,000	8
Santaka, Chiltepin	50,000-100,000	9
Habanero, Bahamian	100,000-300,000	10

■ ABOUT ARIZONA LODGING

The list of hotels in "Hotels and Restaurants by Town" is not a comprehensive list, but rather a few hotels, motels and B&Bs in different price ranges that I have particularly liked. In a few outlying areas I am simply listing what is available. For stays at dude and guest ranches, refer to "Guest Ranches," which follows this section. If you'd prefer lodgings at a hotel or motel chain, consult the 800 numbers which follow. Keep in mind that you may get a better nightly rate by using these numbers to request the local hotel phone number, then calling directly.

Best Western. (800) 528-1234	**Loews Hotels.** (800) 223-0888
Days Inn. (800) 329-7466	**Marriott Hotels.** (800) 228-9290
Doubletree. (800) 222-TREE	**Quality Inns.** (800) 228-5151
Hilton Hotels. (800) HILTONS	**Radisson.** (800) 333-3333
Hyatt Hotels & Resorts. (800) 233-1234	**Ramada Inn.** (800) 2-RAMADA
ITT Sheraton. (800) 325-3535	**Stouffers.** (800) HOTELS-1
La Quinta. (800) 531-5900	**Westin Hotels.** (800) 228-3000

■ ABOUT ARIZONA RESTAURANTS

The first meal I ate in Arizona was a Papaburger at the A&W in Benson, not an auspicious introduction to the state's cuisine. But back then, in the early 1970s, Arizona's cuisine wasn't terrifically distinguished. Every small town like Benson, I quickly learned, would have one good Mexican restaurant and one bad Chinese restaurant, plus the usual assortment of fast feeders and everyday cafes. Phoenix and Tucson each had many good Mexican restaurants and many bad Chinese restaurants. "Continental" menus groaning with hoary standards like Veal Oscar were what passed for fine dining. As a major tourist destination, Arizona seemed to deserve better. In the intervening decades it got better, much better, echoing the revolution in culinary adventure all across the land. Places such as Vincent on Camelback in Phoenix and Cafe Terra Cotta in Tucson have earned national acclaim for their New Southwestern cooking, and they deserve it. "Continental" is as dead as the A&W in Benson, and scores of excellent ethnic restaurants, from Catalonian to Cuban, provide a parade of intriguing tastes. But I still don't know of a good Chinese place.

Mexican food is Arizona's specialty and the culinary passion of every native. There's both good and bad news on this front. Good: the variety and sophistication of Mexican cooking in Arizona has improved greatly in the last decade. Bad: the Center for Science in the Public Interest issued a report in 1994 accusing Mexican food of being outrageously high in fat and cholesterol.

Arizonans rightly were outraged. The best response, which came from the owner of Tucson's El Charro: "They should get a life."

Maybe they should just get a chimichanga—a tortilla filled with stewed spiced beef and deep-fried until golden. Mmmm.

The restaurant selections—listed in "Lodging and Restaurants by Town"—are completely subjective. As a food columnist and constant Arizona traveler, though, I eat out a lot, and I have a pretty good idea what's out there. Other restaurant guides are Harry and Trudy Plate's *100 Best Restaurants in Arizona* and the *Zagat Survey of Southwest Restaurants*. In Phoenix, the weekly *New Times* publishes a critical and reliable guide in every issue.

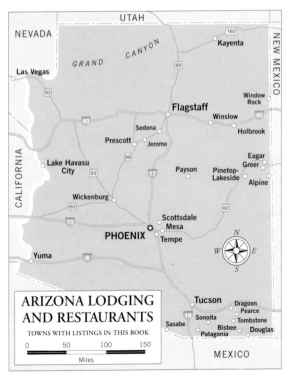

■ LODGING AND RESTAURANTS BY TOWN

> *Room rates:*
> Per night, per room, double occupancy:
> $ = under $70; $$ = $70-130; $$$ = over $130
>
> *Restaurant prices:*
> Per person, not including drinks, tax and tips:
> $ = under $10; $$ = $10-20; $$$ = over $20

Alpine

🛏 **Alpine Cabins.** At junction of US 191 and US 180; (520) 339-4440 $
Cabins featuring fireplaces, four-poster beds, and small kitchens. Open March to November.

🛏 **Judd's Ranch.** 0.5 miles north of Alpine; (520) 339-4326 $
Several small wood-frame cabins with kitchenettes and weathered hardwood floors. Fishing lake and miles of forest trails. Open April to October.

Bisbee

(also see Tombstone)

🛏 **Bisbee Grande Hotel.** 57 Main St.; (520) 432-5900 or (800) 421-1909 $-$$
Elegantly furnished 11-room Victorian hotel, with red carpeting and brass beds. Downstairs is an old saloon, a theatre for melodramas, and a billiards room. Light breakfast included.

🛏 **Bisbee Inn.** 45 OK St.; (520) 432-5131 $
Overlooking Brewery Gulch is this nice renovation of a historic miners' rooming house, with sinks and homemade quilts in the 18 rooms. Guests must share baths, but an all-you-can-eat breakfast is included.

✕ **Cafe Roka.** 35 Main St.; (520) 432-5153 $ - $$
It used to be impossible to find a decent dinner in this quirky old mining town, but no more. A few years back Rod Kass, the sous-chef at Phoenix's swank Registry Resort, opened this contemporary Italian/eclectic cafe here, serving delectable concoctions such as shrimp in angel hair pasta with brown garlic, sweet peppers and cream. "We're just trying to keep ourselves from getting bored," says Kass.

🛏 **Copper Queen Hotel.** 11 Howell Ave.; (520) 432-2216 $$ - $$$
This five-story brick building was the

Bisbee (cont'd)

swankiest hotel in town when it opened in 1902. Former guests include John Wayne and Teddy Roosevelt. Rooms are small but have private baths.

Douglas

Gadsden Hotel. 1046 G Ave.; (520) 364-4481 $ - $$
The stunning lobby of this 1907 hotel, now on the National Historic Register, boasts a white marble staircase and stained glass skylights. (The headless ghost inhabiting the basement is also historic.) Douglas residents used to gather on the hotel's roof to view Pancho Villa's army fighting the Federales at Agua Prieta—despite an occasional stray bullet.

Flagstaff

The Inn at Four Ten. 410 N. Leroux St.; (520) 774-0088 $$$
Bed-and-breakfast in a splendidly

THE INN AT FOUR TEN

restored 1907 home. Nine guest suites, decorated in a variety of themes.

Little America. I-40 at Butler Ave.; (520) 779-2741 or (800) 352-4386 $$
Flagstaff's premier motel: large, unexpectedly luxurious rooms with comfortable sitting areas. Pool, tennis courts, golf, and many other amenities. Set in a woods ponderosa pine.

LITTLE AMERICA

Flagstaff also has many inexpensive motels along East Santa Fe Street, the famous old US Route 66. However, the Southern Pacific railroad tracks parallel this street, and patrons of motels near crossings will be serenaded by train whistles all night.

Cafe Express. 16 N. San Francisco St.; (520) 774-0541 $
All the food at this trendy café/bakery is homemade, natural, and dished out in generous portions. Try the Greek salads, pita pizzas, or one-of-a-kind veggie burgers.

Chez Marc Bistro. 503 N. Humphreys St.; (520) 774-1343 $$ - $$$
Owner/chef Marc Balocco describes his country French cuisine as "classic but

modern, with a flair." Indeed: ravioli stuffed with lobster and bathed in a sun-dried tomato sauce; duck breast bathed in juniper berry-sauce or whatever occurs to maestro Marc on a given day. Refreshingly informal.

✕ **Macy's European Coffee House and Bakery.** 14 S. Beaver St.; (520) 774-2243 $
Gourmet café food.

✕ **New Delhi Palace.** 2700 S. Woodland Village; (520) 556-0019 $ - $$
Superb East Indian cuisine.

☖ **Embassy Suites.** 706 S. Milton Rd.; (520) 774-4333 $ - $$
Includes breakfasts in sunny dining room, adjacent to Northern Arizona University.

Grand Canyon: North Rim

⚐ **Campgrounds.** Camping inside the canyon requires a permit, call park headquarters (520) 638-7888.

☖ **Grand Canyon Lodge.** Reservation number: (303) 297-2757 $
Twelve miles from the park boundary and overlooking the canyon is a 1930s-vintage main lodge, built out of native sandstone and ponderosa beams. Lodge guest rooms are motel-like and moderately priced, or you can choose from rustic to modern cabins.

☖ **Jacob Lake Inn.** 40 mi. from the North Rim along US 89A.; (520) 643-7232 $
Very plain but a good alternative to the crowded lodges closer to the Grand Canyon.

☖ **Kaibab Lodge.** Five miles outside the park on Kaibab Plateau, off AZ 67; (520) 638-2389 $$
A lovely wooded setting surrounds these 25 cabins with motel-style furnishings.

✕ **Vermilion Cliffs Restaurant.** Lee's Ferry Lodge, US 89A near Marble Canyon Bridge; (602) 355-2231 $
One of the only restaurants along US 89 en route to the North Rim. Standard American fare in a rustic, stone-walled dining room.

Grand Canyon: South Rim

☖ **Grand Canyon National Park Lodges.** Box 699, Grand Canyon, AZ 86023; (303) 297-2757
Use the above address to reserve space at all South Rim lodges, plus Phantom Ranch on the canyon floor. Descending in cost are **El Tovar** ($$-$$$), designated a National Historic Landmark, dramatic and luxurious; **Thunderbird** and **Kachina lodges** ($$); **Yavapai Lodge** ($$); **Bright Angel Lodge** and cabins ($-$$$); and **Maswik Lodge** ($). All except Yavapai and Maswik lodges are very close to the rim. Best value: Bright Angel.

☖ **Phantom Lodge.** (520) 638-2401 $
Located at the bottom of Grand Canyon, the lodge is accessible only to hikers and mule riders. The dormitory is reserved for hikers; cabins are exclusively for mule riders.

Jerome

⊞ **Rose Garden Bed and Breakfast.** 120 Juarez Ave.; (520) 634-3270 **$$** Built around 1900 is this small old miner's home, with period antiques.

ROSE GARDEN BED AND BREAKFAST

✕ **House of Joy.** 416 Hull Ave.; (520) 634-5339 **$$$** Lots of eccentricities lurk around Jerome, but none is odder than this highly regarded Continental restaurant installed in (what used to be) a bordello. There are just seven tables, it's open only on Saturday and Sunday nights, and you'll need reservations months in advance. No credit cards (what did you expect in a cathouse?)

Kayenta

⊞ **Wetherill Inn.** US 163; (520) 697-3231 **$$** Pleasant 54-room motel with Southwest decor, in town. Navajo gift shop.

✕ **Amigo Cafe.** US 160 at US 163; (520) 697-8448 **$** For all its other attractions, it's almost impossible to find a good meal on the Navajo Reservation. Richard and Esther Martinez's unassuming little cafe is, well, the place. All the Mexican food is good, particularly the steak picado (chopped beef sauteed with green chile), and the appetizer salsa was at last taste the hottest in Arizona.

Lake Havasu City

⊞ **Nautical Inn.** 1000 McCulloch Blvd.; (520) 855-2141 **$$$** Situated on the three-square-mile island in the center of Lake Havasu is this deluxe resort with private dock and a golf course located nearby. All units are on the water, and have patios, double beds and many have kitchenettes.

NAUTICAL INN

⊞ **Ramada London Bridge Resort.** 1477 Queen's Bay Rd.; (520) 855-0888 or (800) 624-7939 **$$ - $$$** Luxurious Olde English theme resort, with golf course, tennis courts, pool, and modern guest rooms. Overlooks lake and London Bridge.

Patagonia

🛏 **Stage Stop Inn.** 303 W. McKeown (520) 394-2211 $ - $$
Clean and comfortable 43-room hotel in the center of town. Popular with film crews shooting scenes in the area.

Phoenix

(also see Phoenix and Tempe)

🛏 **Arizona Biltmore.** 24th and Missouri; (602) 955-6600 or (800) 950-0086 $$$
Built in 1929 and designed by Frank Lloyd Wright's colleague Albert Chase McArthur, this remains the Valley's most beautiful resort. The lobby is decorated in gold leaf, teak, and marble. Several good restaurants, as well as a dozen tennis courts, two full golf courses and five pools.

ARIZONA BILTMORE

🛏 **Best Western Executive Park Hotel.** 1100 N. Central Ave.; (602) 252-2100 or (800) 528-1234 $$
This eight-story hotel boasts spacious and quiet rooms, as well as a pleasant restaurant, pool and health club. It's centrally located a half-mile north of downtown, yet outside the most congested area. Good value.

✕ **Christopher's/The Bistro.** 2398 E. Camelback Rd.; (602) 957-3214 $$$
Two superb restaurants under the direction of the highly regarded Chris Gross: the less formal Bistro has Mediterranean-American food; Christopher's is contemporary French.

✕ **El Bravo.** 8338 N. Seventh St.; (602) 943-9753 $
Unassuming Sonoran-style Mexican food that's won every media award in town. The succulent *chile colorado* tastes like it's been simmered for a week. Green corn and chicken tamales braid the prickly flavor of green chiles with sweet corn masa. Prices are barely higher than fast food.

✕ **Eliana's.** 1627 N. 24th St.; (602) 225-2925 $
Never had El Salvadoran food? It's delicate and delicious, and this is one of the few places save El Salvador where you're sure to encounter it. Small, friendly, very informal.

✕ **Greekfest.** 1940 E. Camelback Rd.; (602) 265-2990 $$
Sophisticated Greek cuisine such as *exohiko,* a melange of lamb, cheese and vegetables baked in phyllo. Pleasant surroundings, good service.

✕ **Havana Cafe.** 4225 E. Camelback Rd.; (602) 952-1991 $$
The fare here is "pre-Castro" Cuban cuisine, in which every region of Spain is filtered through Caribbean influences. Small and informal.

Phoenix *(cont'd)*

✗ **Lombardi's.** Arizona Center, 455 N. Third St.; (602) 257-8323 $$
A convivial but very noisy downtown place with big crowds and excellent pasta, pizza, veal and seafood. Try the *cioppino Livornese,* an Italian-accented bouillabaisse.

✗ **Roxsand.** Biltmore Fashion Park, 2495 E. Camelback Rd.; (602) 381-0444 $$$
It's called "New American fusion cuisine," which means dishes like "Confit of African pheasant with Evil Jungle Prince sauce." What?! Nevertheless, it's superbly conceived and executed. One of the best restaurants in Phoenix.

✗ **San Carlos Bay Seafood Restaurant.** 1901 E. McDowell; (602) 340-0892 $$
Most of the staff seems not to speak English, but who cares?—this is absolutely authentic Mexican seafood. Beware any dish with the word "diablo" in the title—that means "devil," and the sauce will indeed be satanically spicy.

✗ **Steamers.** Biltmore Fashion Park, 2576 E. Camelback Rd.; (602) 956-3631 $$$
Seafood in Arizona used to be shrimp trucked up from the Sonoran coast and not much else, but that's ancient history now. Steamers has some 20 different fresh fish on the menu, plus eight shellfish entrees—and of course, an oyster, clam and mussel bar.

✗ **Such is Life.** 3602 N. 24th St.; (602) 955-7822 $$
The best Mexican restaurant in Arizona, very possibly the best in the country. Forget tacos and enchiladas; this place demonstrates the seriousness of Mexico City cuisine—things like shredded lamb wrapped in the leaves of a maguey cactus, roasted for six hours, and served with a *pasilla chile* sauce. Upstairs is a separate kitchen and an authentic Spanish menu. It's a small place; make reservations.

✗ **Vincent on Camelback.** 3930 E. Camelback Rd.; (602) 224-0225 $$$
Roasted loin chops with chipotle chile beurre blanc. Grilled sea bass with chimayó chile. Duck tamales. Would you believe owner Vincent Guerithault is a classically trained French chef? Exceptional and imaginative New Southwestern cuisine.

Prescott

🏨 **Hassayampa Inn.** 122 E. Gurley St.; (520) 778-9434 $$
Built in 1927 and listed on the National Historic Register, this elegant downtown hotel, now nicely renovated in period style, features a lovely lobby and guest rooms with private baths.

🏨 **Marks House Inn.** 203 E. Union St.; (520) 778-4632 $$
A Queen Anne Victorian mansion built in 1894, now a four-room B&B. Family-style breakfasts.

HASSAYAMPA INN

⊞ **Prescott Pines Inn.** 901 White Spar Rd.; (520) 445-7270 or (800) 541-3574 **$$** A pleasant B&B, where some of the 13 rooms have fireplaces or kitchens. Impressive full breakfasts.

✕ **Murphy's.** 201 N. Cortez.; (520) 445-4044 **$$** This has been the hot dining and drinking spot in town since it opened in 1984. Part of the appeal is the setting, an 1890 mercantile building beautifully renovated. American menu: prime rib, steaks, shrimp. Big room, often noisy.

Scottsdale

(also see Phoenix and Tempe)

⊞ **The Boulders.** 34631 N. Tom Darlington Dr., Carefree (12 mi. north of Scottsdale); (602) 488-9009 **$$$** This secluded luxury resort has 160 casitas, 34 patio homes, and two celebrated golf courses.

⊞ **Hyatt Regency Scottsdale at Gainey Ranch.** 7500 E. Doubletree Ranch Rd.; (602) 991-3388 **$$$** Ultra-luxurious 475-room resort with verdant grounds. Guests enjoy 10 pools, two golf courses, a little lake with a beach, a three-story water slide, Venetian-style gondolas, and two good restaurants. The spectacular lobby, which opens out to flower-lined walkways and lawns, has a three-story-tall sculpture and an inviting bar.

CAMELBACK INN

⊞ **Marriott's Camelback Inn Resort.** 5402 E. Lincoln Dr.; (602) 948-1700/ (800) 24-CAMEL **$$$** Very deluxe resort , with over 400 spacious and luxurious rooms in casitas, many of them two-story with patios, fireplaces, and even private pools. Set on 125 acres with three pools, with poolside dining; saunas, 36-hole golf course, spas upon spas, concierges.

⊞ **The Phoenician.** 6000 E. Camelback Rd.; (602) 941-8200 **$$$** Covering 130 acres of Camelback Mountain and heavily landscaped with tiers of waterfalls and pools (one is tiled with mother-of-pearl), this ultra-deluxe resort offers over 440 lavish rooms, suites and casitas. Golf, tennis courts and health spas.

Scottsdale (cont'd)

⊞ **Scottsdale Conference Resort.** 7700 E. McCormick Pkwy.; (602) 991-9000 $$$
This excellent establishment has it all: 325 guest rooms and suites, two 36-hole golf courses, sports, and fitness center, five lighted tennis courts, recreational pool and exercise pool, horseback riding, and a respected dining room famous for its Sunday brunch.

✕ **Avanti.** 3102 N. Scottsdale Rd.; (602) 949-8333 $$$
Only open for dinner (there's another location in Phoenix open for lunch and dinner), this northern Italian/Continental eatery is renowned for both exceptional food and service. Try the cioppino or osso bucco.

✕ **Franco's Trattoria.** 8120 N. Hayden Rd.; (602) 948-6655 $$ - $$$
Mouthwatering Italian cuisine. From bistecca Fiorentina, to risotto, to veal, to heavenly zabaglione, the food is the thing at Franco's.

✕ **Malee's on Main.** 7131 E. Main; (602) 947-6042 $$
Set amid art galleries in downtown Scottsdale, Malee's offers excellent Thai fare in an inviting atmosphere. Try the Evil Jungle Princess—a mix of chicken, straw mushrooms and lemon grass in coconut milk—or Ped Yahng, roast duck over spinach with soy-ginger sauce.

✕ **Marquesa at the Scottsdale Princess.** 7575 E. Princess Dr.; (602) 585-2723 $$$
A destination resort restaurant with a Catalonian menu? Bold idea, but it certainly works. The paella is sheer art. Very expensive and rather formal.

✕ **Mary Elaine's.** 6000 E. Camelback Rd. (at the Phoenician Resort); (602) 423-2530 $$$
First-class contemporary cuisine, plus great service and a room with a view make Mary Elaine's one of the Valley's top restaurants. Check out the roasted duck breast or the garlic and herb crusted rack of lamb.

✕ **Oregano's Pizza Bistro.** 3622 N. Scottsdale Rd.; (602) 970 1860 $ - $$
Arguably Scottsdale's best pizza place, Oregano's specializes in thin-crust and stuffed Chicago-style pizzas.

✕ **Razz's Restaurant and Bar.** 10321 N. Scottsdale Rd.; (602) 905-1308 $$$
No one is bored with chef Erazmo Kamnitzer's inventive international cuisine. The menu features dishes ranging from South American bouillbaisse to Asian bath mie goreng.

✕ **Such is Life.** 7000 E. Shea Blvd, at the Promenade Mall; (602) 948-1753
See page 244 for description.

Sedona

⊞ **Canyon Villa B&B.** 125 Canyon Circle Dr.; (520) 284-1226/ (800) 453-1166 $$$
Six miles south of town, this modern B&B rivals Sedona's big resorts for luxury. Attractive library; some rooms are done in Victorian, others in Santa Fe style.

CANYON VILLA

🛏 **Forest Houses Resort.** 9275 N. Hwy. 89a, Oak Creek Canyon; (520) 282-2999 $$
Thirteen rustic cabins 10 miles north of Sedona in Oak Creek Canyon. The Lower Sycamore cabin cantilevers dramatically over the creek.

🛏 **Junipine Resort.** 8351 N. US 89a; (520) 282-3375 or (800) 742-7463 $$$
Condo-like resort nine miles north of Sedona in Oak Creek Canyon. Wood and stone "creekhouse" units have full kitchens and redwood decks overlooking the canyon.

🛏 **L'Auberge de Sedona.** 301 L'Auberge Ln.; (520) 282-1661 or (800) 272-6777 $$$
Lovely resort beside Oak Creek in a sycamore forest. Rates include six-course dinner at L'Auberge's excellent French restaurant *(see page 252).*

🛏 **Los Abrigados Resort and Spa.** 160 Portal Lane; (520) 282-1777 or (800) 521-3131 $$$
A deluxe resort set on 22 acres in the heart of town. The charming, modern

architecture is a delightful twist on the standard hacienda-style. Luxurious suites include fireplace and patio or balcony. Tennis courts, swimming pool.

LOS ABRIGADOS

✕ **The Coffee Pot.** 205 West Hwy. 89a; (520) 282-6626 $
A friendly omelette parlor, bustling with business weekend mornings.

✕ **Garland's Oak Creek Lodge.** Eight
🛏 miles north of Sedona on US 89a; (520) 282-3343 $$$
Fixed menu with eclectic gourmet fare changes nightly. Superb dining. Overnight reservations at the lodge must be made a year in advance. Open April through November.

✕ **The Heartline Cafe.** 1610 W. Hwy. 89a; (520) 282-0785
Charming and private, away from the bustle of shoppers and red-rock gawkers. Lunches are wonderfully eclectic: unusual salads, sandwiches, and entrees. For dinner choose between pastas and other vegetarian dishes, fish, and a variety of grilled or roasted red meats. The garden patio is a delightful.

Sedona *(cont'd)*

✕ **Loaves and Some Fishes II.** Bell Rock Plaza on AZ 179. (520) 284-1145 $
Wonderful homemade soups, salads, pastas, desserts, and gourmet coffee. Breakfast and lunch only.

✕ **L'Auberge de Sedona.** 301 L'Auberge Ln.; (520) 282-1667 $$$
Pining for Paris? The superb French cuisine and stratospheric prices here will relieve the most ardent Francophile's homesickness. The secluded creekside setting is reminiscent of an elegant French country inn.

✕ **Pietro's.** 2445 W. US 89A.; (520) 282-2525 $$-$$$
Arizona's most attractive resort town has become a real mecca for foodies, as exemplified by this excellent little Italian restaurant.

Sonoita

✕ **Er Pastaro.** 3084 Hwy. 82; (520) 455-5821 $$
After being maitre d' at Regine's in New York, Giovanni Schifano wanted out —way out, as in the rolling grasslands of Arizona's primo ranch country (Sonoita is an unincorporated crossroads 45 miles southeast of Tucson). Excellent pasta, without pretensions. Schifano loves it because, as he said, "out here the millionaires drive pickups."

Tempe

(also see Phoenix and Scottsdale)

⌂ **Westcourt in the Buttes.** 2000 W. Westcourt Way; (602) 225-9000 or (800) 843-1986 $$$
Luxury 350-room hotel dramatically built into the top of a small mountain. Tennis courts, pools, nightclub and two restaurants. Located near Arizona State University and airport.

Tombstone

(also see Bisbee)

✕ **Crystal Palace Saloon.** 420 E. Allen St., Tombstone; (520) 457-3611 $$
Furnished with old wood tables and faded red drapes, the saloon looks just as it did in the 1880s. The kitchen serves up deli sandwiches and BBQ.

Tucson

⌂ **Arizona Inn.** 2200 E. Elm St.; (520) 325-1541 $$$
Cypress and orange trees cover the 14-acre lawns of this 1930s-vintage resort The 80 guest rooms are decorated in period style, all have patios, many have fireplaces. Pool, tennis courts and restaurant. Conveniently located.

⌂ **El Presidio Bed & Breakfast.** 297 N. Main Ave.; (520) 623-6151 $$
Lovely B&B in an 1879 Victorian adobe.

La Posada Del Valle. 1640 N. Campbell Ave.; (520) 795-3840 **$$**
This Southwest-style adobe, ca. 1920, offers five guest rooms, each named after a famous woman from the '20s (many guests prefer "Zelda's Room"). Afternoon tea is served in a common room furnished with art deco antiques.

Loews Ventana Canyon Resort. 7000 N. Resort Dr.; (520) 299-2020 or (800) 234-5117 **$$$**
Tucson's most beautiful destination resort: 93 acres nestled in a saguaro forest at the foot of the Santa Catalina Mountains. The 400 Southwest-style rooms feature private balconies, dark pine furniture, and artwork. In addition to restaurants, tennis courts, pools, and quiet paths through mesquite and blue palo verde is an 80-foot waterfall spilling into a picturesque lake.

LOEWS VENTANA CANYON RESORT

Boccata. 5605 E. River Rd.; (520) 577 9309 **$$**
A wonderful menu combining southern French and northern Italian cuisines. If you're lucky, *fettuccine Genovese* with pesto and grilled scallops and shrimp will be on the menu. Dine on the deck to get a lovely view of the city lights.

Cafe Terra Cotta. 4310 N. Campbell Ave.; (520) 577-8100 **$$**
The fountainhead of New Southwestern cuisine in Tucson and a favorite with locals and visitors since 1986. An excellent place to graze on appetizers, which sometimes are more intriguing than the mains. There's a Scottsdale location also: 6166 N. Scottsdale Rd., (602) 948-8100.

Daniel's. 4340 N. Campbell Ave.; (520) 742-3200 **$$$**
This northern Italian restaurant is very expensive, very sophisticated, and very good. Superb wine list and even an extensive single-malt scotch list.

El Charro. 311 N. Court Ave., (520) 622-1922 **$**
Located in a historic downtown house, this Mexican restaurant is famous throughout Tucson for its succulent *carne seca* (sun-dried beef).

Tucson (cont'd)

✗ **Janos.** 150 N. Main Ave.; (520) 884-9426 $$$
Tucson's best restaurant, no matter that Mobil gives the venerable Tack Room one more star. They're wrong. Owner-chef Janos Wilder presides over kitchen and dining rooms in a tastefully but not pretentiously decorated 1865 adobe home. Cuisine is eclectic and imaginative, drawing on French, Mexican and American traditions and techniques. Inexpensive summer specials are a startling bargain.

✗ **Kingfisher.** 2564 E. Grant Rd.; (520) 323-7739 $$
Eclectic decor and refreshingly diverse. New American menu is always tasty. Good grilled seafood, spit-roasted chicken. Mashed potato infused with rutabaga may be an idea whose time hasn't come, however.

✗ **Le Bistro.** 2574 N. Campbell Ave.; (520) 327-3086 $$
Somehow overlooked in some travel guides, this pretty but unassuming place offers very good classic French bistro cuisine at reasonable (for French) tariffs. Great desserts.

✗ **Mi Nidito.** 1813 S. Fourth Ave.; (520) 622-5081 $
A local institution since 1954 and the best Mexican food in town. Most tourists never hear about it because of its location in mostly Hispanic South Tucson. Always jammed at normal mealtimes; go at an odd hour or be prepared for a long wait. Try the green chile enchiladas and a Bohemia, Mexico's best beer.

✗ **Presidio Grill.** 3352 E. Speedway; (520) 327-4667 $$ - $$$
This sleek, lively restaurant serves New American fare with a Southwestern accent. Two appealing examples: prickly-pear marinated pork tenderloin with seasame noodles and chicken pasta with poblano chiles, prosciutto, and fresh basil.

✗ **Ventana Room at Loews Ventana Canyon Resort.** 7000 N. Resort Dr.; (520) 299-2020 $$$
This is an aerie with a view—the night lights of Tucson, sprawling halfway to Mexico. The very expensive New American cuisine presents itself elegantly, and service is formal and professional. The manager must be from another planet, however; this is the only restaurant in ever-casual Tucson requesting male patrons to don jacket and tie.

✗ **Vivace.** 4811 E. Grant Rd.; (520) 795-7221 $$
Owner-chef Daniel Scordato, who hails from a venerable Tucson restaurant family, serves up four-star food at two-star prices in this contemporary trattoria. Excellent pasta, a fabulous seafood soup.

White Mountains

▦ **Greer Lodge.** US 373, Greer; (520) 735-7515 $$$
The ponderosa pine and aspen main lodge and eight cabins here was built by

GREER LODGE

hand 50 years ago as a church retreat. The dining area features huge windows, vaulted ceilings, and a massive fireplace.

🛏 **Lakeview Lodge.** 2251 White Mountain Blvd., Pinetop-Lakeside; (520) 368-5253 $$
Built in 1916, this lodge offers nine homey rooms and cabins (each comes with a bottle of wine), and a rustic lounge with a fireplace and a high, beamed ceiling.

🛏 **Molly Butler Lodge.** US 373, Greer; (520) 735-7226 $
Oldest lodge in Arizona. The rooms are tiny and a bit run-down, but plaques of local historic pioneers hang on the walls, lending a certain charm to this lodge.

Window Rock

🛏 **Navajo Nation Inn.** AZ 264, (520) 871-4108 $
Pleasant hotel with Southwest-style decor, catering to visitors and Navajo businessmen and women. Located just east of shopping center.

Yuma

🛏 **Best Western Coronado Motor Hotel.** 233 Fourth Ave.; (520) 783-4453 or (800) 528-1234 $$
Built in 1938, this Spanish tile-roofed hotel hosted Bob Hope when he came to entertain the troops training here during World War II. Today the inn is run by the original owner. The rooms have all the amenities, and suites with kitchens are available.

SHILO INN HOTEL

🛏 **Shilo Inn Hotel.** 1530 S. Castle Dome Ave.; (520) 782-9518 $$$
Marble and mirrored columns greet guests in the three-story lobby of this modern hotel. Over 130 very comfortable rooms and suites decorated in pale colors, with patios and couches. Fitness rooms, swimming pool and saunas.

Winslow and Vicinity

🛏 **Adobe Inn.** 1701 North Park Drive, Winslow; (520) 289-4638 $
A two-story Best Western motel with modern decor. Cafe and indoor pool.

Winslow and Vicinity *(cont'd)*

▥ **Best Western Arizonian Inn.** 2508 East Navajo Blvd., Holbrook; (520) 524-2611 $$
Pleasantly decorated, English-style motel with all of the modern amenities. Swimming pool and coffee shop on the premises.

✕ **Casa Blanca Café.** 1201 East 2nd St., Winslow; (520) 289-4191 $$
Known for tacos, chimichangas, cheese crisps, and burgers. Ceramic-tiled establishment with booths and tables.

✕ **Romo's Cafe.** 121 West Hopi Dr., Holbrook; (520) 524-2153 $
A storefront cafe with tasty Mexican fare.

■ GUEST RANCHES

For a taste of the cowboy lifestyle, you might consider staying at a guest or dude ranch. While ranches range from family-run businesses where guests are expected to help out with the chores to deluxe resorts where guests can saddle up or just lounge by the pool, all offer rustic lodging, horseback riding, and hearty meals in a quiet, unspoiled setting. The minimum stay at ranches is usually one week, and because meals and activities are usually included, ranch stays can be pricy. Many ranches are closed in the summer, so call ahead.

Douglas

Price Canyon Ranch. P.O. Box 1065, 85607; (520) 558-2383

PRICE CANYON RANCH

This working cattle ranch in the Chiricahua Mountains houses guests in small cabins. Meals (included in the moderate rate) are served in a 100-year-old main house. Horseback riding and overnight pack trips.

Dragoon

Triangle T Guest Ranch. P.O. Box 218, 85609; (520) 586-7533
Cottages and RV hookups. American Plan for meals. Horseback riding, hiking, birdwatching, pool. Open year-round.

Unusual rock formations fire the imagination.

Eagar

Sprucedale Ranch. P.O. Box 880, 85925; (520) 333-4984
Working cattle and horse ranch, where guests participate in trail rides, rodeos, branding, bonfires, and horse roundups (driving horses from winter to summer range). Cabin lodging with all meals included. Open June to September.

Mesa

Saguaro Lake Guest Ranch. 13020 Bush Hwy., 85205; (602) 984-2194
Accommodations in cabins and rooms. Horseback riding, hiking, river recreation. Open year-round.

Patagonia

CIRCLE Z RANCH

Circle Z Ranch. P.O. Box 194, 85624; (520) 394-2525
Teddy Roosevelt stayed in one of this ranch's 1920s-vintage adobe cottages. Decorated with colorful Mexican craftwork and casual wicker furnishings, altogether they accommodate no more than 45 at a time. Guests gather by the main lodge's huge fireplace to read classics from the well-stocked bookshelves. There is a three night minimum stay.

Payson

Kohl's Ranch. AZ 260, 85541; (520) 478-4211
On the banks of Tonto Creek, 17 miles (27 km) east of Payson. About 50 rooms and cabins with outdoor grills and patios; cabins have stone fireplaces and vaulted ceilings. Lodge rooms are less authentic, but have their own light-hearted appeal. Swimming pool and horseback riding.

Pearce

Grapevine Canyon Ranch. P.O. Box 302, 85625; (520) 826-3185
American Indian and rustic pieces furnish the cabins on this working cattle ranch. Guests enjoy relaxing in the cozy sitting room, as well as swimming, hiking, birdwatching, but best is the horseback riding. Open year-round; however, the ranch takes no children under 12.

Sasabe

Rancho de la Osa. P.O. Box 1, 85633; (520) 823-4257
The buildings on this quiet, 250-year old Territorial-style ranch are of handmade adobe bricks, with fireplaces and colonial Spanish-style furnishings. Ride pure-bred quarterhorses or swim in the pool on warm days. Open year-round.

Tucson

Elkhorn Guest Ranch. Sasabe Star Route, Box 97, 85738; (520) 822-1040
Accommodation in cabins, with meals included. Horseback riding, pool, tennis. Open November through April.

Lazy K Bar Ranch. 8401 N. Scenic Dr., 85743; (520) 744-3050
The adobe main house (built in 1933) is situated on 160 acres of beautiful desert and mountain trails. Meals are served family-style, or at picnics and cookouts. Guests enjoy mountain bikes, hayrides, rodeos, and trapshooting; there's also a library, a pool, and a whirlpool. Open September through mid June.

Tanque Verde Ranch. 14301 E. Speedway, 85748; (520) 296-6275
This super-deluxe ranch, dating from the 1880s, offers 70 adobe casitas and main lodge rooms, furnished with antiques and beehive fireplaces. Swim indoors or out, go horseback riding, play tennis, and take a course in nature studies. Open year-round.

TANQUE VERDE RANCH

White Stallion Ranch. 9251 W. Twin Peaks Rd., 85743; (520) 297-0252
An informal ranch on 3,000 acres, with 29 rooms in cottages and lodge. Family-style meals; tennis, golf, trap and target shooting. Hayrides, rodeos, bonfires. Open September to May.

Wickenburg

Flying E Ranch. 2801 W. Wickenburg, 85390; (520) 684-2690
Seventeen rooms in the main house on a 21,000-acre working cattle ranch. Heated pool, sauna and whirlpool; family-style meals, chuckwagon dinners, hay and trail rides, and a gym. Golf is located near by. Open November to April.

Kay El Bar Ranch. P.O. Box 2480, 85358; (520) 684-7593
Room for 20 guests in these territorial-style adobe buildings, which have been placed on the National Historic Register. Charming stone fireplace in the lobby; pool, horseback riding. Open October to end of April.

Wickenburg *(cont'd)*

Rancho Casitas. P.O. Box 1150, 85358; (520) 684-2628
Minimum stay one week, open September to May. American Plan for meals. Horseback riding, pool, hiking.

Rancho de los Caballeros. 1551 S. Vulture Mine Rd., 85390; (520) 684-5484
Wickenburg's super-deluxe guest ranch, with 79 Southwestern-style rooms and suites. Owned by the same family since 1947, the ranch offers a swimming pool, tennis courts, championship 18-hole golf course, skeet and trap shooting, plus programs for children. Full American Plan. Open October to early May.

Merv Giffin's Wickenburg Inn. 34801 N. Hwy 89; (520) 684-7811
Nine rooms in lodge plus 54 casitas, many with fireplaces and beamed ceilings, on a 4,700-acre wildlife refuge. Eight tennis courts for guests. When you tire of tennis, visit the Desert Nature Center, play sand volleyball, go horseback riding, take a whirlpool, or make jewelry in the arts and crafts center. Dining room open to public by reservation. Closed in August.

LOS CABALLEROS

■ FESTIVALS AND RODEOS

JANUARY

Scottsdale: Phoenix Open. The PGA's best tee off at the Tournament Players Club.

Tempe: Fiesta Bowl. Nationally televised New Year's Day football game between two selected college teams.

FEBRUARY

Scottsdale: Jaycees' Parada del Sol Rodeo. Rodeo, parade, and daredevil ride by the Hashknife Pony Express. (602) 990-3179

Tubac: Festival of the Arts. Oldest arts and crafts fair in Arizona, mostly visual arts. (520) 398-9201

Tucson: La Fiesta de los Vaqueros. Rodeo and parade. (520) 294-8896

Yuma: Jaycees' Silver Spur. Rodeo and parade. (520) 783-3641

MARCH

Phoenix: Jaycees' Rodeo of Rodeos. Known best for its parade. (602) 263-8671

Tempe: Spring Festival of the Arts. More than 600 artists, crafters and food vendors. (602) 967-4877

APRIL

Cave Creek: Fiesta Days Weekend. Rodeo and parade. (602) 488-3637

Globe: Copper Dust Stampede. Rodeo and parade. (520) 425-4495

Tucson: International Mariachi Conference. North America's largest festival of mariachi performances and workshops. Always a sellout; obtain tickets in advance. (520) 884-9920

MAY

Flagstaff: Native American Arts and Crafts Festival. The Museum of Northern Arizona celebrates the Zuni, Hopi, and Navajo cultures with dancing, artwork, and exhibits one weekend each month from May to July. (520) 774-5211

JUNE

Flagstaff: Pine Country Rodeo. Rodeo and parade. (520) 526-9926

Prescott: Bluegrass Festival. Big crowds turn out for this music festival held annually at Watson Lake Park. (520) 445-2000

Prescott: Territorial Days. Rodeo, golf tournament, 10k run, dancing, carnival. (520) 445-3103

Safford: Gila Valley Pro Rodeo. Rodeo and parade. (520) 428-2511

JULY

Flagstaff: Festival of the Arts. Classical, jazz, pops, chamber, and symphony music. Late July to August. (800) 332-9444 (in Arizona only) or (520) 774-7750

Prescott: Frontier Days. One of the world's oldest professional rodeos. (520) 445-3103

AUGUST

Williams: Festival in the Pines. Arts and crafts, food booths. (520) 625-4061

Payson: Payson Annual Rodeo. The country's top cowboys compete in calf- and steer-roping contests. (520) 474-4515 or (800) 6-PAYSON

SEPTEMBER

Bisbee: Brewery Gulch Days. Mining contests, dancing, parade. (520) 432-5578

Cottonwood: Verde River Days. Sand castle building, rubber duck race, live music, canoe rides, nature walks, geological and archaeological tours. (520) 634-7593

Flagstaff: Coconino County Fair. Pig races, lumberjack show, magicians, carnival, horse show tournament. Labor Day Weekend. (520) 774-5139

Grand Canyon: Chamber Music Festival Evening concert series feature classical and jazz. (520) 638-9215

Payson: Old-Time Fiddlers' Contest. Storytellers, food, crafts, fiddle makers. (520) 474-4515

Phoenix: Music in the Garden. Concert series held at the Desert Botanical Gardens. Concert goers may also make reservations for a Champagne brunch. (602) 941-1225

Sedona: Jazz on the Rocks. The state's top jazz festival. A full day of outdoor performances. Always a sellout; request tickets several months in advance. (520) 282-1985

Window Rock: Navajo Nation Celebration and Rodeo. One of the largest American Indian fairs and rodeos in the country. Intertribal powwow, concerts, parade, traditional singing, free barbecue, arts and crafts. (520) 871-6702 or (520) 871-6478

OCTOBER

Kingman: Andy Devine Days. Rodeo and parade. (520) 753-6106

Phoenix: Arizona State Fair. Rides, concerts, Native American and cowboy dancing, 4-H Club events—a classic American state fair. (602) 252-6771

Sedona: Fiesta Del Tlaquepaque. Includes Mariachi bands, piñatas, folklorico dance performances, and flamenco guitarists. (520) 282-4838

Tombstone: Helldorado Days. Shootouts, 1880s fashion show, rodeo, parade, and other entertainment. (520) 457-2211

Willcox: Rex Allen Days. Rodeo, fair, and music concert. (520) 384-2272 or (800) 200-2272.

DECEMBER

Wickenburg: Cowboy Christmas. Cowboy poetry, live music, crafts, and breakfast. (520) 984-5479

Tempe: Old Town Tempe Fall Festival of the Arts. Downtown streets shut down for a three-day fair of music, food, and local arts. (602) 894-8158 or (800) 283-6734

(opposite) A mariachi band entertains festival goers. (Kerrick James)

(following pages) Indian children light bonfires during the Spring Festival at Mission San Xavier in Tucson. (Kerrick James)

■ MUSEUMS AND CULTURAL ATTRACTIONS

BISBEE

Bisbee Mining & Historical Museum. 5 Copper Queen Plaza, (520) 432-7071. For underground mine tour call (520) 432-2071. *See page 163*

DRAGOON

Amerind Foundation. (520) 586-3666. Take I-10 to exit 318, 58 miles east of Tucson. Founded for research in Mexican and Southwestern archaeology. Outstanding artifact collection. *See page 90*

FLAGSTAFF

Lowell Observatory. 1400 W. Mars Hill Rd., (520) 774-2096. Guided tours on weekdays. *See page 177*

Museum of Northern Arizona. 3101 North Fort Valley Road, (520) 774-5211. Natural history and human settlement of Colorado Plateau. *See pages 90, 177*

GREEN VALLEY

Titan Missile Museum. 1580 W. Duval Mine Rd., (520) 625-7736. Take I-19 to Duval Mine Road exit, 20 mi. south of Tucson. Guided tour of disarmed ICBM in underground silo. *See page 161*

PHOENIX

Arizona Science Center. 600 E. Washington St., Phoenix; (602) 256-9388. Complex includes planetarium, Iworks theater, and a waterplay exhibit. *See page 147*

Desert Botanical Garden. 1201 N. Galvin Pkwy., Phoenix; (602) 941-1225. 10,000 desert plants and a demonstration garden of watersaving landscaping. *See pages 38, 149*

Hall of Flame. 6101 E. Van Buren St., Phoenix; (602) 275-3473. Museum of antique fire trucks and firefighting equipment.

Heard Museum. 22 E. Monte Vista Rd., Phoenix; (602) 252-8840. Artifacts and artworks from prehistoric and modern Native American cultures. *See page 148*

Phoenix Art Museum. 1625 N. Central Ave., Phoenix; (602) 257-1222. Exhibits include European painters and the American West collection. *See page 148*

Phoenix Zoo. 5810 E. Van Buren St., Phoenix; (602) 273-1341. More than 1,000 animals. *See page 149*

Pueblo Grande Museum. 4619 E. Washington St., Phoenix; (602) 495-0900. Ruins from the Hohokam civilization. *See page 90*

Out of Africa Wildlife Park. 2 S. Fort McDowell Rd., Fountain Hills ; (602) 837-7779. Located 2 mi. north of Shea Blvd. and AZ 87.

Wildlife World Zoo. 16501 W. Northern Ave., Litchfield Park; (602) 935-WILD. Kangaroos, wallabies, and other exotic species in privately owned suburban Phoenix zoo.

PRESCOTT

Sharlot Hall Museum. 415 W. Gurley St.; (520) 445-3122. History of Prescott and Arizona Territory, housed in historic building. *See page 171*

SCOTTSDALE

Fleischer Museum. 17207 N. Perimeter Dr., (602) 585-3108. Art museum featuring American Impressionists. *See page 151*

Scottsdale Center for Fine Arts. Off Second St. in the Scottsdale Civic Center Mall; (602) 994-ARTS. Changing exhibits and various performances. *See page 151.*

Taliesin West. From Scottsdale Road take Shea Blvd. 4.6 mi. east to Frank Lloyd Wright Blvd., turn left and follow signs. School of Architecture and former home of Frank Lloyd Wright; (602) 860-8810 *See page 151*

SUPERIOR

Boyce Thompson Southwestern Arboretum. 37615 US 60; (520) 689-2811 (4 mi. west of Superior). 1,000-acre arboretum includes cacti from around the world. *See page 39*

TEMPE

University Art Museum. Nelson Fine Arts Center, on the corner of Mill Ave. and tenth St., Arizona State University, (602) 965-ARTS. American, Latin American, print, and craft art. *See page 154*

TUCSON

Arizona Historical Society's Museum. 949 E. Second St.; (520) 628-5774. Exhibits of Arizona history: Hohokam Indians, Spanish explorers, mining and cattle ranching.

Arizona-Sonora Desert Museum. 2021 N. Kinney Rd., (520) 883-2702. Zoo, arboretum, natural history museum. *See page 38*

Arizona State Museum. University of Arizona, (520) 621-6302. Exhibits are divided between two buildings flanking the main west campus entrance at Park and University.

Center for Creative Photography . University of Arizona, (520) 621-7968. Superb photographic museum conceived by Ansel Adams. *See page 201*

Flandrau Planetarium. University of Arizona, (520) 621-7827. Star Theater, Interactive meteor exhibit, and a small mineral museum. *See page 161*

Mission San Xavier del Bac. Take I-19 mi. south of Tucson; (520) 294-2624. Beautiful monument to Spanish baroque architecture. *See page 160-161*

Pima Air Museum. 6000 E. Valencia Rd., (520) 574-9658. Collection of historic aircraft. *See page 161*

Reid Park Zoo. 900 S. Randolph Way, (520) 791-4022. Small zoo includes South American rainforest section.

Tucson Museum of Art. 140 North Main Ave., (520) 624-2333 Free on Tuesdays. Pre-Columbian and Western art as well as changing exhibits and a block of restored historic buildings.

University of Arizona Museum of Art University of Arizona, (520) 621-7567. Small museum with wide-ranging European collection of paintings. *See page 161*

YUMA

Yuma Territorial Prison State Historic Park. Take Giss Pkwy. to Prison Hill Rd.; (520) 783-4771. *See page 184.*

Arizona Historical Society Museum. 240 South Madison Ave.; (520) 782-1841. 1870 adobe structure exhibits artifacts from territorial Yuma.

■ SPECTATOR SPORTS

After a decade of local debate and abandonment at the altar of the big leagues, Phoenix at last is about to see real baseball. The Arizona Diamondbacks—great name; can't wait to see the uniforms—will debut as one of two expansion teams in 1998, playing in a $275 million stadium with a retractable roof. Traditionalists cheer: this will be the first domed stadium with real grass on the field. Whether the Diamondbacks will be National League or American League hasn't been decided.

For long years Phoenix has languished as the largest city in North America without major-league baseball. It has had a wildly popular NBA team, the Phoenix Suns, since 1968; and a generally disliked NFL team, the Arizona Cardinals, since 1988. The Cards moved from St. Louis, which infuriated that city; then owner Bill Bidwill promptly set Phoenix afume by charging the highest ticket prices in the league—for a perennially losing team. The Cards play in Arizona State University's 72,000-seat Sun Devil Stadium and rarely sell out; the Suns occupy America West Arena and always do.

Eight major-league baseball teams hold their spring training in Arizona; they're collectively called the Cactus League. Their exhibition games attract more than 600,000 fans every year. The Oakland A's play in Phoenix, Milwaukee Brewers in Chandler, Chicago Cubs in Mesa, San Francisco Giants in Scottsdale, Anaheim Angels in Tempe, Colorado Rockies in Tucson, and Seattle Mariners and San Diego Padres in Peoria. (See essay "Spring Training," pp. 184-185.)

For the last decade the consistently hottest sports franchise in Arizona has been the University of Arizona's Wildcat basketball team. The Cats went to the NCAA Final Four in 1988 and 1994, and won the PAC-10 championship in 1986, 1988, 1990 and 1991.

Moreover, Wildcat coach Lute Olson's program is so clean it squeaks like a gym shoe: virtually all the players graduate, and there's never been even a hint of recruiting violations. A Tucson reporter once described the team as "St. Lute and His Leaping Apostles." The only discouraging word is that you cannot get a ticket. McKale Center's 13,800 seats sell out long in advance to the same season ticket holders every year. All games, fortunately for fans, are televised locally.

■ DESERT PHOTOGRAPHY

Arizona's landscapes and various human cultures form a photographer's dream, but there also are a few difficulties.

The light is one. Except on overcast days, the Arizona sky is brighter than in most places in North America. A modern camera's metering program doesn't realize that it's *supposed* to be bright, and often will choose a smaller aperture or higher shutter speed than it should. Then the rest of the picture will be underexposed. The solution is to point the camera a bit downward, at what appears to be an average brightness level in the scene, and use that meter reading. Also, remember that in the deserts, broad daylight is flat light. It bleaches color and nuance out of your pictures. The best landscape photos are shot in the early morning, late evening, or when a storm is threatening.

Another problem is overexposure—not of your film, but of the state itself. Arizona has been photographed so extensively (and so expertly) that it is quite a challenge to come up with a fresh image of a familiar attraction such as Monument Valley. Keep alert for unusual details—say, a rattlesnake on a boulder that could be used for a foreground—and pray for unsettled weather.

Finally, Arizona's natural environment is not particularly gentle with camera equipment. Camera repair shops warn customers not to leave cameras in a car parked in the sun on a hot day; the heat can melt lubricants and allow them to ooze onto components where they don't belong. The heat will not affect unexposed film, but do have it processed promptly after shooting.

Light and shadows play along the Redwall Formation of the Grand Canyon's South Rim. (Kerrick James)

■ How to Look Like a Native

Arizona is largely an informal state, although Phoenix, sad to say, is growing steadily less so (See the "PHOENIX" chapter for a discussion). In the smaller towns and cities, only the lawyers ever wear suits. For the pleasure visitor, casual, comfortable clothing is recommended—especially shorts in summer. Only a handful of restaurants in Phoenix require jackets for men at dinner; in Tucson, at this writing, only one does.

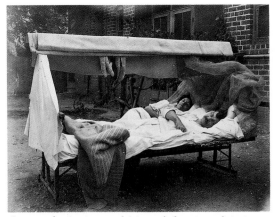

Summer sleeping in central Arizona before air conditioning. (Arizona Historical Society)

One important accessory, summer and winter alike, is sunblock with a protection factor no lower than 15. This is not only to prevent sunburn: southern Arizona has the world's second highest rate of melanoma, a deadly skin cancer, and cumulative exposure to sun is the prime cause. As enticing as sporting a well-bronzed body may seem, Arizona doctors speak as one in this recommendation: forget sunbathing.

■ Arizona Publications

Arizona's most famous publication is, interestingly, owned by the state of Arizona itself: *Arizona Highways* magazine has a circulation of 410,000, about 80 percent of it out of state, and a nonpareil reputation for spectacular photography.

It was founded in 1925 as a newsletter published by the Arizona Highway Department and sold for 10 cents per copy. It chronicled highway construction and administrative humdrum within the department, and its purpose was to promote roadbuilding in the young state. The modern concept of *Arizona Highways* began in 1938 with the editorship of Raymond Carlson, which lasted three decades. Carlson introduced four-color photography, which was rare at the time, and rhapsodic prose. Today the photography is better than ever, the writing more journalistic than promotional. But its mission remains the same: to promote tourism in Arizona. It does so with great success. For a one-year subscription write *Arizona Highways,* 2039 West Lewis Avenue, Phoenix, AZ 85009.

The state's largest newspaper, the *Arizona Republic,* is available in every town and hamlet. Its daily columnist, E. J. Montini, is worth the price of the paper; he's one of the few columnists anywhere who still bases his commentary on solid reporting. The *Arizona Daily Star,* published in Tucson, is available all around southern Arizona. Once a fine newspaper, it has been in a deep slumber since the mid-1980s. Its evening competitor, the *Tucson Citizen,* will give a visitor a better feel for the city.

Other publications of use to the visitor include *Tucson Guide* and *Valley Guide,* both quarterly magazines with features and entertainment suggestions; *Phoenix* magazine, which has some excellent writing and provocative features; *Tucson Lifestyle,* which is relentlessly upscale; and Phoenix's *New Times* and the *Tucson Weekly.* The latter two are available free in street boxes and stores on Wednesdays; they offer the best guides to dining and entertainment.

■ GENERAL INFORMATION

Arizona Game & Fish Department
2221 W. Greenway Rd.
Phoenix, AZ 85023
(602) 942-3000

Arizona Golf Association
7226 North 16th St., Suite 200
Phoenix, AZ 85020
(602) 944-3035

Arizona Office of Tourism
1100 W. Washington St.
Phoenix, AZ 85007
(800) 842-8257/(602) 542-8687

National Parks Service
202 E. Earl Dr., Suite 115
Phoenix, AZ 85012
(602) 640-5250

Native American Tourism Center
4130 N. Goldwater Blvd.
Scottsdale, AZ 85251
(602) 945-0771

Phoenix Convention & Visitors Bureau
400 E. Van Buren, Suite 600
Phoenix, AZ 85004
(602) 254-6500

Sierra Club
516 E. Portland St.
Phoenix, AZ 85004
(602) 253-8633

Tucson Convention & Visitors Bureau
130 S. Scott Ave.
Tucson, AZ 85701
(520) 624-1817

RECOMMENDED READING

ARIZONA'S PHYSICAL CHARMS AND CULTURAL INTRIGUE have been luring painters and photographers to the state for more than a century, and the result is uncommonly rich documentation of this land through the visual arts. Less obviously, this is equally true of its literature. Writers are smitten with Arizona for precisely the same reasons as artists.

The literature of the Sonoran Desert begins in the 18th century with the meticulous chronicles of Spanish explorers such as Diego Pérez de Luxán, and continues with the accounts of soldiers and evangelists over the next two centuries. These journals are invaluable to historians, but some also offer entertaining insight to the casual reader. One in particular crackles with immediacy and lucid detail: Father Ignaz Pfefferkorn's *Sonora* (see below), which has been translated into English and is currently in print.

This tradition of perceptive journalism continues into the period of early Anglo occupation. Some remarkably good writers, curious about the remote frontier, came to Arizona between 1860 and 1900. While their prose may seem excessively florid by today's standards, the meticulousness with which many described their encounters is (or ought to be) a model for journalism in any age. John G. Bourke's *On the Border With Crook* is an indispensable account of 1870s Arizona, written by an aide to Gen. George Crook, most successful commander of the Apache campaigns. Bourke's high respect for the Apaches is revealing, and he insightfully observes that "The moment (the Indian) concludes to live at peace with the whites, that moment all his troubles begin. Never was there a truer remark than that made by Crook: 'The American Indian commands respect for his rights only so long as he inspires terror for his rifle.'"

In modern times Arizona has been tamed—some believe—but its endangered beauty, continuing cultural conflict and very rapid pace of change generate more words than ever. Some come from unexpected sources. Former Gov. Bruce Babbitt, originally educated as a geologist, edited and annotated a superb anthology on the Grand Canyon. William K. Hartmann, an astronomer, recently authored the definitive work on the Sierra Pinacates, the remote black volcanic mountains in the heart of the Sonoran Desert. Eva Antonia Wilbur-Cruce, a woman who grew up on a ranch near the Mexican border in the first two decades of this century, finally has

Havasu Falls in the Grand Canyon at the Havasupai Indian Reservation is a Shangri-la still unreachable, fortunately, by car. (Kerrick James)

transformed that experience into a personal history graced with lovely and softly lyrical prose. (All these are listed below.) And there are books that are anything but lovely and soft, that instead glow with outrage over the depredations that humankind has visited on this fragile land. Of these, the works of Edward Abbey and Charles Bowden lodge at the top of any list.

This bibliography of 32 books on Arizona and its neighboring lands is colored without apology by this author's own tastes and convictions. A few of the titles listed below are out of print but still worth searching out in used bookstores and libraries.

■ MODERN DESCRIPTION AND TRAVEL

Miller, Tom (ed.): *Arizona, the Land and the People.* University of Arizona Press, Tucson 1986. Not the pretty but superficial coffee-table volume it appears to be, but an authoritative and literate anthology of articles covering the state's natural history and human cultures.

Weir, Bill: *Arizona Traveler's Handbook.* Moon Publications Inc., Chico, California 1996. An exhaustively detailed general guide for the traveler.

■ ESSAYS

Abbey, Edward: *Desert Solitaire: A Season in Wilderness.* University of Arizona Press, Tucson 1988 (reprint). Originally published in 1971, this is the earliest and most treasured of Abbey's collections: passionate, combative, keenly focused, and achingly beautiful in its use of the English language. Much of the book describes Arches National Monument in Utah.

Abbey, Edward: *The Journey Home: Some Words in Defense of the American West.* E. P. Dutton, New York 1977. A more quixotic, irritatingly self-indulgent Abbey lurks in this collection, but it remains a flinty and entertaining read.

Banham, Reyner: *Scenes in America Deserta.* Peregrine Smith Books, Salt Lake City 1982 (out of print). The late Reyner Banham, an architectural historian, shaped these essays around human beings' impact on the Mojave and Sonoran deserts. They are not academic, but sharp-eyed, passionate, and occasionally eccentric.

Bowden, Charles: *Blue Desert.* University of Arizona Press, Tucson 1986. As is true of his friend Abbey, the earliest of Bowden's collections is also the best. These prickly essays cover an astonishing range, but the constant thread is decline and death—of animals, humans, and ways of life.

Bowden, Charles: *Frog Mountain Blues.* University of Arizona Press, Tucson 1986.

Shelton, Richard: *Going Back to Bisbee.* University of Arizona Press, Tucson 1992. Shelton has lived in Southern Arizona since 1958, and this gracefully written and entertaining book is a memoir of his encounters with the region's natural history, critters, and people.

Wilbur-Cruce, Eva Antonia: *A Beautiful, Cruel Country.* University of Arizona Press, Tucson 1987. *(See comments on page 272.)*

■ NATURAL HISTORY

Alcock, John: *Sonoran Desert Spring.* University of Chicago Press, Chicago 1985. A biologist writes both authoritatively and lyrically about the life of the Sonoran Desert. A highly readable and informative personal journal.

Alcock, John: *Sonoran Desert Summer.* University of Arizona Press, Tucson 1990. A wonderful second volume in what evidently will be a tetralogy.

Babbitt, Bruce (ed.): *Grand Canyon: An Anthology.* Northland Press, Flagstaff, Arizona 1978 (out of print). A perfect dip into the immense body of literature on the Grand Canyon, including trenchant commentary by former Arizona Governor Babbitt himself.

Hartmann, William K.: *Desert Heart: Chronicles of the Sonoran Desert.* Fisher Books, Tucson 1989. This superb book centers on the volcanic Sierra Pinacate that sprawls, black and malevolent, across the Arizona-Sonora border. But it manages to elucidate much of the natural and cultural history of the entire Sonoran Desert—from Hohokam to modern *narcotraficantes.*

Van Dyke, John C.: *The Desert.* Peregrine Smith Books, Salt Lake City 1987 (out of print). The classic 1901 work on the Southwest deserts, written by a New Jersey art historian and librarian who for three years explored this land, in his words, "as a lover."

Whitney, Stephen: *A Field Guide to the Grand Canyon.* Quill, New York 1982. The perfect companion for the amateur canyon naturalist, with exhaustive information and illustrations covering its geology and biology.

■ PREHISTORY

Lister, Robert H. and Florence C.: *Those Who Came Before.* University of Arizona Press, Tucson 1983. The best single volume encompassing all the prehistoric cultures of the Southwest.

Matlock, Gary: *Enemy Ancestors.* Northland Press, Flagstaff, Arizona 1988 (out of print). A short but comprehensive non-academic book on the Anasazi.

Bronze bells in the patina curing room at the foundry in Arcosanti. (Kerrick James)

Modern Navajo rugs and blankets wear searing colors and aggressive geometry.

■ HISTORY

Bourke, John G.: *On the Border With Crook*. University of Nebraska Press, Lincoln 971 (reprint). The most essential book on the Apache wars and life in Arizona Territory.

Byrkit, James: *Forging the Copper Collar: Arizona's Labor-Management War of 1901-1921*. University of Arizona Press, Tucson 1982 (out of print). The title does this superb book no favor. It is no dry and arcane navigation of an obscure historical narrows, but a dramatic story of Arizona's painful political puberty. Byrkit is both a careful historian and a fine, bold writer.

Luckingham, Bradford: Phoenix: *The History of a Southwestern Metropolis*. University of Arizona Press, Tucson 1989. The only available comprehensive history of the Southwest's largest city.

Officer, James E.: *Hispanic Arizona, 1536-1856*. University of Arizona Press, Tucson 1987. Definitive and fascinating.

Pfefferkorn, Ignaz: *Sonora: A Description of the Province*. University of Arizona Press, Tucson 1989 (reprint). A book about Sonora, not Arizona, but the two were culturally and politically one during Fr. Pfefferkorn's ramblings between 1756 and 1767. His curious and observant eye records details as fine as the Piman bowstrings: ". . . made by twisting the intestines of various animals, and about as thick as the quill of a raven's feather."

Sonnichsen, Leland: *Tucson: The Life and Times of an American City*. University of Oklahoma Press, Norman, Oklahoma 1982. Informal, but written by a man who takes a lover's care of the English language. Prime among the several available Tucson histories.

Summerhayes, Martha: *Vanished Arizona*. University of Nebraska Press, Lincoln 1979 (reprint). The fascinating memoir of a cultivated Massachusetts woman who came to Arizona as an Army bride in 1874.

Trumble, Marshall: *Arizona: A Cavalcade of History*. Treasure Chest Publications, Tucson, 1989. Bursting with anecdotes, this history is written in a tone that occasionally crosses the line from informal to cloyingly folksy.

Tuscon: A Short History (Anthology). Southwestern Mission Research Center, Tucson 1986. Engaging writing by six experts; more depth than one would expect in 150 pages.

■ NATIVE AMERICANS

Fontana, Bernard: *Of Earth and Little Rain.* University of Arizona Press, Tucson 1989. An intimate and affectionate portrait of the Tohono O'odham of southern Arizona, written by a field historian who has lived at the reservation's edge for 25 years.

Iverson, Peter: *The Navajo Nation.* University of New Mexico Press, Albuquerque 1983. A history of the Navajo people, with emphasis on the last 50 years.

Waters, Frank: *Book of the Hopi.* Penguin Books, New York 1977. Waters lived among the Hopis: he writes about their religion and ceremonies with insight.

Yetman, Daivd: *Where the Desert Meets the Sea.* Pepper Publishing, Tucson 1987. A jewel-like book, sparkling with warmth, insight, and gentle humor, about the scarcely known Seri Indians of the Sonoran coast.

■ MISCELLANY

Griffith, James S.: *Southern Arizona Folk Arts.* University of Arizona Press, Tucson 1988. Griffith is the walking encyclopedia on the folk arts of Native American, Hispanic, and Anglo Arizonans; this book offers a well-researched introduction to many different traditions.

Watkin, Ronald J.: *High Crimes and Misdemeanors.* William Morrow & Company, New York 1990 (out of print). For political junkies, this is the only thorough and relatively objective chronicle of Gov. Evan Mecham's chaotic 1987-88 administration and impeachment—a story with more drama and strange characters than most works of fiction.

(following pages) December snowstorm descends on the south rim of the Grand Canyon. (Kerrick James)

I N D E X

COMPASS AMERICAN GUIDES

Available at your local bookstore, or call (800) 733-3000 to order.

COMPASS AMERICAN GUIDES are available at special discounts for bulk purchases for sales promotions or premiums. Special editions, including personalized covers and corporate imprints, can be created in large quantities for special needs. For more information call Special Markets at Fodor's Travel Publications, (800) 800-3246.

Arizona (4th Edition)
0-679-03388-2
$18.95 ($26.50 Can)

Chicago (2nd Edition)
1-878-86780-6
$18.95 ($26.50 Can)

Colorado (3rd Edition)
1-878-86781-4
$18.95 ($26.50 Can)

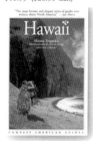

Hawaii (3rd Edition)
1-878-86791-1
$18.95 ($26.50 Can)

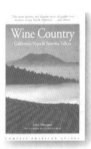

Wine Country (1st Edition)
1-878-86784-9
$18.95 ($26.50 Can)

Montana (3rd Edition)
1-878-86797-0
$18.95 ($26.50 Can)

Oregon (2nd Edition)
1-878-86788-1
$18.95 ($26.50 Can)

New Orleans (2nd Edition)
1-878-86786-5
$18.95 ($26.50 Can)

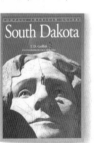

South Dakota (1st Edition)
1-878-86726-1
$16.95 ($22.95 Can)

Southwest (1st Edition)
1-87866779-2
$18.95 ($26.50 Can)

Texas (2nd Edition)
1-878-86798-9
$18.95 ($26.50 Can)

Utah (3rd Edition)
1-878-86773-3
$17.95 ($25.00 Can)